COMMO   ...DS

COMMON THREADS
Women, Mathematics and Work

Mary Harris

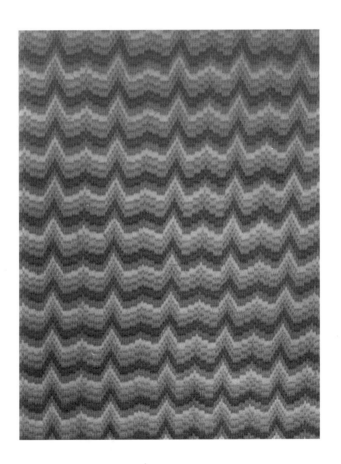

Trentham Books

First published in 1997 by Trentham Books Limited

Trentham Books Limited
Westview House
734 London Road
Oakhill
Stoke on Trent
Staffordshire
England ST4 5NP

British Cataloguing in Publication Data
A catalogue record for this book is available from the British
Library
ISBN: 1 85856 015 2

Designed and typeset by Trentham Print Design Ltd., Chester
and printed in Great Britain by Qualitex Printing Limited, Cardiff

Contents

Acknowledgement of sources of illustrations

Cover: The textile that forms the base of the design was worked by the author's daughter Jane Harris, when aged fifteen and attending a special school. Although Jane had very great difficulty in manipulating number, she worked the design in wool on canvas, under the guidance of her teacher Mrs Jessup, by following its visual symmetry.

Figure 2: Reproduced by permission of Punch Ltd.

Figure 3: Reproduced by permission of the British Library. MS. Add. 27695, fol. 8r.

Figure 5: Reproduced by permission of Liverpool Record Office.

Figure 6: Reproduced from the archive of the North London Collegiate School, by permission of the Headmistress.

Figure 7: Reproduced by permission of Punch Ltd.

Figure 11: Reproduced by permission of Paulus Gerdes.

Introduction

The word 'mathematics' no longer has a single meaning and schools and universities can no longer be seen as the only places where mathematics is learned and taught. Children who go to school develop a substantial part of their mathematical knowledge outside school. It is different from school mathematics, but there are overlaps and its qualities influence their learning in school. People who have never been to school can also develop and use mathematics, inventing or inheriting their own ways of measuring, or counting, or of finding their way around, to suit their particular needs. Even in schools there is no unitary mathematics, nor is there a unitary workplace mathematics. The mathematics that is taught in schools has varied in time and between cultures, though there is now an international hegemony of mathematics education that includes very similar syllabi and examinations worldwide. Mathematics is both a creation of social groups and a personal construction, but control of access to the mathematics of the former can restrict the development of the latter, for it cannot reach the full wealth of mathematics on its own.

The social control of mathematics and mathematics education has had severe negative effects on the majority of people, and on women in particular. Throughout the 2000 years of the history of Christian education the lives of women have been subordinated to and separated from the lives of men. Mathematics has been a masculine pursuit and a mark of men's high intellect and high social status. The equivalent activity that has marked the femininity, status and empty-headedness of women has been needlework.

Common Threads was the name of an exhibition that drew together a number of views of mathematics, and displayed them operating in the activity deemed most devoid of them. It demonstrated and challenged both gender stereotypes with its evidence that needlework is full of mathematics. The exhibition was very much a child of its time. I devised and produced it when issues of gender, class and race were high on the agendas of mathematics education, itself a relatively new profession. Since everyone, at least in England and Wales, wears clothes most of the time, and since most cloth and clothes are most frequently the results of the work of women the world over, Common Threads addressed simultaneously most of the chief issues in mathematics education.

After a week at its home base, the University of London Institute of Education, Common Threads toured England for two years, as a learning resource in school, adult, craft and vocational education, and its impact was such that a number of requests were made for it from outside England. By then my largely office-made original was worn out, but in an act of courageous imagination on the part of its Mathematics Advisor David Martin, the British Council took it over and redesigned it, and in two copies of its new version it visited a total of twenty three countries between 1991 to 1994 before it finally wore out again.

This book tries to place Common Threads and its influence within the historical context of the development and spread of mathematics education in England and beyond, while tracing the history of the education of girls and women and the effects of their work with textiles on their school curricula. The first two chapters sketch the 2000 years of the history of how needlework and mathematics came to be stereotypes in polar opposition. Chapters 3 and 4 trace the effect of these histories in the curriculum of working class and middle class girls respectively during the period when the national system of education was first set up in England and Wales. Chapter 5 tries to bring the story up to date. In Chapter 6 I introduce my own attempts to demolish the stereotypes and take forward an educational programme that developed mathematics from within traditional feminine skills and Chapter 7 discusses some of the effects of this work in class-rooms. In Chapters 8 and 9 I explore some of the international hegemonies of mathematics education and discuss the work of the Common Threads tour. Chapter 10 tries to bring all the threads together again.

Gender and class structures in society have developed in interaction. Until about 150 years ago, the formal study of mathematics was an extreme minority occupation of upper class males, though the society that sustained them could not have functioned without a wide range of mathematical activity among the lower orders of both sexes. Until about 30 years ago, history was written as if it only happened to men: all feminist historians since then, who have worked to redress this crude imbalance, have remarked on the virtual absence of women from history's records. The painstaking revelation of their presence is now beginning to change the nature of the record. The history of education, however, is still largely the history of patriarchal politics. The education of girls is a highly political matter and the forces upon it are extremely complex.

Even without such a complexity of interlinking historical events and inter-pretations, the study of theory and practice of education involves the crossing of borders and the plundering of the concepts of other disciplines, notably history, philosophy, psychology and sociology. The Maths in Work Project that produced Common Threads was itself set up to work across the boundaries between school mathematics and work mathematics, which at the time included discordant voices within further education and further education research, and disparate views of employers. It was my job to be fair, to far too many issues at once.

The book itself is a more than usually personal one from an academic stable, not only because the Maths in Work Project was always a one person operation but because it took place over ten years leading up to my formal retirement from mathematics education. Everyone brings a unique life experience to a job and mine has given me a rich, and wide-ranging one. Like many of my age, my childhood was war-torn, but it had taken me on a circuit of the world by the time I was nine years old, in a wide variety of cultures and living conditions. From the beginning of my life I have lived in the global village, in conditions of both comfort and economic hardship, in the company of people who are Asian, African, European and American, whose faiths are Christian, Jewish, Moslem, Buddhist or none, and whose work has ranged from domestic servant to university Vice Chancellor. Such experience makes for people who do not belong anywhere, but who can fit everywhere, while equipping them with a multitude of experiences, attitudes and skills that are useful when running a project like Maths in Work. And as is well known, the experience of being a refugee from a lost war can instil powerful feelings about social injustices and the motivation to amend them. Maths in Work and my previous work in special education were about the mathematical education of underdogs.

Through my work in curriculum development in special schools, I evolved a complete rejection of the idea of any person prejudging the eventual intellectual development of any other person. Through Maths in Work I learned to respect more than ever the skills of those usually classified and treated as unskilled, and by the time I had finished researching Common Threads, my mild feminism was rather less mild. Like many working women I have been hurt by harassment and marginalised by power groups within my own working hierarchy, and I remain appalled at much utterly masonic behaviour still evident in mathematics education. All these influences feed my motivating belief that mathematics goes on mainly in people's heads, that everyone has one of these, and that several heads are better than one when it comes to tackling a problem. I do not subscribe to the argument that widening access to mathematics, or any other knowledge, somehow dilutes that knowledge or 'lowers its standards', any more than I believe that when a few more people sit in the sunshine they dilute it for those already there.

In a piece of work that consciously, though not perversely, woollies the edges of disciplines and concepts, there can be no tight definitions. To argue definitions for each of the concepts that the book considers would require another book. The best I can do for *mathematics* is something like 'the ability to abstract patterns and handle them symbolically'. *Gender* is now well and widely defined in the literature as referring to social conditioning or social expectations that may include biology but are not determined by it. The meaning of *patriarchy*, originally the socio-legal status of the Classical male over his family, has changed since the granting of legal rights to married women, and is now used to describe the 'fatherly' controls of commerce, economics or politics that act to female disadvantage. By *hegemony* I mean the successful way in which a dominant group manages to maintain its position while unifying potentially different interests within its own ranks, thus creating allies and persuading them that the dominant view is universal and best, even when it works to the allies' disadvantage. In my years of running Maths in Work I found that *skill* has a multiplicity of meanings, all with behaviourist overtones that I reject, but which I use casually. The word *numeracy* drives me to despair, for it is overloaded with nineteenth century values and assumptions. It is widely used in practice to mean pencil and paper sums and as such is reputed by many who should know better, notably politicians and industrialists, to be the basis of mathematics. Chiefly because of the way it has too often been taught, it comes across to me as the opposite of the relaxed ability to understand and deal with the uses and abuses of number that it should be. Finally, *mathematics educators* are people who are professionally concerned with the learning and teaching of mathematics. The cumbersome category label includes mathematics teachers and lecturers but also those who do research in the many disciplines that try to understand the learning of it. Thus a mathematics educator like me need not be a mathematician: I came into the field to find out what it is about mathematics that makes it difficult to learn.

Though the book takes a strong personal line – and the reader will detect where the voice of frustrated experience may have overstated its case – I have received much professional help and support. During the tours I met hundreds of exceptional people often working under very difficult conditions and feel honoured to have done so – but there were far too many for me to name here.

In the preparation of the text I am particularly grateful to Pat Drake and Leo Rogers who read drafts of Chapters 4 and 2 respectively and gave me the benefit of their advice. Mrs Joan Glancy, Headmistress of North London Collegiate School kindly gave her permission to use the School's archive, and read Chapter 4.

To Anna Davin, I record particular thanks for her advice, encouragement and the loan of many books. Anne Watson, and the Association of Teachers of Mathematics, kindly gave me permission to quote, in Chapter 7, from the Association's journal, *Mathematics Teaching.* Will Morony generously gave his permission for me to quote from his feedback after the visit of Common Threads, in Chapter 9. As well as my professional debt to Teresa Smart, acknowledged in my citation of her work in Chapter 10, I am grateful for consistent, supportive friendship in trying times. While I was preparing this book my life was more than usually stressed by another expectation on women's work, that of carer, and I am deeply grateful to my brother Ken Alexander and my sister Bernice Jones, the other two thirds of the war-torn trio, for their time-honoured and characteristic appearance in time of trouble, to share the load. I am enormously grateful too, to my multi-talented friend and builder Lisa Ridley who deconstructed and reconstructed parts of my new home as I worked.

All my work leading up to and supporting the Common Threads tour was done in or from the University of London Institute of Education where I was privileged to be a Research Officer in the Department of Mathematics, Statistics and Computing under the support and guidance of Professors Celia Hoyles and Harvey Goldstein. My time at the Institute of Education was the happiest and most productive of my career in mathematics education, and I am immensely grateful to this lively and demanding institution for its professional hospitality and support, the daily contact it provides with people from all walks of life and from all corners of the world, its technical and media services and its excellent library and staff. The latter includes Stephen Pickles whose knowledge of the archive was extremely helpful. Finally, although she bears no responsibility for its contents, I dedicate this book to Marion Walter, a brilliant mathematics educator and a good friend, whose gentle nagging made me write it and place it in the hands of my ever patient publisher, Gillian Klein and her skilled editors, Jack and Stella Hyams.

Special Acknowledgement

I am grateful to the University of London Institute of Education for my Visiting Fellowship during the period of the Common Threads tours overseas, and for a grant towards helping with the production of this book. The Institute of Education however carries no responsibility for its contents.

Chapter 1

The Gendering of Needlework

Introduction

There is nothing in the biology of the Western European male that
prevents him making his own trousers. The idea that there should be
some biological disposition, or some social necessity for him to do such a
thing is ludicrous. Yet for hundreds of years, the equivalent idea for
women was seen to be so natural that it came to define their very femininity, and to justify every sort of social, economic and intellectual constraint placed upon them. By the time education for the masses became a
reality, sewing so dominated the schooling of girls that it caused distortions in their education that have effects to this day.

Women, Cloth and Economies

In the Mediterranean regions of the world, making cloth and weaving
baskets has been women's work for 20 000 years (Barber, 1994). Such
work consists largely of making perishables, and it becomes invisible in
the decay of passing time. Modern ethnographic methods of archaeology
no longer discard the small scraps that do survive however, but preserve
them and reproduce them in the technology of their time to reveal
considerable details of the lives and work of the people who made them.
Exploration and reproduction of designs woven into textiles can retrace
patterns of thought in action, for making textiles is not a mindless activity.
Woven textiles have a particular structure of crossed threads, that dictates
which patterns can be made by eye and which have to involve skills like
tallying or counting. Weavings of 3000 years ago, preserved in mud in
what is now Switzerland, show sophisticated geometric designs of
'stripes, checkers, triangles: braided fringes, knotted fringes, bead work
and fancy edges' (Barber, 1994:91), systematic work that requires
systematic thought. It also requires considerable time. Until the last two
or three hundred years, most items of clothing worn by most people were
the result of such hard, time-consuming and mindful labour. Until the
arrival of the sewing machine, and for long afterwards, every hour that

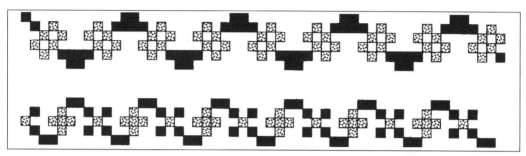

Figure 1: 'Thought in action'. Systematic
patterns worked in textiles, over many centuries.

Top: Design found on a neolithic linen cloth in
Switzerland. After Wayland Barber (1994:92)

Middle: Traditional cross stitch designs from the
Holy Land, two of many recorded by Heinz Edgar
Kiewe (1964). Many of these designs were
revived by Victorian cross stitch embroiderers.

Bottom: From designs worked by Hannah Canting
in 1691, on a sampler now in the Fitzwilliam
Museum, Cambridge.

could be spared of a woman's daylight hours was spent on one textile activity or another.

Male weavers appear towards the end of the bronze age, weaving for prestige and for profit, and men entered the textiles business in a big way in the late second or early first century BC, in work that is associated with towns, and the beginnings of urban specialisation (Barber, 1994). The first differentiations of male and female work with cloth were economic, and as economies developed, so work of women began the long process of being rendered less visible to contemporary eyes.

The home-based economies of the Middle Ages were dominated by cloth making; cloth for domestic use, or for surpluses to be sold as a side-line, or cloth made for commercial disposal in the workshop that was the clothmaker's home. Whether in workshop, or farm or field, men and women worked side by side in economic partnership, for there were no independent people: everyone's work was directed inwards to the economy of the household, or outwards to the lord of the manor, town government or the monarch (O'Day, 1992:179). Marriage was an economic arrangement, a property relationship to which the woman brought a dower, however small, and domestic skills, and the man brought physical support and provision for widowhood (O'Day, 1992: 182). The role of women in the household or outside it, was as important as that of men, indeed it was believed impossible for a man to head a household successfully without a wife, whereas it was regarded as per- fectly possible for a widow to continue to run it and the farm or business, without remarrying. The Guilds that controlled economic life made special arrangements for such *femmes soles*.

All the professional work of the workshops of medieval trades was organised through the Guilds. As religious and fraternal organisations these were a survival from Roman times and they retained their religious character when they assumed their closer connections with trade, com- merce and the crafts in the eleventh and twelfth centuries. As hard- headed business organisations, they knew well that women's work was essential in the economy, even though they gave it no formal recognition, for it was seen as underpinning the economic function of husband or father. Womanhood was always, in Hufton's nice phrase (1995:501) 'refracted through a male prism.' Even where Guild regulations expressly excluded women from participation in a trade, they regarded this un- professional labour as a matter of course, and made exceptions for wives and daughters (Power, 1975: 55). As the Guild system developed, the wife's role continued to be both complementary to the husband's and an economic necessity, though she remained socially subordinate. Thus, though a Guild might require a workshop master to be married, as a guarantee that the business would be run both efficiently and with impeccable morality, and though a wife and daughter were expected to take part in workshop activities, the labour of women was the first to be dispensed with when jobs were needed by men (Hufton, 1995:63). The main reason given was that of today, that women's wages were low and the threat of undercutting was very real.

It seems that women were only rarely admitted as full members of guilds in their own right, and never to the rungs of the hierarchy that determined policy. According to Power (1975:60), references to women as masters in guilds do exist, and regulations for *femmes couvertes* (those 'covered' by their husband's craft) make it clear that married women practised crafts independently, but it likely that they were wives or widows, and shared only in the Guilds' social activities. Even in textiles trades exclusively in the hands of women, there is no evidence of their recognition as a craft. This is especially so in the case of the silk industry (Power, 1975:61) where silk-women took apprentices and registered their indentures in the usual way, becoming sufficiently strong to petition the Crown against the invasion of the trade by Lombards. Power suggests that a reason for the absence of a silkworker's guild could be the number of bye industries in which a woman worked, for in addition to their duties to the husband's, brother's, or father's work, women made and sold, or bought and sold, everything that anyone would want to buy. As Hufton remarks of a later period (1995:494), a farmer's wife could also be a lace maker, a commercial spinner, a maker of gloves or shoes, but she would still classify herself as a farmer's wife. Under such circumstances a woman's work in a particular trade may have been for a supplementary wage, and it was unlikely that she would have had time, even if she had had the inclination, for the ceremonies and rituals that accompany the processes of the building of masculine power hierarchies. There were already considerable differences in gender and power relations in the textiles industries.

In the lay workshops where the famous embroidery of *Opus Anglicanum* was carried out, differences in gender and power seem to have begun when increased demand brought greater capitalism, though there is little evidence that women were pushed out of the craft altogether. The embroidery workshops continued to employ women, though by the end of the fourteenth century the Guilds had been reconstructed and the more powerful and exclusive livery companies formed. Women were still not barred from the workshops, but increasing regulation circumscribed their access. As the companies became more rigidly hierarchical, the number of amateur women workers outside them rose, but the companies still controlled the trades. Professional male embroiderers, protected by their livery, continued to receive commissions and were supplied through trades associated with the work, for example the gold thread that they needed. The production of metal thread had been in the hands of women, but was now forbidden to all except but members of the Company of Gold Wire Drawers: membership of the company may still have been possible for women, but specialised training and other privileges were not, and women were beaten down to the ranks of the sweated industries.

The purpose of the Guilds was control, control of the craft or trade, its standards and training, and the machinery, literally and figuratively, of its economic power. Control of larger looms, too big for a cottage, controls who is de-skilled by their use, and the history of the textiles industry records the details of how such control always sidelines and downgrades the work of women (Holland, 1991 and Cockburn, 1985 for example). These processes took longer in the craft of knitting than in the crafts of weaving however, for machines for knitting took longer to develop high speed and reliable sophistication than did those of weaving.

There is debate about the earliest knitting, confused by myth, wishful thinking and the existence of textiles very similar to knitting in appearance, but different in construction (Rutt, 1987). In England, knitters were making caps by the thirteenth century, but there was no mass development until the manufacture of drawn steel wire in the days of Elizabeth I made it possible to produce knitting needles of consistent diameter and smoothness (Rutt, 1987:65). Knitting then centred on stocking making, an activity that was still large part of women's domestic life in the first half of the twentieth century. Originally stockings had been cut and sewn from woven cloth, but such material and such construction cannot take the continual movement of ankles without wrinkling, nor remain snugly fitting round the rest of the leg, for woven cloth lacks the capacity of knitting to reform after stretching. Knitted silk stockings imported from Spain were immensely flattering to the Elizabethan male calf, but local wool provided a cheaper and warmer alternative for those who could not afford the bought articles. Elizabethan hose included both stockings and breeches and both were knitted with mathematical ingenuity in a range of colours that were to shock Puritan taste. Grey or blue were the preferred colours and later 'blue stocking' became an epithet of academic women, not so much for their sober behaviour as for the eccentricity of the eighteenth century author Benjamin Shillingfleet, who arrived at one of the literary ladies' clubs of the day, wearing his comfortable worsted stockings, instead of formal black silk and leaving the memory of the episode attached to the name of the clubs (Rutt, 1987:84).

Although knitted hose dominated the knitting market, many other equally ingenious garments were made including gloves, caps, sleeves, gaiters, mittens and socks, indeed all the small, warm serviceable garments of working people, most skilfully fashioned. Knitting was a widespread occupation of poor people and a significant part of the country's economy. By the end of the Tudor period, it occupied nearly half the spare time of Midland cottage farmers and Thirsk, quoted by Rutt (1987:77) records that during the last third of the sixteenth century, about 200 000 knitters in England and Wales were producing about 20 million pairs of stockings for the home market. In the seventeenth century the export trade built up to about one and a half million pairs a year, with England recognised as the leading producer.

The advent of the knitting frame, and the incorporation of the Guild of Framework Knitters in 1657 did not kill the craft of hand-knitting for several centuries, neither did it do it on its own. Although Defoe reported in 1704 that 'men on the knitting frame could perform that in a day which could otherwise employ a poor woman eight or ten days' (Rutt, 1987:86), the early framework knitters barely competed with a good hand-knitter who could make six pairs of stockings a week: up to about 1750, the speed advantage was not enough to make serious competition. Neither could a frame match the quality of hand-knitting, at least not until the advent of high-quality machine fibres, nor could machines respond swiftly to the frequent changes in fashion of the time.

Although in some districts and in some seasons knitting became a full time occupation, it was also a perfect side-line activity. Like hand spinning, it was portable, could be done while doing something else, could be taken up seasonally for example when there was no agricultural work, could be learned by the very young yet still be done by the elderly and infirm, and it could also be done in the dark, saving the expense of candles. Both men and women knitted, indeed Henry Brougham, campaigning for parliament in the Yorkshire Dales in 1826, noted women labouring in the fields while their canny menfolk 'sat knitting stockings under the hedges, basking in the sun' (Rutt, 1987:102). The fact that men knitting is recorded as some-thing unusual, however, implies that the craft was generally gendered. The Dales were known to be exceptional, and a fuller gendering of knitting took place later in the nineteenth century at a time when the feminisation of the domestication of women was at its height. Knitting had always been an occupation of the poor and remained a domestic necessity long after rates of pay finally became so low as to make knitting for sale uneconomic, even for the very poorest. Not least because young children could be taught to knit stockings for sale, it became a strongly urged task in measures to alleviate child poverty.

The textiles work of women (and of young children) was always essential in the economy but had no intrinsic value to the societies that needed it, for the economic status of women made what they did marginal, however skilled it was. The more modest the family, the more essential to it was the labour and ingenuity of its womenfolk. They were, again in the words of Hufton (1995:495), 'at the centre of the economy of makeshifts', a whole gender full of unacknowledged problem-solvers.

Women, Cloth and Social Judgment

Church and aristocracy were often at odds with each other and among themselves, but between them they established women as subject to men in economy, marriage and law. In real life, a woman could run a business but marriage demeaned her: she may have had some protection under the law, but it was still possible, as late at the nineteenth century for a man to sell his wife for cash or beat her in public (Klein, 1946:8). Recorded comments on women's reactions and on their lives exist are rare but, as we have seen, much can be deduced from reworking the structure of decoration in their textiles (Barber, 1994). Recently too there has been some published work on the generally unregarded intellectual skills without which it would be impossible to weave a basket or knit a sock (Gerdes, 1986 and 1995, Harris, 1987). Through embroidered images, Parker (1984) has traced the history of the development of ideals of femininity, how women reacted to them and how they came to dominate masculine perceptions of what women should be, to the extent that needlework came to represent not only women's economic invisibility but their intellectual vacuity.

Of the few items of early English art that survived the iconoclasm with which the Church of England was born, the clerical vestments of *Opus Anglicanum* are probably the most complete. From the tenth century, this richly worked embroidery of silk and metal threads, pearls, jewels and beaten gold, on linen and velvet, was a leading English art with high export value, and a status that was shared with painting and sculpture. Under commissions from both Church and nobility, it was worked by both men and women in religious houses and lay workshops. Early medieval art was the Church's exclusive property and was used to demonstrate spiritual and secular power and the solemnity of its liturgy. The very form and substance of the embroidery however, reveals conflicts of interest between those of the ecclesiastical patrons and those of the embroiderers themselves (Parker, 1984:50). The images worked on the copes had a strong narrative line, intended to convey meaning to illiterate congregations, well-versed in interpreting pictures, and the opulent, light-catching materials and three-dimensional techniques of the embroidery of

Opus Anglicanum showed the images to maximum advantage. In the gothic period the embroiderers seem to have had some leeway in the designs they sewed, for in spite of the Church's attempts to ensure that depictions of women's lives conformed to its own ideals, the women themselves worked into them some of their own daily concerns.

Most copes were dominated by pictures of the Virgin Mary, in images that could be read in several ways: ascetic virgin, idealisation of women under patriarchal authority, confirmation of feudal hierarchy or fertility symbol. The difficult and dangerous business of childbirth was women's work and the expertise of midwives was an honoured theme of the women who worked the pictures. Favourite apocryphal figures were the midwives Zelenie and Salomie who attended the divine birth and testified to the miraculous virginity after the event, but such images however placed the midwives in too powerful a position for Church authority. In one of their periodic affirmations of authority, Zelenie and Salomie were banished, and licensed midwives, no longer independent operators, were made directly responsible to the Church hierarchy. The equally popular image of the feisty St Margaret, who hacked her way out of the belly of a dragon to become the patron saint of childbirth proved more enduring, though Popes had tried to ban her too. She survived in the symbolic characteristics of womanhood of which the Church did approve, not the tough contender with masculine aggression in human or dragon form, but in chastity, humility, virtue, meekness and mildness.

The embroidery workshops of the Renaissance still worked images of Mary and St Margaret, but the world had changed and a more scientific age was changing its view of womanhood. No longer was woman seen as a mistake of nature, but a mirror to the perfectibility of mankind, a deviation from the male masterpiece (Hufton, 1995:40). In defining him, much of the debate concerned differences between the sexes and the proper role of women in man's maintenance. A man of public affairs required the balance of a properly domesticated woman, he of the world, she out of it. Protestant theology glorified marriage and love within it, but by subcontracting patriarchy to the husband, circumscribed the wife's love as humble duty to the head of the family. Much literature was devoted to how a woman should behave. No longer was it 'becoming for women to handle weapons, ride, play the game of tennis, wrestle or take part in other sports that are suitable for men, for as Castiglione himself had remarked ; it is well for a woman to have a certain soft and delicate tenderness, with an air of feminine sweetness in every movement' (Parker, 1984:62). The image of an ideal woman sewing or spinning at the hearth, now included the head bowed humbly and delicately over her needle, a less robust, more submissive image of femininity than that of the previous partner in trade. Some women still worked in embroidery work-shops, where Mary was still enthroned on copes, but now depicted feeding the baby. St Margaret, the erstwhile dragon slayer, is now a help-less young girl about to be martyred.

The medieval workshop view of embroidery had been of patient, persistent and skilled labour within a working group of both designers and embroiderers, both male and female. There had been no distinction of status between art and craft. The Renaissance cult of the individual however, developed the view of the artist as an intellectual working swiftly and alone, fired by some divine or less high-powered inspiration. The new economy and domestic philosophy now rendered the female embroiderer an amateur, working at home at one of her domestic tasks, literally 'for love'. Embroidery began to evoke a fresh version of femininity that pro-vided evidence of the status of the household. For individual women it suggested modesty, but for the household it provided a man of affairs with an appropriate grandeur.

> Embroidery combined the humility of needlework with rich stitchery. It connoted opulence and obedience. It ensured that women spent long hours at home, retired in private, yet it made a public statement about the household's position and economic standing. (Parker, 1984:64)

To hang on their tapestries, the wealthy required paintings; painters' fees rose and artists began to be able to free themselves from direct com-mission and aspire to the class to which the amateur embroiderers belonged, that associated with intellectual in contrast to manual skills, and with individualism. For the women of the class though, their own creative work was seen not as emanating from artistic intellect but as illustrating a feminine presence, for embroidery, now separated from art, represented the virtues of femininity. Professional embroiderers still worked but in what was now perceived as craft. Art became increasingly masculine and powerful, embroidery a public craft or an unintellectual, feminine, and purely domestic art.

These freshly defined social and intellectual differences were enhanced and maintained in the training of the next generations, for that is the socialising role of education. Upper class families may have given their daughters the classical education they gave their sons, but for girls its expression was confined to the house, and it was distinguished from that of the boys by the requirement of needlework. Elizabethan domestic embroideries had represented flora and fauna through a limited range of stitches. The seventeenth century samplers of a girl's education became exercises in stitchery itself, with increasingly complex rows of symmetrical designs, every stitch systematically placed, representing stages in the training of a skill. A girls' impending domesticity began to be seen as a calling, for which sewing was disciplined preparation. With her moral control vested in her family, and a matter for the authority of her father as first reserve for her priest, moral sentiments were carefully stitched into the work. Embroidered pictures show Adam and Eve, Abraham and Sarah, standing with hands clasped, celebrating the new ideology of the conjugal bond. St Margaret and St Mary are replaced in religious embroidery by older biblical heroines and by contrasting views of womanhood. Parker (1984: 8) notes the choice of male workshop embroiderers of Delilah, Salome and Jezebel, and women amateur embroiderers of Judith, Sarah and Esther.

By the eighteenth century few women of the upper classes could escape an education in femininity through embroidery. No longer taught simply to differentiate a girl's from a boy's education, embroidery was now taught so as to inculcate obedience and patience, as girls sat quietly for long hours, their heads bowed over work whose technical complexity became submerged in the submissiveness it was expected to instil. To protest was to earn the label of a 'hoyting girl' a 'tomboy', though occasional complaint appears in the embroidery itself. 'Polly Cook did it' embroidered one child on her sampler 'and she hated every stitch she did in it' (Parker, 1984:132). Submissive femininity never came naturally to little girls, nor was it welcomed by their new, rather better educated elder sisters. Increasingly the concentration of so much time and effort on sewing was rejected both for the stereotype of femininity it perpetrated, and because the time spent on it kept women from better things. As Parker points out (1984:103), it became almost axiomatic that women in pursuit of a less trivial education in a more literate age, should first repudiate embroidery, thereby entering another gender trap, for extreme rejection meant siding with the masculine lobby now openly sneering at sewing because it was deemed mindless. The cycle of destructive stereotyping was well established. Women were expected to sew in compliant domesticity, then condemned for compliant domesticity because they sewed. Addison's Spectator was of course deliberately provocative on the subject, and it did not confine itself to the sewing needle. Addison's hero, Sir William Wimble, was a friend of Sir Roger de Coverley and one 'extremely well versed in all the little handicrafts of an idle man.' The eponymous wimp presented garters of his own making to various ladies and raised mirth by his frequent inquiries as to how well they wore' (Rutt, 1987:8).

With the arrival of Rousseau's Émile, and his trainee mate Sophie, embroidery acquired the symbolic dependence of the clinging vine. Sophie had all the characteristics of an appropriately mindless femininity, as defined by one whose influence on educational theory became pervasive. Her 'shame and modesty, love of embellishment and finery, the desire to please and be polite to others' were, said Rousseau, entirely natural (Parker, 1984:123). The manufacture of her finery is also entirely natural for

> dress making, embroidery, lace making come by themselves... This spontaneous development extends easily to drawing, because the latter art is not difficult – simply a matter of taste: but at no cost would I want them to learn landscape, even less the human figure. Foliage, fruits, flowers and drapery is all they need to know to create their own embroidery pattern, if they can't find one that suits them. (Rousseau quoted by Parker, 1984:124).

Thus was Sophie's model brain emptied of any complicity in the work of her hands, in the skill above all others that made her feminine. Reared only to please a man, the height of her intellectual achievement became a sly seductiveness. As Hufton (1995:501) notes, it was still a fact that women required husbands, but methods of getting them had now changed from practical planning for a joint economic future, to dissi-mulation and animal cunning.

The model of domestic idyll presented by Émile and Sophie wrong-footed women again, for so much concentration on the feminine by the feminine was soon to be decreed an excessive vanity. An imposition of guilt was laid upon those required by their prescribed nature to embroider. Any amount of embroidery at all was too much for Mary Wollstonecraft, whose tart response to Rousseau was an argument of nurture not nature. Other women reformers were more circumspect. Hannah More's way out of the guilt trap was to persuade women of the virtues of needlework, but carried out for somebody else. Embroidery for moral purposes joined the other virtues of femininity, and prepared the way for the excesses of the Victorian angel of the home and her interminable Berlin work.

By the nineteenth century embroidery and femininity were fused as one. 'Women embroidered because they were naturally feminine, and were feminine because they naturally embroidered' (Parker, 1984:18). The eighteenth century had asserted a femininity that was natural, with embroidery as its natural expression, but it had at least allowed women some satisfaction in it. Now femininity through the needle had heavy moral implications. It was to be performed as duty to husband and home, as moral crusade to rescue the poor from what was seen as their own inadequacies, or as a solace, a comfort rag against the unspecified, weakening complaints to which Victorian ladies were so prone. Sewing was a necessary characteristic through which a girl learned to take and endure her place in the dual hierarchy of class and sex. Dr Gregory John spelled it out in his *Father's Legacy to his Daughters*:

> The intention of you being taught needlework, knitting and such like is not
> on account of the intrinsic value of all you can do with your hands, which is
> trifling... but to enable you to fill up, in a tolerably agreeable way, some of the
> many solitary hours you must necessarily pass at home. (quoted by Klein,
> 1946:20)

It was charitable and moral concern for the poor that brought knitting,
the traditional practice of the poor, into the drawing room in a newly
feminised version. Ladies began knitting in the eighteenth century, both
for sale and for charity but in the nineteenth there was an explosion of
activity sustaining an enormous amount of published advice and instruction. Knitting suited the ethos of the time, that of a high moral tone made
suitable for the drawing room by the invention of a new style of holding
the needles. The fast and efficient method, used by knitters who knit for
a living, is to hold the needles under the palms, but this involves much
coarse movement of the elbows. By holding the needles like pens, the
work is slowed down considerably but pretty hands and fingers are
displayed to much advantage. Although now a drawing room activity,
knitting never earned the epithets of frivolity that were placed on other
drawing room needlework however, for its products were nearly always
made to be immediately useful. Even the knitting and refooting of stockings, the stock in trade of working-class knitters, now became a universal
skill. Knitting was certainly more feminised but its gendering was rather
more subtle than the symbolisms of the drawing room and the increasing
exploitation of women and girls in factories and workshops.

In the twentieth century, male apologia for knitting continues to
emphasise the acceptance of the femininity of knitting by stressing the
work of the few men who confess to doing it, and who earn fame not only
for the skill but for their unusualness. James Norwood the designer, is
described by Rutt (1987:151) as 'the strongest single influence in British
knitting during the twenty-five years after the second world war.' With
masculine authority he was able to establish, at least in part, that there is
more to knitting than the by-then universal assumption of a trivial,
feminine pursuit. He could also get away with being 'colourful and self-
centred, with more than a little of the showman about him' a characteristic that is unlikely to have been tolerated so benignly in a woman.
Rutt also quotes a number of male knitters who, like himself are clergy-
men, noting that the reason that Geoffrey Fisher, Archbishop of Canterbury from 1945-1961 had his sons taught knitting was because it is
'reflective and repetitive. Whenever you are engaged in doing a pure
repetitive thing, your mind can reflect on life' (Rutt, 1987:157). Reflection can take on more sinister connotations in a woman however: there
are dual standards even in knitting. According to Freud, such reflection in

women is merely daydreaming, and induces in her 'the dispositional hypnoid states' that render her 'prone to hysteria' (Parker, 1986:11). Women cannot be allowed to be thoughtful.

For nearly a thousand years, changing views of femininity, reflecting social and economic change and the perennial distrust of woman unconfined, gradually tightened round women like a noose. In the progress of Parker's detailed review, there is an accumulation of epithets that describes the masculine view of what the feminine should be, as demonstrated by her needlework. In summary alphabetical order they label a truly feminine woman as one who is chaste, delicate, dependent, devoted, docile, domestic, dutiful, frail, frivolous, humble, innocent, meek, modest, moral, obedient, patient, pure, sedentary, seductive, selfless, shameful, silent, spiritual, still, subjugated, subservient, subordinated, trivial, vain and virtuous. Records of the feelings of women themselves include at least some of the distress their heavy repressions caused them. They suffer from: ambivalence, boredom, debilitation, demoralisation, distress, ennui, guilt, hate, intellectual starvation, lassitude, living death, loneliness, melancholy, monotony, penance, unhappiness and weariness. Although there are claims by many needlewomen that the work is satisfying, the cumulative stereotype empties it of any mental stimulation or intellectual reward. In the work itself, there is little recorded analysis of anything systematic in design without which most of the work could not have been done, or of ingenuity of technique, or of skill in construction, but rather a blanket denial, within the stereotype itself, that such things are possible. When their existence is undeniable, then the stereotype decrees that they are of no account.

Women, Cloth and Work

From about the sixteenth century, embroidery was increasingly a drawing room activity: outside the drawing room, women sewed and knitted because they had to. By the mid fifteenth century, the textiles industries had become organised under capitalist clothiers, employing out-workers in their own homes, providing them with the raw materials and collecting the products. Until it began to pass into factories at the end of the eighteenth century, cloth production remained one of the chief occupations of women, and they remained involved in all stages of it. Spinning was both a domestic occupation and a side industry, weaving still a home industry, and even in grand houses, it was still usual for garments and for household linen to be made at home by women of all classes. Economic life continued to centre on marriage. Regardless of perennial imbalances in the male-to-female population, marriage remained the prescribed goal of all girls, and their young lives consisted in learning the skills and acquiring the dower on which it depended. A girl's skill with a needle was an essential domestic requirement, and it also increased her chances of developing an economic sideline. However little she brought to her marriage, she always brought some cloth and the skills necessary for repairing it: though the husband might bring more assets in money, cattle or kind, towards helping stock a small farm, it was unthinkable to marry a woman who could not spin, knit or sew.

From the late Middle Ages, the largest category of female employment available to young women until after the first world war, was domestic service. Skill with a needle, along with good presentation, a reputation for honesty and the ability to do the shopping, could improve a girl's chances of entering service at a higher level than scrub or scullery maid. In the sixteenth and seventeenth centuries a good mistress would see to the improvement of her maids' skills but by the eighteenth, pressure for jobs made this responsibility unnecessary. Many of the initiatives of charity schools aimed to take over this responsibility for training servants, in an enterprise that made girls employable but offered them little else, and both employers and future husbands shared the charity school recipe for what a young woman should be: sober, industrious, thrifty, obedient, competent, clean and neat.

> The girl who could present herself as the product of such an establishment, with needlework skills attested to in sampler or specimen darn, with her hair tucked neatly under her cap, her apron cleanly starched and the appropriate 'yes ma'am' at her command, was on the way to success. (Hufton, 1995:83)

As lighter boned corsets, elaborate underwear and silk drawers replaced the leather stays and flannel petticoats of ages that never washed, demand for girls who could sew increased. The fashionable demand for millinery, loose mantuas and complex undergarments provided work indeed, but created pauper trades for those with no capital to set up their own workshops. Hufton paints a picture of the beginnings of the gendering and down-grading of urban working women that was to become the sordid problem of the nineteenth century for 'the seamstresses and makers of stays and bodices, of bone lace and embroidery, of lingerie and shawls, of gloves and bonnets and lace caps, and all those who provided the paraphernalia of a girls on a swing in a *fête galante* were towns-women' (Hufton, 1995:94). Though tailors clung to their monopoly of outer garments which are relatively immune to changes in fashion, they abandoned claims to making dresses and mantuas to the female dressmakers whose role was assured by royal precedent. Even if she did not have a formal apprenticeship, a dressmaker would certainly spend a couple of apprentice years in a workshop on a non-resident basis, and her parents would either have to pay for it or accept that she would not be paid while training. 'Even when experienced, very few, unless patronised by the high aristocracy, made a comfortable living' (Hufton, 1995:94).

In some areas of the country, the proto-industrialisation of the old cottage industries offered girls a greater diversity of employment, though less security than domestic service. Women and children were always the cheapest labour in the transitional textile industries that bridged agrarian and industrial economies. In the pre-industrial economy of cottage industry textiles work, the male head of the household was its supervisor and had had considerable autonomy over the hours worked and how it was apportioned. The advent of factory-based machinery however brought with it a realignment of traditional jobs. As work that had previously been done in homes shifted to factories, male authority went with it, with a man frequently employing his wife or other family members as assistants: in such a way the centuries old work of spinning became a man's job in one generation. This control by men over the occupation of spinning was consolidated in the early nineteenth century by the development of unions and the exclusion of women from membership, training and jobs (Holland, 1991:232).

It is not easy to assess the economic activity of women in the nineteenth century, for the process of industrialisation affected different groups of people in different ways, but reasonable patterns can be deduced (Purvis, 1989: 26). Skill with a needle was ubiquitous and domestic service was still the most common employment by far, followed by millinery, dress-making and stay-making together in one category, and cotton and cotton goods manufacture in the next. Textiles work was often all that was available to women trapped in their homes by young children, elderly relatives and the new concept of a husband's family wage. The very mark of their femaleness, their assumed skill with a needle, became a snare that kept working women locked in a vicious cycle of poverty. A married woman with dependents, previously part of a home-based, mixed sex, home production unit, was now employed as an individual at take-in rates notoriously among the lowest.

Widows and single mothers, as single wage earners could fare worse. For many, slop work, the taking in of sewing, was the only option. Its essence was the contract system, with orders given to the contractor asking the lowest price, and filled by women under the system appropriately called 'sweating'. In 1852 it was claimed that three of every four of all the garments sold in the country were made under the slop system (Purvis, 1989:33). Outwork, like lace-making, knitting or slopwork suffered all

Figure 2: 'A dress for an occasion could and did not put pressures on workshop sewing women that could quite literally, and far from seldom, kill them'. *Punch* Cartoon of July 4th 1863.

the abuses that kept its pay below poverty limits: mislabelled unskilled, treated as casual, known to be overstocked, it was both unorganised by trades unions and unprotected by law.

An unmarried woman could, in theory, fare better in the sewing workshops, but the range of needlework available to them carried its own forms of constraint. Apprentices had to pay for their place; day work required long hours, was poorly paid and was precarious, but both offered a marginally better deal than that of 'improvers,' often country women working in a town workshop to improve their skills, for a limited period but for no pay at all (Purvis, 1989:32). All grades of needlework in both millinery or dressmaking shared excessively long hours. The Workshops Act of 1867 imposed some control over hours but was not always effective. As late as 1896, when a statutory ten-hour limit was imposed, employers could still impose overtime at no extra pay. Factory workers in cotton mills could achieve better pay, though silk workers earned less, and hours there too were punishingly long. An 1844 Act of Parliament limited them to 12 and forbade night work, and Acts of 1850 and 1853 achieved a ten hour day for women and children, but there were frequent abuses.

Such abuses of women's work is rendered more poignant by the fact that many employers in the sweated fashion workshops were women themselves, with just enough capital to set up on their own and survive, if only by exploiting other women who desperately needed the work. It was in the dress-makers' and milliners' workshops that the crudest exploitation of women by women occurred, for they supplied fashions at the best price they could get for the lowest outlay. Before the arrival of sewing machines all the processes of constructing the multiple layers of long-skirted garments were made by hand, and for long afterwards so were all the processes of decoration with lace, ribbons, frills and flounces, and of fixings with buttons and button holes, hooks and eyelets, tapes and laces. It is difficult for late twentieth century women not brought up to do fine backstitch, to recognise both the skills and the time it requires to work just one accurately place and spaced, undecorated seam and to neatly finish the cloth on each side of it so that it does not fray. Very rich women still pay Paris couturiers five figure sums for one garment, not just for the name but for the skill of their handmaking. A ball dress for a Victorian lady, even a simpler house-dress, required a total of days and weeks of hand-sewing. A wedding, or a collection dresses for some other occasion, could and did put pressures on workshop sewing women that could quite literally, and far from seldom, kill them (Neff, 1996).

Though there may be little enough hard evidence on the work of women that has survived from the Middle Ages, and though it would be wrong to assume that the times saw complete female independence, it is difficult not to see a pattern of spiralling downwards of women's work opportunities, in parallel with the constraints of feminine domesticity, both controlled by the tool that above all others makes the public perception of woman as woman. With the double-bind circularity that occurs so frequently in the history of girls and women, a girl could not get by without her needle skills even though they condemned her to a life of economic deprivation, social submission and intellectual inferiority.

It comes as no surprise therefore that, by the time the State belatedly began its interest in the education of all its children, it simply endorsed the established view of the day, already in place in the charity and Church schools, that the education of girls both as future women and as future workers should be to sew. In a society that believed that social stability depended on proper relationships between social classes, the femininity identified by needlework was social class specific. What was considered as appropriate, relevant and attainable for middle class ladies was certainly seen as inappropriate, irrelevant and unattainable for working class women. As the supply of cheap servants grew, the lady of the house that employed them became less directly involved in household management and more a manager of personnel. With this role, and increased leisure in which to pursue it, she could see herself as expert in the lives of working class women, whom it was her moral and philanthropic duty to improve. Selected characteristics of working-class life; poverty, squalor, poor housing conditions, lack of hygiene, and intermittent patterns of work, were seen as characteristics of individuals themselves. 'Overall, the image of the working class woman, as articulated by the middle classes, was that of a degraded human being' (Purvis, 1989: 64). As such, working class women presented a dilemma, which the middle classes resolved by an appropriate modification of the ideals already applied to themselves.

Thus came about the ideal of the 'good worker' for the working class girl, and the 'good wife' and 'good mother' for the working class woman. The good worker was of course a good domestic servant, and her training was happily convenient and advantageous to her mistress: her waged labour remained where it had always been concealed, in the most suitable place for it, the home. A steady supply of drudges, albeit trainable drudges, was assured: and the skills acquired during service would ensure that sound, middle class, domestic values would be transferred as a softening working-class influence when the trained servant later married. The good woman could necessarily sew, not embroider of course, but enough to keep her mistress' linen in order, or run up a pinafore for a child, and later to furnish her suitably humble home.

The whole scheme of things could have been laughed off by the robust, indeed regrettably coarse sense of humour of working-class women themselves, had it not been for the long tentacles of middle-class influence on the education of their daughters, for middle-class women were heavily involved in ideas of what the education of working-class girls should be, and in seeing them put into practice. So strong was the association of sewing with the right sort of femininity, and the right sort of femininity with domesticity, and domesticity with a girl's vocation in the natural scheme of things, that all that needed to be decided was what particular needlework was to be taught in the church schools to which the ladies subscribed. What working-class girls faced, when legislation at the end of the nineteenth century finally required them to attend schools of the church tradition, was the aftermath of a millennium of heavily gendered control attached to the one, consciously limited, skill that was permitted. Oozing with piety and loaded with their own learned guilt, the devisers and approvers of the curriculum for the country's girls, placed them in a double bind from which it was impossible to escape. The fact that they were biologically female and of a low economic and social order condemned them to a needlework curriculum that ensured their lack of intellectual progress, while their lack of intellectual progress justified both their femaleness and their social class.

References

Barber Elizabeth Wayland (1994) *Women's Work: The First 20 000 Years*. New York: Norton.

Cockburn Cynthia (1985) *Machinery of Dominance: Women, Men and Technical Know-How*. London: Pluto Press.

Gerdes Paulus (1986) How to Recognise Hidden Geometrical Thinking: A Contribution to the Development of Anthropological Mathematics. *For the Learning of Mathematics* Vol 6 No 2 June p 10-12.

Gerdes Paulus (1995) *Women and Geometry in Southern Africa*. Mozambique: Universidade Pedagógica.

Harris Mary (1987) An Example of Traditional Women's Work as a Mathematics Resource. *For the Learning of Mathematics*. Vol 7 No 3 November p 26-28.

Holland Janet (1991) The Gendering of Work. In Mary Harris (Ed) *Schools, Mathematics and Work*. Basingstoke: Falmer Press.

Hufton Olwen (1995) *The Prospect Before Her: A History of Women in Western Europe. Volume I 1500-1800*. London: Harper Collins.

Kieve Heinz Edgar (1964) *History of Folk Cross Stitch*. Nuremburg: Sebaldus-Verlag

Klein Viola (1946) *The Feminine Character. History of an Ideology*. London: Harper Collins.

Neff Wanda F (1996) (first published 1929) *Victorian Working Women. An Historical and Literary Study of Women in British Industries and Professions 1832-1850*. London: Frank Cass

O'Day Rosemary (1982) *Education and Society 1500-1800: Social Foundations of Education in Early Modern Britain*. Harlow: Longman.

Parker Rozsika (1984) *The Subversive Stitch*. London: The Women's Press.

Power Eileen (1975) *Medieval Women*. Edited by M M Postan. Cambridge: Cambridge University Press.

Purvis June (1989) *Hard Lessons: The Lives and Education of Working Class Women in Nineteenth Century England*. Cambridge: Polity Press.

Rutt Richard (1987) *A History of Hand Knitting*. London: Batsford.

Chapter 2

The Gendering of Mathematics

Introduction

English education in any formal sense, goes back 1500 years, and from the beginning it was by and for the Church. It was the Church that decided what education was and who should have it, and for long periods it was the Church who sanctioned what knowledge itself was. Until the twentieth century, even when it was not directly involved, the Church insisted on its right of supervision. Throughout this history, three strong distinctions that affect women, mathematics and work, have been maintained with varying degrees of clarity at any one time, but always with an underlying presence: that between speculative, academic and practical, vocational mathematics; that between the content of the education of the upper and lower social classes, and that between the education of males and females. All three were most hotly contended during the period in which education for the masses became a reality, and the Church view predominated. A mere 100 years later, the distinctions are still with us: the particular union of women, mathematics and work has a long and triply destructive past in which the notion of mathematics as the subject of middle and upper class men is very deeply embedded.

Mathematics and Education

Among the many minority Jewish sects of the Hellenistic world, one was pigeon-holed as Christianity by a Roman administrator of Antioch. Christianity developed its philosophy and practice in several centres on the Mediterranean rim over many years and with much contention, through a unique reconciliation of Hellenistic and Hebrew culture, experience and philosophy. The most influential early reconciliation for the development of Christian education, was that of Philo Judaeus of Alexandria (c25BC-50AD), by religion orthodox, by philosophy a Platonist. From the Judaic tradition he took the concern for extensive study of the scriptures and the possibility of it leading to direct revelation, together with the insistence on the family as the training ground for morality. From the Hellenistic tradition came the idea of a true, literate education as progression through the study of the Liberal Arts, towards *areté*, usually translated as 'virtue' but meaning something more like 'ideal value.'

In Philo's synthesis, Christian ideals became areté and the literary methods of the liberal curriculum the precursor to the study of the scriptures, through which two-fold revelation could be achieved, that of the bible itself and that of divine inspiration of individuals. Having no schools of its own, the early Church used the existing Hellenistic ones. There was of course a clash of values between those of the pagan culture and those of the new religion, but the latter were expected to be taught at home and by the Church, and to override all other values. For its religious education, the Church developed catechitical teaching and the preaching of the clergy, and in the monasteries it dealt with its own internal needs.

The number and content of the liberal arts changed over the centuries, but seven were formulated in about the middle of the first century BC, as a *trivium* of the three literary arts of grammar, rhetoric and dialectic, followed by the four subjects of the mathematical *quadrivium*: arithmetic, geometry, music and astronomy. Simply put, the quadrivium represented the most profound human thought of the time, while the trivium provided the wherewithal for speculation. The arithmetic of the quadrivium was the science of numbers for which Pythagoras had been honoured for raising it above the level of sordid commerce. Geometry was the abstract propositions, theorems and proofs of Euclid, certainly not the geodesy and metrics of the architect or artisan. Music was the science of interval, rhythm and acoustics founded in Pythagorean philosophy, and astronomy was speculative, but with a practical application and a tendency to astrology. Education through the liberal arts was for the social élite, and it remained disdainfully aloof from the more mechanical arts of those whose labours were of the world. Euclid became and remained the mark of a gentleman until well into the twentieth century.

To Platonists like Philo (and, as Davis and Hersh point out (1983: 231), most mathematicians still are Platonists most of the time), mathematics is still attributed features usually attributed only to God. The position leads to certain philosophical difficulties, not least that of challenge to God himself, for if mathematics has its own laws and powers, it either places limits on the power of God, or faces mankind with the unnerving possibility that the rules could be changed by divine whim. Philo had overcome this problem by arguing that God would suspend the physical laws of the universe in the case of a salutary miracle for example, but that there would be no point in changing the laws of thought and the laws of mathematics. Mathematics retains its special relationship.

Christianity was its own areté. In Hellenism, the thinking man's religion was what Marrou (1956: 320) calls 'the cult of the muses'. Every revival of the classical tradition, has been accompanied by an upsurge of neo-paganism and a Church reaction in restatement of its values but the Platonic aspiration in pure mathematics remains the achievement of a lasting work of art. 'If on occasion, a beautiful piece of pure mathematics turns out to be useful, so much the better. But utility as a goal is inferior to elegance and profundity.' (Davis and Hersh, 1983:86). In fact it is possible, and not infrequently done to retreat into statements about the beauty of mathematics rather than to confront the fact, also noted by Davis and Hersh (1983:87) that in a number of respects, it is harder to work in applications than in pure mathematics, for 'the stage is wider, the facts are more numerous and are more vague'. Regardless of the mathematical ability of the engineer with grease under his finger nails, he remains in the company of rude mechanics, in safe social distance from those who sit on the right hand of omniscience.

In the Western Christianity of the late Roman Empire, lay education was the Roman version of the liberal arts curriculum. For Rome, educational interest centred on the trivium; her interests in mathematics lay more in the direction of the mechanical arts. A version of the quadrivium was retrieved by Boethius and Cassiodorus, in a renaissance of their own day that tried to preserve at least some of the mathematics on which classical liberal education had been founded, but historians are scathing about its content. As works of mathematics, wrote Boyer (1985:12), Boethius' texts were no more than 'jejune and exceedingly elementary abbreviations of earlier classics' and 'of mathematics as a logical structure there is little trace.' Nevertheless it was almost all there was, and it eventually re-emerged in the post-graduate study of the medieval universities. Significantly for mathematics education however, and regardless of the reduction in the content of the quadrivium, what was confirmed within the institutions of those who defined and controlled knowledge, was mathematics as the way to truth, at the highest level of intellectual functioning, below direct revelation itself.

Versions of the mathematics of the mechanical arts also survived, but until recently they have been of little interest to historians of mathematics and of education, who tend to come from and speak to the liberal arts tradition. Some of the mathematics without which the great gothic cathedrals could not have been built, is to be found in the works of Vitruvius, architect, engineer and surveyor to the Emperor Augustus. As a man of the mechanical arts he had had little formal education, but like many since he had pursued what mathematics he needed for his work. Also like many since, he recorded his resentment at the lack of esteem through which the liberally educated perceive those whose use of mathematics is merely practical.

In the political void left by the disintegration of the Roman Empire, the secular system collapsed, leaving liberal education ideals to survive in the houses of the powerful, as society descended into feudalism. By force of circumstances, the reading and writing of the religious schools became the only institutional means through which educated culture could be acquired and passed on. The work of the monasteries, cut off from a hostile world became increasingly degenerate, inward-looking and defensive, and increasingly distanced from pagan educational influence. Literary learning and religious education became one, and it was the material components of the classical tradition which reemerged in the new synthesis of English medieval culture.

The history of mathematics education in England is the history of the social distance between liberal and mechanical mathematics, with occasional narrowings to actual co-operation, followed by bursts of separation and status retrieval. The two came together for example with Roger Bacon's advocacy of the practical experience of working people in the renaissance of the thirteenth century, in the work of the Elizabethan practitioners, in the making of the rift between Newton and Hooke, in the building of fresh ideas of curricula in the eighteenth century. The most extreme insistence on the separation however came from the Church and State Establishment in the period when State education for all was grudgingly conceded. More than any other subject, it was mathematics that defined the *social* differences that were built into English education from the beginning.

Work and Numeracy

At least two other sorts of mathematical activity went on in the early seats of learning, for the Church calender required the prediction of the dates of Easter, and the clergy needed to be housed, clothed and fed. *Computus*, the study of the calender was essential to the functioning of the Church and its main textbook was another survival contemporary with Boethius. Little remains of the detail and conceptual difficulties of the computation of lunar events under Church insistence on a flat earth and a geocentric universe, but the chosen methods were formidable, and inordinately difficult for most students (Boyer, 1975:15). The practical business of monastery management was conceptually more accessible, for it is not possible to effectively house, clothe and feed any community, through unrefrigerated summers and deadly winters, without being numerate, whatever methods are used and whether or not they are recorded. People who work the land for a living have always had ways of gauging it. Nobody ploughs a furrow without some idea of how long it will take, how many furrows can be ploughed before dark and an estimation of yield. Nobody keeps chickens or a cow without some calculation of expected yield, and nobody spins or weaves without some good idea of how much yarn and fabric can be obtained from the raw material in hand.

The assumption that such practical activity is unsystematic, even mindless, is a legacy of the power of the liberal education tradition. Today an additional assumption remains in obsessions with written sums of archaic algorithm as a measure of numeracy, and the unsubstantiated idea that to be numerate, a person must first be literate. Chaucer made such a point in an age that had less use of literacy, while introducing the Manciple, the domestic bursar of one of London's Inns of Court, in his fourteenth century *Canterbury Tales*.

> The Manciple came from the Inner Temple;
> All caterers might follow his example
> In buying victuals: he was never rash
> Whether he bought on credit or paid cash.
> He used to watch the market most precisely
> And got in first and so he did quite nicely.
> Now isn't it a marvel of God's grace
> That an illiterate fellow can outpace
> The wisdom of a heap of learned men?
> (Chaucer in Coghill's translation, 1971:18)

In Chaucer's day, England was still a developing country at the end of an era of great invention. Agriculture and power sources had come under more sophisticated control, landowners and financiers had grown fat on capitalism supported by new banking and accounting methods, and the textiles trade was Europe wide (Gimpel, 1988:15). As Europe had descended into feudalism, trading empires had been built. By the eleventh century the North Sea rim, now at peace, was trading again, drawing in the skills of Italy, notably Venice, where the customary low esteem of merchants had been reversed, for Venice had been built on trade and its merchants were supported by a literature in the skills of commerce. It was Italy that supplied vernacular trade and business manuals that introduced to commerce the revolutionary mathematical idea of the use of the Indian numerals in calculation.

There were of course applications of the idea in both commerce and academe, and no denial that, once understood, they were profoundly useful. Conceptually demanding, they stood alongside the continued use of the more concrete but well understood use of the exchequer board and the Roman numerical system. But the main preoccupations of academe in the new universities was the assimilation of the newly emerging Graeco-Arab sciences into Christianity, for the universities were the craft guilds for professional training for the Church. The study of Aristotle's works overshadowed the mathematical quadrivium and it was his natural philosophy that stimulated the research of Grosseteste and his pupil Roger Bacon into mathematics and optics. Bacon's oft-quoted remark that mathematics is the 'gate and key to all sciences' arose in his expression of its joint philosophical and practical importance. In one of the earliest recorded efforts to reconcile liberal and mechanical mathematics, Bacon wrote warmly of his colleague Peter de Maricourt's research in what today would be called ethno-science and ethno-mathematics, motivated by his self-confessed ignorance of things 'known to laymen, women, soldiers [and] ploughmen.' He had looked closely 'into the doings of those who work in metals and in minerals of all kinds: he knows everything relating to the acts of war, the making of weapons and the chase: he has looked closely at agriculture, mensuration and farm work: he has even taken notes of the remedies, lot-casting and chances of the wise people of the day.' (Gimpel, 1988:194).

But Bacon's metaphysical explorations, and his open criticism of the Church for its archaic methods of computus, were among the errors for which he was condemned. In one of its periodic reactions to threats to its own metaphysics, the Church was retreating into scholasticism by the time the plague began to close down much of life. The institutions of education withdrew into themselves again, while the world carried on in an era of plagues and wars. War however has always been a stimulus for mathematical and technological advance, and the industries of war as well as those of commerce and peace, prepared the stage for the next mathematical joint venture.

The Educability of Women

Peter de Maricourt had included the work of women in his research for, at the time is was normal for men and women to work side by side, even though the work of women had little economic recognition. All aspects of working life were dominated by the values of the Church. Church laws ruled society, its doctrines decreed morality, its schools offered what formal learning was available and its senior clerics constituted almost the entire body of the literate. It was the universally visible authority – and it was blatantly misogynist.

Fear, resentment and vilification of women were already active within the cultures from which the early Church grew its own philosophies. The origins of monotheistic, patriarchal religions and their responses to the gynocentrism of the old religions are well recorded and discussed elsewhere (Anderson and Zinsser, 1988 for example). The very nature of monotheisms is power relations. Any 'one god' idea had a built-in, institutional notion of primacy and supremacy which inevitably created hierarchy (Miles, 1993:92). All monotheisms too, are built on the idea of men and women as complementary opposites, a system under which women must necessarily lead a second order existence, for if males are to embody one set of characteristics, and if they arrogate to themselves all the strengths and virtues, then women must necessarily be the opposite. Contrastive and derogatory views of women permeated all the philosophy and work of the early Church. Philo in a comment on Genesis, noted that the soul had a dwelling place with men's and women's quarters. For the men, there was a place 'where properly dwell the masculine thoughts. [These are] wise, sound, just, prudent, pious, filled with freedom and boldness, and kin to wisdom.' As for the female sex, it is 'irrational and akin to bestial passions, fear, sorrow, pleasure and desire from which ensue incurable weakness and indescribable diseases.' (quoted by Anderson and Zinser, 1988:27).

In an institution that developed an asceticism that condemned all biological functions as diversions from the path of spiritual growth, ignorance of the reproduction system and fear of the rumbustuous celebrations of fecundity of the old religions, that were still part of the lives of the populace, presented the Church with severe problems of control. As the new religion became codified and philosophies developed, increasing numbers of pronouncements on women appeared, varying from the mildly admonitory to violent scatological onslaught. Diatribes against women were conspicuous in the Middle Ages (Power, 1975:11) and were still common during the arguments from which arose the compromise that is modern English education. Woman as the instrument of the devil originated in Christianity and was the judgment embodied in the ethic of the monasticism from the beginning (Power, 1975:11). The myth of Eve and her dual crime as disobedient seeker of knowledge, expanded to embrace Eve the seducer, whose very sexuality was responsible for poor innocent Adam's loss of self-control. In body and in mind woman was a disaster, though as scapegoat she has proved a wonderfully useful prop to masculine ambition. The same patriarchs, the same philosophies, the same preaching and the same practices that confirmed mathematics as the highest form of human intellect, placed woman as the lowest form of human life.

There was of course the problem that Jesus had a mother, but that was dealt with, in solemn convocation, by the happy agreement that she remained a virgin after the event, as Zelenie and Salomie testified to the unconvinced. The result of institutionalising two extremes of female stereotype however was that the ordinary people were fed both messages together, in role models that were at one extreme unlikely and the other impossible. Workers, male and female alike, 'went to their churches on Sundays and listened while preachers told them in one breath, that women was the gate of hell and that Mary was Queen of Heaven.' (Power, 1975: 11). There is no need to invoke the use of conspiracy theories in feminist history: violent and abusive misogyny was preached from every pulpit in the land and the outcome, that whatever a woman did she was likely to be morally wrong, had the sanction of the highest authority.

This ideological misogyny was periodically reinforced in the evidence of the most respected scientific opinion of the passing years. From the fourth century until the sixteenth, Aristotle was the authority. Bio-logically-based invective becomes drearily familiar to any who trace the course of women's educational and social development, at any stage. During the energetic campaigns of the National Association of Schoolmasters in the 1920s and 30s, against the threat to their jobs of the increasing number of women teachers in schools, some of the language of complaint reveals the same fears as those of the early Church fathers. Women teachers were accused of having 'a castrating effect' on the 'nascent virility of boys' of 'nipping out' the 'budding shoots of young manhood.' (Dyhouse, 1987: 37). The bud-nipping proclivities of women were a constant source of anxiety to the holy fathers since the beginning of English education, and in every age there is a consistency of emotional masculine response to any attempt at women's intellectual advance, in some form of sexual vilification.

The yo-yo model of womanhood could have been completely ignored by the women themselves, had not all formal aspects of their lives been controlled by masculine expectations, and women have always been sickened by what has been thrown at them. It was revulsion at the relentless testimony of 'so many notable men' and the quest for a more reasoned judgment, that drove the fourteenth century Christine de Pisan to discover for herself 'impartially and in good conscience' whether such stuff could possibly be true (Anderson and Zinsser, 1988:xiii).

Then as now, the vast majority of women just got on with their work. But women's work is judged differently from men's. 'A woman's paid occupation is a dimension of her femininity... Moreover her work takes a back seat – by definition it must – in the scheme of things: it recedes in the service of the greater vocation – the reproduction of family life. And with it of course, the reproduction of patriarchal relations.' (Chisholm, 1987:6). No matter what a woman's work contributed to the economy, in the retail activities of so many of her side-lines, it was still woman's work and took on the values ascribed to women. As we have seen, these were not high. Such work however included mathematical skills, in the working numeracy that is recognised the world over, for there is nobody more numerate than a market trader with a survival interest in the product. One medieval complaint testifies to such expertise:

> ...if a woman be at it she in her stinginess useth much more machination and deceit than a man: for never alloweth she the profit of a single crumb to escape her, nor faileth she to hold her neighbour to paying his price. All who beseech her do but lose their time, for nothing doth she by courtesy, as anyone who drinketh in her house knoweth full well. (quoted by Power, 1975: 68)

Trades carried on by women ranged from big business with overseas connections to that of small workshops, and there is no reason for assuming that they were any less numerate than men, as the work required. Like men, women were able to deal financially, in the methods of the day, with everything from foreign currency to petty cash.

In a large household, practical numeracy would have been a necessity for a community that made everything it needed, and had always to be prepared for large numbers of guests. The lady of the manor supervised the making and preserving of foodstuffs and clothing, and laid in stores bought in markets, shops, the nearest city, or sent from London. The Paston letters (Bennet, 1991) contain many commissions to husbands in London, giving precise instructions and carefully budgeted costs of fabrics not obtainable locally. Christine de Pisan's suggestions of budget headings were made for women expected to be numerate. In the institutional control of the wider economy however, there was neither the will nor the means through which women could achieve recognition of their numerate ability. The corollary was that there was no institution which had either the will or the capability of recognising the intellectual content in anything that women did.

The only way in which a medieval woman could acquire an institutional education on something resembling a par with that available to men, was to abandon altogether what made her a woman and become a nun. As a bride of Christ, she was freer of the grosser taints of Eve and could concentrate on the virtues of the celestial mother in law. A well-endowed nunnery could give her access to the same literature as her male colleagues, and to the approval of Church fathers who, while continuing

Figure 3: 'Trade carried on by women ranged from big business with overseas connections to that of small workshops'. Women queuing at the bank, children fidgeting. Italy, fourteenth century.

to preach women's inferiority, believed that 'through such a masculine education a woman could become literally more 'virile', more like a man and thus more holy.' (Anderson and Zinsser, 1988:185).

Such a high and masculine education was available to very few women however. The number of convents was always small, they were less well-endowed than monasteries, the women who entered them came from a small social class and the reasons they entered them were more likely to be economic than educational for they were a refuge for respectable young women whose families could not afford a suitable marriage dowry. Some, but not by any means all, ran schools which took girls as well as boys, but fees were charged and there is scant knowledge of their curricula.

Any convent of any size was of course a business, run by women for women. There are records of continuing financial problems in the nunneries, which can no doubt be partly blamed on poor management, tempered a little perhaps by recognition of the nuns' relative lack of education, but a lot by remembering that they never had the capital of the richly endowed monasteries. A powerful Abbess however would necessarily be a business woman as well as an academic, for she would have been responsible for the management of land, institution, products and people. By the end of the thirteenth century however, the learning that could take place under such relative independence was in decline, for the Church was reactivating its old values in response to current threats to its metaphysics. The convents went through administrative reorganisation and increasing centralisation, which finally closed some of the less financially viable ones. They became subject to more direct supervision of male ecclesiastics and restrictions were placed on nuns preaching and teaching (Anderson and Zinsser, 1988:I:190). Some English Abbesses were still independent in the fourteenth century, but they lost their internal access to the luxury of learning as study. Disputation and explication moved from the monastic centres to the all male enclaves of the new universities, where only masters and doctors of theology could teach, and where the prerequisite to study was the intention to become a priest. As education available for boys expanded, that for girls closed down. It is no coincidence that the decline in the nunneries parallels the increase in grammar schools, the feeder schools of the universities. And the Church is still troubled by the idea of women as priests.

Moving to Modern

The sixteenth century Renaissance reaffirmed the classical tradition in education, but had less effect in England than did the Reformation. Direct power over the universities had already shifted from the Pope to the university chancellors by the time Henry VIII took over as Head of the Church. The rise of the Tudor state required a new kind of public servant, and increasingly the universities became the training ground for young gentlemen, in addition to their continuing role in the training of the clergy. The masculine status of higher education acquired a social as well as a religious dimension. The reformation of the Church radically changed the university curriculum, particularly with the abolition of Canon law; there was more emphasis on Greek, and the classical quadrivium was restored. Grammar schools continued their classics courses and sixteenth century students arriving at Oxford were unlikely to be familiar with either the numerals or the elementary operations of the arithmetic of the working man (Howson, 1982: 29). The same situation still held in the middle of the eighteenth century (Lawson and Silver, 1976:176). There was debate about mathematics in the curriculum, however. At Cambridge, the Edwardian statutes of 1549 had required all undergraduates to do mathematics as a foundation for the liberal arts course, but even the minimal amount specified was removed by the Elizabethan statutes of 1570, for the university commissioners 'thought that its study appertained to practical life, and had its place in a course of technical instruction rather than in the curriculum of a university' (Howson, 1982:12). The study of the classics and the virtual canonising of Aristotle was no lasting defence against commercial demand and empirical effort however, and the pursuit of secular and empirical knowledge could no longer be held back, subdued or condemned as error: it developed a more productive life of its own, in the vernacular, outside university walls.

Personal connections between advocates of educational reform, university academics and commercial entrepreneurs were already working for change by the time the intellectual climate of the Civil War universities provided encouragement for such a fertile union. Meetings in London seeded meetings in Oxford and fed an era of scientific inventiveness. Gresham's College, one of the meeting places, had been established by merchant finance in 1596 and its professors of geometry and astronomy had the task of making university learning available to merchants and tradespeople in London.

The English equivalents to the Italian vernacular manuals on bookkeeping and accounts, weights and measures, credit and exchange, appeared in the early sixteenth century to meet demand. Robert Recorde's

Grounde of Artes (published in 1543) was not the earliest of such books, but was the most genuinely educational of its time in that it attempted, as good mathematics educators have always done, to bring relevant application, with mathematical development from the application, into the same learning experience: like Bacon, he was concerned not just to apply knowledge but to add to it. The real mathematical activity of the day took place in time measurement and navigation, as academics and instrument makers worked together in resolving problems of competitive world trade and colonial ambition. Every navigator of the day consulted John Dee in his library at Mortlake: Raleigh consulted Thomas Harriot: the East India Company consulted Edward Wright. The instrument makers John Goodwin and John Trapp joined the freelance university mathematicians, working from their own homes. Gresham Professor Briggs is credited with the rapid dissemination of the very useful logarithms of Mr Napier, and Henry Lyte's book informed the public of the usefulness of decimal fractions in measuring and dividing land into acres, and measuring cloth, glass, board and timber (Charlton, 1965:285).

The liberal arts claimed the route to virtue however, and with the new humanist philosophy, it was particularly associated with the male virtues. Colet's new school became the model for sixteenth and seventeenth century grammar schools in an era in which it was repeatedly preached that the liberal curriculum, in Latin, had the power within it to counteract the evil influence of the family and society on boys. Throughout Western Europe women still 'epitomised the ignorant and the superstitious, the sexually lax and the profane' (Hufton, 1996:27). Women still worked in small and large scale trade, in both their invisible economies, but work and the mathematics associated with it, were now further gendered. Commerce had had its mathematical revolution: the action now was with the very masculine merchant adventurers.

A woman was still expected to be numerate however. Sir Anthony Fitzherbert's aptly named manual for wives, the *Book of Husbandry*, was among many of its time, and declares the duties of the wife

> to go to market, to sell butter, cheese, milk, eggs, chickens, capons, hens, pigs, geese, and all manner of corn. And also to buy all manner of necessary things belonging to the household, and to make a true reckoning and account to her husband what she had received and what she hath paid (quoted by Miles, 1988:159).

The skills of people like the fifteenth century Margery Haynes of Castlebrook, who had taken over three mills from her husband and expanded the holding, were still in evidence. Joan Dent, a seventeenth century weaver's widow sold cloth and haberdashery door to door and amassed £9,000 before her death. Edith Doddington was a licensed trader of wheat, butter and cheese throughout four counties in Southern England. Mary Hull, Barbara Riddle and Barbara Milburn owned and administered collieries (Anderson and Zinser, 1988:I:426). Merchants were expected to be literate, highly numerate and they used sophisticated commercial techniques (Charlton, 1965:255), and the vernacular advisory literature for merchants had been directed at both men and women. Edmund Cootes' *The English Schoolmaster*, first published in 1596 (and last in 1702) was directed to such 'men and women of trade' as tailors, weavers and teachers.

Religious reform had involved both sexes but in females it had focussed on chastity and obedience, the predictable old values to which the Church, albeit a different one, returned with the new interest in classicism. The Spaniard Jan Luis de Vives, whom Henry VIII had hired as tutor to his daughter Mary, is a hero of mathematics education, for he set out the case for university mathematics as the subject above all others that displays 'sharpness of mind', while warning of the danger that its study can lead people away from 'the things of life and estrange men from the perception of what conduces to the common weal.'(Howson, 1982: 5). His work on the education of women however, written for Catharine of Aragon, presents a feminine ideal more of clinical depression than of sharpness of mind. Even with the more accurate rendition of the 'sad' of the day, with the 'sober' of today, it makes miserable educational reading. Maidens should be full of prayer and piety, humbleness and obedience and must above all things, learn to control their tongues. The chapter on what a wife should do at home is summarised in the quintessentially gloomy pronouncement that 'great sadness of behaviour and arrangement is required in a wife.' (Hufton, 1995:33). The view of women as in need of constant guidance from a man fails Vives when he comes to widows however, for lack of reliable men to turn to. They are advised against the company of priests, it is not too clear why, and against remarriage, but are advised to spend the rest of their lives in cloistered prayer, going out only in the company of 'some good and sad woman'.

Men were still dreadfully at risk from woman uncontrolled, indeed it was not long before a fresh outbreak of bud nipping was reported. The classical legacy resurrected for the newly scientific exploration of the perfection of man, revived evidence of women's inferiority, from which all parties in the newly splintered Christianity selected. The views of the ancients on female anatomy, never as profound as their views on mathematics, reappeared in the spectre of the voraciously wandering uterus, and selective evidence (ignoring washer women for example) of the smaller and weaker female physique. By the eighteenth century, anatomists were demonstrating that a woman's cranium contained not only a smaller brain than a man's, but a weaker one, particularly at risk from the errant uterus. It was inconceivable that such a creature could have an intellect, indeed the concept of rationality itself excluded women from the possibility.

It was against the background of the involvement of the Renaissance man of affairs in the mathematics of their work that the philosophy of Descartes and Newton developed (Charlton, 1965:295). Without the work of people like Robert Recorde, John Dee and the Gresham professors, Descartes could not have written 'it is possible to attain knowledge which is useful in life, and instead of that speculative philosophy by means of which ... as distinctly as we know the different crafts of the artisans, we can in the same way employ them in all those uses to which they are adapted, and thus render ourselves master and possessors of nature' (Charlton, 1965: 296). The Cartesian concept of reason was deeply involved with controlling 'mother' nature. Rationality had a motive and a situation. It was taken to be a kind of rebirth of the thinking self and this rational self, this 'thinking' subject, was emphatically male: the female role was to provide the biological prop to procreation, and to service the possibility of idealised man (Walkerdine, 1989:27). Reason itself was gendered.

Education and Mathematics

The initiatives of the Elizabethan mathematical practitioners had been some of the most open and lively in the history of mathematics education, and the Restoration and Act of Uniformity did not entirely quench them. Not only was the monarchy restored but the House of Lords, the Bishops and the Established Church in a defensive if not vengeful union. By the Act, all clergy, dons, schoolmasters and tutors were required to declare conformity to the Church of England or be banished from the business of education. As a consequence non-conformists were banned from professions which required a university education, forcing them to earn their keep as practical, not gentle-men. By doing so, they 'changed sides' from an élite already beginning to react against the recent extension of academic education beyond the traditional, small, selective circle, to join those already critical of the relevance of classical education to the needs of other sectors of society (O'Day, 1982:196). Although the statutory provisions of most grammar schools were for a classical education only, some were already providing some other subjects, including mathematics and arithmetic, for they were failing to recruit on classics alone. While unendowed schools began to offer military, commercial and technical curricula, the education of the sons of the powerful in both Church and State, remained firmly classical. An increased public interest in mathematics and science was catered for by popular day and evening lectures, attended by both men and women and all social classes. Weavers, already working in what is a very mathematical craft, showed particular interest in mathematics. The best known of the public lectures and courses however were those specifically designed for gentlemen (O'Day, 1982: 212) for the social distance between the study of mathematics for its usefulness, and its dilettante pursuit 'for its own sake' remained. The Anglican hierarchy retained its pessimistic view of the people outside its enclaves, and continued to operate in corporate immunity from outside opinion, fearful that too much education would cause social unrest. It was from the curricula of the dissenters that the industrial revolution drew its intellectual responses and that modern curricula derive. The Church continued to fight its rearguard action until well into the twentieth century.

Increasing literacy amongst women is more fully recorded in women's literary output than in mathematics and the sciences, not least because more research has been done there. In addition, it is difficult to properly gauge women's interests in either practical or academic mathematics, for historians of mathematics and of mathematics education have tended to write not just from the classical, liberal view of mathematics but, until very recently, in a discourse that is also masculine. So gendered was the study, its philosophical bases and more recent applications, that women were as absent from its records as they were from the economy. As Burton comments (1986:9), in Bell's *Men of Mathematics* (sic), the reader finds that discussion of Sophie Germain's work in the chapter called 'The Prince of Mathematicians', is prefaced by the remark that the discussion shows the liberality of Gauss's views on the subject of women scientific workers. The unattributed Sonya Kovalevska, noted as 'the most celebrated woman mathematician of the nineteenth century', gets her anonymous recognition in a chapter called 'Master and Pupil'. It is such dismissive portrayals that have provoked modern women in mathematics education into pursuing heroines and role models for their pupils, rather than into exploring the working lives of women for the mathematics they routinely do, that is routinely glossed over or ignored.

Mostly what women did achieve was by courtesy of men on whom they were dependent. A well-placed woman, with access to her father's time and library, or her brother's tutor could follow her interests, indeed many of the women who did work in mathematics came into it through this route. By the end of the eighteenth century, 'corresponding gentle-women', lampooned by Addison in the Spectator were communicating directly with men of science in pursuit of their own studies, and some-times submitting their own contributions. The philosopher Henry More acknowledges his own intellectual exchanges with Ann Conway and her influence on Leibniz, and published her notes after her death. John Norris, the Cambridge neo-Platonist, became known for responding to questioning women, and sought to publish his correspondence with Mary Astell. Astell is thought to have been educated in philosophy, logic and mathematics by her uncle, but moved on to open criticism of the role of women in society as the result of the hardship she endured in having to earn her own living in a very restricted field. It was bitter experience of the only options available to educated but penniless women that fuelled Mary Wollstonecraft's *Vindication of the Rights of Women*.

In an extension to the medieval tradition of the upper classes of sending their children to better established homes for their education, an increas-ing number of boarding schools were founded in the eighteenth century, some of which followed the line of Astell and Wollstonecraft by offering a more academic curriculum in addition to the usual array of domestic sub-jects and feminine accomplishments. Mrs Makin of Westminster and Mrs Meribah Lorrington of Chelsea both offered arithmetic and astronomy: Mrs Margaret Bryan kept a school at Blackheath and one at Hyde Park corner where she delivered lectures on astronomy and mathematics. Mrs Florian Jolly modelled her school on her husband's academy for boys in Bath and included arithmetic, geometry, trigonometry and astronomy as well as general science (O'Day, 1982:69).

As the Industrial Revolution developed however, the role of women was progressively closed down, so in an increasingly scientific age there were new theories to explain intellectual inferiority and domestic necessity. The masculinity of mathematics meanwhile received another boost in the enthusiasm for competitive examination. It is not surprising that Victorian middle-class prosperity and self-consciousness, coupled with Darwinian ideas of the survival of the fittest, should support the idea of competitive examination so wholeheartedly. Their original motivation may have been to check nepotism and patronage, but they were also seen as a way of stimulating exertion and raising standards through the healthy competition of the playing field. The content and process of examinations was jealously guarded by the Universities in their role as guides to what the upper class schools should be teaching, and the Oxford and Cam-bridge Board was set up in 1873 to protect their privilege from possible State intervention. So far as mathematics education was concerned however, the Universities remained obdurately locked in liberal education mode, out of touch with the industrial world outside.

By 1870, and the first Education Act permitting the extension of education to all, Cambridge was still clinging to Euclid in the dying embers of the quadrivium, in a manner that was the laughing stock of Europe. No less than 73 new editions of Euclid had been published in the 1840s (Price, 1994:20). How such a peak of Greek culture was seen as the best education for the Victorian, middle-class, small boy can only be explained in terms of adherence to liberal education as mental and moral exercise. When in 1868, the Taunton Commission on the education of the middle classes divided mathematics into layers considered appropriate for the professional aspirations of three levels of the class, it left Euclid safe in principle and practice in the upper class layer, well out of sight of the minimal arithmetic of the entirely separate elementary school system, far below. In a formal coding of general practice, the social classes became defined by the mathematics they were to be taught, and the mathematics to be taught defined the different gradations of society.

The first intensive curriculum development of the era of the modern profession of mathematics education, centred on the place of Euclid in the mathematics curriculum, and inevitably took place in a discourse that was masculine and middle-class. Cambridge clung to the requirement of Euclid until 1903. The battle to replace it by more modern geometry is well described in Price's (1994) history of the Mathematical Association, originally the Association for the Improvement of Geometry Teaching (AIGT). In the struggle for modernisation, the AIGT produced its own syllabus, leaving schools who taught pupils with university aspirations the problem of which syllabus to select: AIGT for a better mathematics education, or Cambridge for the entrance requirement. The complacency of the universities had been such that they had remained aloof from mathematics education until the Clarendon Commission of Inquiry into the state of the nine prestigious 'public' schools revealed the real danger that the new and efficiently managed proprietary schools of the middle classes would soon place them in a position of inferiority. Although some of the Public schools had introduced mathematics and science into 'modern' sides, classical languages, history and divinity had continued to dominate a curriculum geared entirely to the wants of the 3% of the already tiny minority, male population heading for Oxford and Cambridge, from which the government of the country was recruited.

The battle of Euclid eventually won, mathematics education moved into what Howson (1982) called the Golden Age of curriculum progress in the first decades of the twentieth century. Although middle class girls could now acquire a mathematics education as honorary boys (see Chapter 4 below) the same era forced the great majority of girls into a repressive prescription of femininity that reaffirmed their position at the polar opposite. Mathematical education continued to grade and exclude people, not only by the examination system, but by the new enthusiasm for psychometric testing and its promise of putting a figure on the educability of individuals, for mathematics featured strongly both within the tests and in the statistical manipulation of their results.

Liberal education aims remained an Establishment ideal, and the careful grading of social and mathematical steps below it, laid out by Taunton, remained embodied in the educational hierarchies, emerging again in the tripartite system of the 1944 Education Act, of grammar, technical and secondary modern schools, their curricula 'determined respectively by tradition, vocational needs and default,' (Howson, 19892: 183). So entrenched within these hierarchies was mathematics as a boy's subject, that as late as 1959, a chapter heading of *Adapting Mathematics for Girls*, in a review of secondary modern schools, could pass without comment (Cooper, 1985:44).

Throughout its 2000 year history in Christian education, mathematics was always a gendered subject, always at one extreme end of a scale of human functioning that, by ideology, maintained women at the other. The advent of state education and an establishment that inherited the ideology virtually without question, institutionalised it and maintained it so that it received its first real challenge only in the latter decades of the twentieth century. The entirely unsubstantiated belief that girls and women do not do mathematics because they cannot, is the result of two thousand years of social conditioning, and remains strongly in public perception, not least in that of many women themselves.

References

Anderson Bonnie S and Zinsser Judith P (1988) *A History of Their Own: Women in Europe from Prehistory to the Present, Vols I and II.* Harmondsworth: Penguin Books.

Bennet H S (1991) (first published 1922).*The Pastons and their England.* Cambridge: Cambridge University Press.

Boyer Carl B (1985) *A History of Mathematics.* Princeton: Princeton University Press.

Burton Leone (1986) *Girls into Maths Can Go.* Eastbourne: Holt, Rinehart and Winston.

Charlton K (1965) *Education in Renaissance England.* London: Routledge and Kegan Paul.

Chaucer Geoffrey *Canterbury Tales.* Modern English translation by Neville Coghill (1971 revision of 1951 translation) Harmondsworth: Penguin Books.

Chisholm Lynne (1987) *Gender and Vocation.* Working paper No 1, new series. London: University of London Institute of Education, Post 16 Centre.

Cooper Barry (1985) *Renegotiation Secondary School Mathematics. A Study of Curriculum Change and Stability.* Lewes: The Falmer Press.

Davis Philip and Hersh Reuben (1983) *The Mathematical Experience.* Harmondsworth: Penguin.

Dyhouse Carol (1987) Miss Buss and Miss Beale: Gender and Authority in the History of Education. In Felicity Hunt (Ed). *Lessons for Life: The Schooling of Girls and Women 1850-1950.* Oxford: Basil Blackwell.

Gimpel J (1988) *The Medieval Machine: The Industrial Revolution of the Middle Ages.* Aldershot: Wildwood House.

Howson Geoffrey (1982) *A History of Mathematics Education in England.* Cambridge: Cambridge University Press.

Hufton Olwen (1995) *The Prospect Before Her: A History of Women in Western Europe.Vol 1 1500-1800.* London: Harper Collins.

Lawson John and Silver Harold (1973) *A Social History of Education in England.* London: Methuen.

Miles Rosalind ((1993) *The Women's History of the World.* London: Harper Collins.

Marrou H I (1956) *A History of Education in Antiquity.* Translated by George Lamb. London: Sheen and Ward.

O'Day Rosemary (1982) *Education and Society 1500-1800: Social Foundations of Education in Early Modern Britain.* Harlow: Longman.

Power Eileen (1975) *Medieval Women.* Edited by M M Postan. Cambridge: Cambridge University Press.

Price Michael A (1994) *Mathematics for the Multitude: A History of the Mathematical Association.* Leicester: The Mathematical Association.

Walkerdine Valerie (compiler) (1989) *Counting Girls Out.* London: Virago in association with the University of London Institute of Education.

Chapter 3

Schooling and Sewing

Introduction

From the beginning of the Charity Schools to the arrival of the compre-hensives, it was needlework, alone or combined with other domestic subjects, that dominated the curriculum of working class girls, sometimes in time, always in significance. It was needlework that differentiated girls' schooling from boys', that confirmed girls' subservience to the needs of the men in their homes, that reduced their access to and attainment in other curriculum subjects, that channelled them into a highly restrictive job market, that ensured that their work was held in low esteem, and that hung a prejudgment of intellectual inferiority over the rest of their lives. It was through needlework that the low expectations of girls were first institutionalised, then systematised.

Schooling for the Poor

The problem of how to educate the masses, if at all, was an old one, and in a country changing from rural to urban societies, it had been difficult to solve. It was not until relatively fixed urban populations made the presence of the poor so visible as to constitute a threat to the established order, that it became necessary to tackle poverty systematically. The specific problem of urban poverty had been considered by the Charity Schools of which there had been an exponential increase in the late eighteenth century. The motivation was Christian, the aim to replace what was seen as a deficient moral environment and the cause of poverty, with a more wholesome, Christian one. The Charity School movement brought in a new kind of of educational intention for an entire social class, not moral instruction but moral rescue (Williams, 1965:155). The schools were mainly supported by charitable subscription, and it was as such a subscriber that the State first became active in the education of the masses in the early nineteenth century. At a time when the whole idea was particularly contentious, State intervention was not through Parliament itself, but for the sake of reducing the heat in the issue, through a com-

41

mittee of the Privy Council. Two strands are prominent in an intensely complex debate. On one hand, a rough grouping of people with very different attitudes to working class organisation and the rise of democracy, argued that the people had a right to education and the State a duty to provide it. In contrast, another grouping opposed to democracy, argued for the spiritual health aim of the liberal tradition.

From at least the year 1500, projects for the education of the poor had fallen into one or another of these two broad divisions, and it was an etiolated version of the latter, that the Charity schools had chosen. This was criticised at the time as a narrow and illiberal idea in practice, and arguments for more technical education remained strong.

At the beginning of the nineteenth century Charity school ideologies and practice were absorbed into a new 'monitorial' system, a mass production exercise that claimed to do the same job as the charity schools but for more children and more cheaply. The method was to employ just one teacher who instructed a group of children chosen to be monitors, who then passed on the lesson to groups of younger children. The system was, indeed it had to be, a highly disciplined affair with quantities of rules both for pedagogy and for behaviour: everything from the alphabet to a child's hand positions was subject to strict control. The method was used in two separate school systems promoted by the established and non-conformist churches respectively. The National Society for Promoting the Education of the Poor in the Principles of the Established Church (the National Society for short) was by far the larger and by 1850 its schools out-numbered those of the non-denominational British and Foreign Schools Society by seventeen to one. By 1870, the year of the first Education Act, the Societies between them provided about 90% of voluntary school places (Purvis, 1989:87).

Provision of a grant by the State as subscriber inevitably brought with it the question of accountability and in 1839 the Committee of Council on Education appointed Her Majesty's Inspectors (HMIs), named as such because they reported to the Privy Council not Parliament. Until the 1860s HMIs covered the country on the developing railway system, encouraging, supporting, criticising and writing reports that reveal a deep and compassionate concern for the condition of the poor within the values of the day. The changed political circumstances of education however began to change their role. Already by the 1830s pressures for social change and franchise reform were prompting a reassessment of the purposes of teaching the poor, and emphasis was shifting from education as moral rescue to education as a means of controlling social change. It was realised that, along with the minimum of necessary skills for its future workers, mass schooling could be used to maintain the structure of society and its moral imperatives by teaching the habits of obedience, industry and punctuality (Gomersall, 1988:42). Social control became and remained a strong if unwritten aim of mass education.

By the 1860s attitudes had hardened from a charitable paternalism to one of rather tougher compulsion, and schooling was becoming an increasingly costly undertaking. Fresh controls over grants, minuted in a meeting of the Committee of Council and published as a Code, instigated direct Committee control over the curriculum through the system that came to be known as 'payment by results'. Subsequent revisions and modifications of the Code brought an increasing tangle of controls and restrictions which eventually quite defeated the original policy of paying for the means (Board of Education, 1912:4). Effects of the Code on schools included extreme financial pressures to teach particular things in particular ways and changed the role of the HMIs from the giving of advice and support to policing a suffocating system of regulations. By the 1870s, education was well recognised as an 'investment in the national interest' (Gomersall, 1988:42). As the system grew, legislation and increasing administration became necessary. By 1856 the Committee of Council was merged with the Department of Science and Art (set up after the Great Exhibition of 1851 to support science and art education) into the Education Department. In 1870, locally elected School Boards were created, much to the chagrin of the Established Church, to fill up the gaps in the voluntary schools provision. In 1899 the Education Department became the Board of Education, which itself became a Ministry in 1944.

The schools usually preferred by the working-class themselves were their own Dame and Gaffer schools, whose quality may have varied enormously, but which provided a service for working parents that was closer to home in location and feel, than the National and British schools and that could teach literacy and other necessary subjects without the Societies' rigid rules, fixed hours, dress requirements or brow-beating morality. The Dame schools reached their peak during the first half of the nineteenth century and, though they declined with the rise of the Societies' schools, some survived into the early years of the twentieth century (Purvis, 1989). At the beginning of the nineteenth century, a variety of other schools also remained: factory schools for example trained children for specific work and a good one also taught a little literacy.

Girls in School

From the outset, voluntary education had had different implications for boys and girls, for the accepted place of working-class children was already heavily gendered, and where it was not, was rapidly becoming so.

So long as the curriculum was limited to religion and a little basic literacy, both sexes learned the same subjects and the experience of schooling should have made little difference to children's working lives. But even in such a limited curriculum, there were hidden messages: most women in the bible for example, are portrayed as wives and mothers (Purvis, 1991:16). The curriculum undoubtedly also contained both explicit and implicit messages about the appropriate place for boys and girls, men and women in society. Patriarchy was not an abstract notion (Purvis, 1984:87) and the patriarchy of the Charity and the Societies' Schools did not suddenly reverse its 1500 years of their own preaching on women's place. Girls were explicitly taught to serve their fathers and brothers, to whom they were taught they were inferior, indeed their whole educational experience taught them that they were not important (Purvis, 1984:91).

In practice, the Societies generally gave priority to boys. Boys and girls were originally admitted at different ages, could be charged different weekly fees, and be taught in different rooms, or separated in one large room by a partition and girls sometimes remained in the infants' class as boys moved on up the school. Family gender roles could also be a major factor in girls' access to schooling, for though both boys and girls were required to work at home, the requirement on girls for regular work like minding the baby or helping on washing day, was so widespread that it was accepted by schools. Truancy regulations were much less heavily imposed on girls than on boys. Whatever the local variation, it is safe to assume that overall, and for very many years, girls got less education, measured in hours, than did boys.

As traditional patterns of employment changed, and the reality of the father working outside the home for a family wage extended, the expectation of working-class males on their girls came closer to those of the middle-class, and though they disagreed in detail, both increasingly saw the future of girls as in the home. In the teeth of the evidence that women needed to supplement family income by work outside the home, the Trades Union movement also asserted a domestic role for women, and discriminated heavily against them (Horn, 1988:71). Girls' domestic destination was reinforced on all sides.

The reality was that education itself had always been a thoroughly male affair and that girls, however numerous, were newly-arrived extras in the expanded system. From then on, in official and educational parlance, there was 'education' and 'girls' education', in a systematic usage that maintained women's economic invisibility and sustained pathological interpretations of their biology. To confirm their vocation, not as a worker but as a female, their curriculum was distinguished by the task that beyond all others signified their feminine, domestic role and where the boys followed the 3Rs, the girls followed 3Rs and 1N. No matter how traditional or radical, no matter how opposed to the domination of education by the Church, needlework for girls was the one thing that everyone agreed must be taught.

In practical terms, the teaching of needlework was fully justified. In theory at least, a girl who could sew could raise herself and her dependents above some of the more obvious degradations of poverty, and could also get a job. Many HMI reports on needlework express a pastoral concern for a domestic skill which could at least put a respectable gloss on poverty. One Inspector, the Rev. Fussell, declared in 1857:

> If we can teach them to darn and mend, and patch with readiness and skill, if we can enable them to master cutting-out to such an extent as is required for the ordinary man's home, we shall have rendered to them, and at the same time we shall have rendered to society, a lasting and incalculable service. (Sutton, 1976:76)

But pragmatics alone did not determine either curriculum content or pedagogy. Whatever the educational philosophy, whatever the school, the requirement for needlework meant that the girls' curriculum had always to be a compromise. In the time-table of the 'literary' curriculum sewing had to be an extra that could only be fitted in by displacing more bookish subjects. An 'industrial' curriculum on the other hand could provide, at least in theory, both a justification for sewing as a vocational subject, and an overall educational theory that could have given it status equal to other subjects. Richard Dawes for example, the proponent of the idea of the *Science of Common Things*, which became fashionable in the 1840s and 50s, spelt out his philosophy of active learning in the context of sewing:

> When a girl has cut out for herself the dress she has made, she has associated her labour, in a natural relation with the exercise of her judgment; she has taken one step towards her emancipation from a state of pupilage, and gratified an instinct which associates the growing independence of her actions with her progress to womanhood. (Ball, 1979:112)

Near universal acceptance of the position of girls in society however, and the Societies' curricula: religion, the 3Rs and 1N, rendered the possibility of any girl exercising judgment and becoming independent unattainable.

The reality for most girls was of 'learning to form neat stitches as fast as possible on whatever materials came to hand' (Ball, 1979: 109).

Hardly less subtle than Code ideology were the two social variables that were the reason for its controls, social class and gender, both energetically pursued by the Ladies Committees of the Societies. Both featured in the insistence on plain sewing, the skills of basic making and mending without the frills, flounces and embroidery that distinguished the garments of the higher classes. So strongly was this requirement seen to be necessary, that it was written into the Code. From 1862 the prescriptions of the Revised Code decreed that children should be examined for grants, according to their age:

> Managers could lose the grant if the premises were not satisfactory: if the teacher was not certificated and duly paid: if registers were not accurately kept: 'if the girls in the school be not taught plain needlework as part of the ordinary course of instruction.' This drastic result which could be shared with only three other misdemeanours is an astonishing commentary on the attitude towards needlework by the controllers of elementary education. (Sutton, 1967:77)

Lady Dukinfield's evidence to the Newcastle Commission confirmed middle-class opinion on plain sewing. 'Knitting, crochet and fancy work are very objectionable in a school, because they occupy the time that ought to be better employed.' (Sutton, 1967:76). Sutton notes only one exception to this insistence, but a striking one. In the Catholic Training Colleges, beautiful ecclesiastical vestments were made (Sutton, 1967:80) and, by long tradition, the humbly dressed congregation could admire their work on the backs of their priests.

But the symbolic use of needlework as feminising agent for working-class girls, was a card played just as strongly in an era in which femininity was being rewritten as domesticity, and where a version of that was being devised by the middle classes for 'good' working class women and workers. Thus Lady Dukinfield could declare to the Newcastle Commission. 'A girl of fourteen . . . may have become proficient in the art of plain needlework ... not only as a means of obtaining her bread in future, not only as making her valuable as a wife and mother, but because proficiency in this art requires patience, perseverance, attention, industry and neatness ... therefore the practice of it is excellent discipline for the mind of a poor girl' (Sutton, 1967: 76). The aims spelt out by the National Society in 1841 had been clear: 'to teach the young women to be sober, to love their husbands, to love their children, to be discreet, chaste keepers at home, obedient to their husbands' (Gomersall, 1988:43). Nearer the end of the century, Mrs Floyer, the London School Board's Inspectress of Needle-work 'found the image of the silent, motionless female, bent busily over her sewing, a pervasive ideal of mature womanhood, and organised needlework instruction accordingly, believing that such a paragon could be moulded from infancy via the needlework curriculum' (Turnbull, 1987:88).

Both Societies ran model schools and the teaching practice of that of the British Society for 1846 was recorded in some detail:

> A signal is given for monitors to examine their girls' hands to see if they are clean, and that each is provided with a needle and thimble... A command is now given for the whole school to show work ... the bell is then rung, each child holds down her work and immediately begins; and the monitors pass down the desks to instruct them ... At half past eleven o'clock the mistress examines the work of each child; those who merit rewards have a tick, and those who have been careless and inattentive forfeit one, or are confined after school. (Sutton, 1967: 74)

The effect on the girls is described by a diocesan Inspector of the 1850s who barely disguises his dismay under an ironic referral to a generic girl as 'it'.

> It works away ... at its puckered production today, and looks forward to finishing tomorrow what, by a stretch of imagination, it has deemed might be turned into some article of apparel for its own doll ... But tomorrow comes, and out of the school work-bag ... is pulled the precious relic, not by any means necessarily to be put in the expectant hands of its former sempstress; chance will give someone else a turn at it, or it will be ruthlessly torn across in some new direction for the reasonable purpose of being sewn together again ... it, and its relation to its former employer, are treated with utter contempt, and it becomes a matter of heartless speculation to the little work-woman, why she was ever employed on it at all. (Ball, 1979: 109)

Pinning Girls Down

It was when overt justifications for teaching needlework as more impor-tant than other curriculum subjects were argued, that the picture became more educationally sinister. An education that included needlework, and a lot of it, was often one that followed the declared, and thoroughly anti-educational aim of actually preventing girls from learning other things. In some Charity schools for example, writing had been considered a poten-tially dangerous skill since 'ignorant parents attached to it the idea of 'scholarship and capacity', ideas which might encourage a rejection of manual work and the low levels of income in domestic service (Purvis,

1989:86). The Ladies Committees of the Societies were in agreement. Inspector Fletcher's report of 1847 recorded that:

> ... it was not unusual to find ladies ... objecting against these branches of instruction [ie. geography and grammar] altogether, as tending to give the children notions above their station, and encouraging an indisposition to the healthy labour and domestic disciplines of household work. (Gomersall, 1988:52)

The message was repeatedly reaffirmed throughout the century. The National Society Monthly Papers of 1861 recorded an opinion that:

> ... it is to be hoped that no desire to make girls little Newtons, little Captain Cooks, little Livingstones, little Mozarts and Handels and little Sir Joshua Reynoldses, will ever take us too low for keeping in sight the object of teaching them to make and mend shirts, to make and mend pinafores and darn stockings and socks. If it does, then from that day the Society will go back. (Gomersall, 1988:43).

To this cruelly exclusive role of sewing was added another piece of mental brutality. The middle-class view of what working-class 'good women' should be, passed on through the Societies' schools some of the guilt associated with the role. Once feminine domesticity was on the curriculum, the ghost of Eve in the role of scapegoat became institutionalised in school. Throughout the century and well into the next, every national, economic or social crisis was met with renewed demands for domesticity from elementary school girls, while their mothers were belaboured for the nation's ills. The general depravity of the poor, their discontent with their God-given station in life, the servant problem, the lack of healthy military recruits for the Boer War, and fears of 'racial degeneration' in a contended Empire, high infant mortality rates and low birth rates were all seen as the fault of incompetent or indolent working-class women. As the curriculum in general slowly expanded through more and more manipulations to the Code, and as more subjects were added, ostensibly for both boys and girls, more domestic subjects were added for girls: for every curriculum advance for boys, the girls were met with curriculum retreat.

Increasing regulations on girls for domestic subjects added further financial burdens for schools, for the plain sewing that was compulsory had also to be self-financing. As one inspector's memoirs noted, the Ladies Committees were happily able to supply,

> for Mrs Squire and Mrs Rector kept vigilant eyes on this branch of education, and the subscribers to the school funds often got back part of the value of their money by sending their household sewing to be done in school.

> [in one school] the schoolroom had become the workroom of the Castle. There was a liberal display of household articles, and while the third class had sufficed to seam and hem them, it had been found necessary to employ the first class to mark them with coronets. (Dyhouse, 1981:87)

Purvis (1989: 90) quotes items that brought in financial benefits for a school 'including men's fine shirts at 2s each, night shirts at 10d, a girl's coarse shirt from 3d to 6d, and a pair of pillow cases from 2d to 4d.' Such commercial practice was accepted as necessary by the Societies and as late as, 1912 the Board of Education agreed that the practice of taking orders from local shops was 'acceptable within limits' (Turnbull, 1987:92). To keep up the supply of the appropriate work, girls were asked to bring in mending from home, something that many parents found objectionable. One mother of the 1890s complained that she would not like to send in her husband's stockings for mending, nor her old shifts (Purvis, 1985: 148). Parents objected too to the fact that such domestic work was on the curriculum at all: education was book learning and that is what they they paid their fees for. Parental complaints were a constant feature of elementary education.

A characteristic of middle-class enthusiasm for plain sewing was its selective blindness to skills that were already obvious in working-class communities. Both the ability to do plain needlework and the ability to decorate it could hardly have been absent from girls and women whose homes and livelihoods had long depended on it. And in a culture where to be neatly turned out was a distinguishing difference between the 'respectable and the rough', sewing was part of girls' upbringing.

> A girls' education at that time consisted principally of needlework of various disciplines, plain sewing to all manner of fancy work and embroidery, including muslin and net, on which we worked on flowered squares for the shoulder, veils, caps, collars and borders: likewise a multitude of things not in wear now, but then considered very necessary. Parents were prouder then of their daughters' pieces of needlework than of their scholarship. (Dyhouse, 1981: 85)

Davin (1996:136) summarises testimonies recorded nearer the turn of the century, of long traditions of ingenuity with the needle. 'Making down' and mending, knitting and refooting stockings, had long been facts of life.

> Patches were normal – 'all we asked was that the patch should be a reasonable match to the rest of the material. 'Whether passed down or bought from a rag stall, old clothes never died. Women and girls unpicked the seams of jackets, dresses, shirts, skirts and coats, then 'turned' them

(remade them inside out) so as to hide where they were worn or stained, or used good parts for some new purpose altogether. They ran up frocks and underclothes from old flour sacks: knitted endless scarves, socks and jerseys, often recycling wool unravelled from something else, and 'made down' adult trousers for small fry. (Davin, 1996:85).

Records of girls themselves show clear resentment of the amount of time spent on sewing. Hannah Mitchell, born in 1871 and the recipient of practically no schooling, left her complaint.

At eight years old my weekly task was to darn all the stockings for the household, and I think my first reactions to feminism began at this time when I was forced to darn my brothers' stockings while they read and played cards or dominoes ... Sometimes the boys helped with rug-making, or in cutting up wool or picking feathers for beds and pillows, but for them this was voluntary work: for the girls it was compulsory, and the fact that the boys could read if they wished, filled my cup of bitterness to the brim. (Purvis, 1984:107)

Another girl confronted with the realities of its teaching in school, took more direct action:

The Headmaster's wife was in charge of the needlework class. She would never allow me to do anything worthwhile. Oddments of wool to knit, unknit and reknit – the same with needlework, just odds and ends to stitch together, unpick and restitch. One afternoon, after taking the same little piece of calico, sewn, unsewn and resewn for the sixth time, I just threw it on the desk, jumped the seat, through the door, jumped the playground wall and away home. (Turnbull, 1987:91)

Political objection too came from the newly confident middle-class feminists. Emily Shireff could not see:

what educational advantage results to the girls ... from furnishing plain needlework to the ladies of the parish at a lower price than would be paid to a poor woman who depends for bread on her needle, or on the machine in which she has invested her little savings. (Dyhouse, 1981: 88).

Probably the most frequently voiced objection however was Hannah Mitchell's. In 1833 the National Society had declared that 'in a well managed school for girls, half the day may be given to needlework or knitting and the other half will suffice for acquiring a knowledge of reading, writing and summing, besides a more familiar acquaintance with the most important religious truths.' (Gomersall, 1988:45). Already by 1846 one Inspector had reported of the British and Foreign Society's girls' schools that 'it may be said that the instruction of the majority ... is not so much in reading, writing and arithmetic, as in reading, writing and needlework' (Sutton, 1967:74). In 1873 sewing was taking up a quarter of the school hours devoted to instruction in the London School Board.

By the end of the century, enormous investment of regulation had been made into the teaching of needlework, and the problem of justifying the space it occupied in girls' schooling was severe. Yet in spite of the mass market for sewing machines and the introduction of paper patterns for dressmaking, there was no question in the establishment of giving it up. But the profession of education was advancing, teachers were better trained, the influence of Froebel was being felt and an educational justification was proving elusive. In the middle-class sector, the Royal School of Needlework was arguing for needlework as art, and William Morris and the Arts and Crafts Movement were preaching the benefits of good design.

One needlework expert of the time (Dodd 1895) marshalled all the current arguments against teaching needlework. Educated women dislike it, hence the girls whom they influence learned to despise it: girls hate it, they loll around over it, risking spinal curvature; the required microscopic stitches damage their eyesight; it is beyond the scope of school life; any girl who wants to learn it can easily do so afterwards; it is useless as an educational training and anyway the sewing machine has removed the necessity for hand needlework. School needlework is useless as vocational training; women who teach it are underpaid therefore it is better not to teach it and, finally, it perpetuates 'irrational dress' because girls are taught to make 'obsolete and unhygienic garments', no doubt for the obsolete skills involved (Dodd 1895: 460).

But, like her contemporaries, Dodd was unable to shake off tradition, its assumptions and confusions. 'A working woman is a blessing to her family' she wrote ' if she can use her needle skilfully and patch, darn and mend, alter garments, reduce them in size to fit a small child, and construct new garments', but she immediately follows this declaration with the traditional disparaging remark, that 'this does not require any special knowledge or skill.' Continuing in pedagogic vein, she offers the prescription of the day, that 'the real object of handwork ... is to develop muscular dexterity'. This however involves 'a sense of proportion, an accurate eye ... together with some skill (sic) in working the various stitches' (Dodd 1895:461). She concludes with her own scheme, which reads like the beginnings of a mathematics curriculum. Infants should fold and cut paper, use squared paper and stitch outlines on perforated cardboard. Standard I children should draw squares and oblongs on squared paper according to scale. They should also cut evenly on lined paper strips, 'squares, oblongs, [and] diagonals, according to scale' (Dodd 1895: 461).

All attempts for an educational justification carried the same stings in their tails. The moment analysis reveals that the work is skilful, the skills are trivialised: obvious mathematical skills are assumed, and abandoned. The Board of Education itself was a master of such specifically gendered language and used it constantly.

Holding Girls Down

At the turn of the century renewed pressures were being placed on the education of girls as the State became increasingly involved in the post-elementary education of the masses, in an era when the need for technical competence and a practically skilled workforce could no longer be denied. The role of girls was to be solely domestic and needlework and other domestic subjects now had the justification of practical work. It was formally endorsed by new regulations of the Board of Education in 1905, that housewifery should be a compulsory subject. In 1908 the Board announced that it was prepared to countenance girls over 15 studying domestic science instead of science and in 1909 the idea was extended to suggesting that they might substitute domestic subjects 'partially or wholly for science and for mathematics other than arithmetic' (Dyhouse, 1977:25).

In personnel, policy and practice, the Board of Education was and remained staunchly Victorian, imposing and maintaining values already seen as outdated, until the end of the second world war. Its permanent secretary, the powerful and persuasive Sir Robert Morant held a strictly hierarchical view of society. He saw elementary schooling as proper provision for the accepted limited ability and required limited aspirations of the masses, and secondary education as the preserve of the élite Public School tradition of the upper classes. All Morant's senior officers were Oxford and Cambridge graduates, many of them distinguished scholars but with a notable lack of experience in the elementary education system, and all were recruited under the exemption of the Board from the public examinations that now controlled entry into the rest of the Civil Service. Until 1940, virtually all senior appointments were made by and from men who had grown up through the Board and were similar in character to their nineteenth century predecessors (Hunt, 1991: 56). In the inter-war years the Board made much of shedding curriculum control through decentralisation to the local education authorities, but the general discretion it retained was an absolute one (Hunt, 1991:91). Time-tables, syllabuses and hours had to be reported annually for every secondary school class, the Board's Handbooks of Suggestions for Teachers were virtually mandatory, and Board administrators sat on the examinations councils that controlled examinations and standards.

From the beginning of the twentieth century until the outbreak of the second world war, the Board developed and maintained a liberal education fiction in the elementary school sector that brought ideals and practices from the early Victorian era into the education of men and women who are grandparents and parents of today's children. While it was perfectly aware of the curriculum content of elementary girls' schools, because it controlled them, it continued to declaim the fiction, writing in 1918 for example that:

> The aim of the Public Elementary School is to provide for children up to the age of 14 or 15, a sound general education free from any specific vocational bias. It is true that a good deal of practical work is included in the curriculum, particularly for the senior scholars, but these activities are included for their educational value and no attempt is made to provide any pre-employment vocational training. (Hunt, 1991: 117)

There was by now a considerable lobby that recognised the weaknesses in most of the claims made of the educational value of needlework, and concerned about the domination of the girls' curriculum by domestic activities, yet the claims of curricular differentiation from that of boys remained strong. In 1920 the Board asked its Consultative Committee to investigate curriculum differentiation, and revealed the confused thinking that surrounded it. Asked whether greater differentiation was desirable, the committee took considerable evidence on psychological and intellectual differences between boys and girls, producing evidence that was both diverse and contradictory (Hunt, 1987:17). No intellectual differences were found between the sexes but many teachers and others declared for psychological and emotional differences, and of course adolescent girls suffered their 'periods of weakness'. The Committee found it impossible to come to a conclusion, and the Board sat on its fence of tradition, deciding that boys and girls 'had different functions to perform' in secondary schools and society. All children must be prepared to earn their own livings and to become useful citizens, but girls also had to be 'makers of homes.'

Once the Board had decided that both gender differentiation and a liberal curriculum were policy, it was locked into a double-think of its own devising which prevented it from even perceiving the inevitable problems of esteem and curriculum overload. Under such circumstances it was quite unable to provide an 'appropriate' curriculum for girls. It had to look backwards to a domestic ideal because it was unable to recognise the changing nature of women's work outside the home, for it was impossible to prepare girls for both work and home careers in a society that saw them as incompatible. It was impossible for the Board to allow domestic subjects the same educational status as other subjects in the curriculum, without undermining the principles of liberal education. It was impossible for girls to achieve the same as boys because of their 'double' curriculum. By insisting, and continuing to insist that education was neutral and available to any child, the crudities of gender differentiation went unrecognised, and because they were unrecognised they preserved the double standard that maintained the intellectual inferiority of girls (Hunt, 1991). It showed clearly in the arts subjects. Because of the traditional accomplishments curriculum of middle and upper class girls, middle class secondary schools had become expert in teaching them. Thus they were clearly a girls' subject and therefore less intellectually demanding than mathematics for example.

The new secondary schools leaving examinations enforced and reinforced the distinctions. In 1917, School Certificate replaced the old University system of 'local' examinations and school subjects were divided into four groups. Group IV contained the aesthetic and practical subjects, and did not count towards the certificates. The 'Group IV controversy' that ensued centred on the academic status of the subjects, for in addition to the subjects that girls were traditionally good at, the domestic subjects were compulsory for them, yet they were not allowed credit for either. The debate continued until 1929 when it was agreed that two Group IV subjects could be regarded as equivalent to one of the subjects of the other groups, but even further modifications in 1938, gave neither aesthetic nor domestic subjects parity in their own right. The most powerful system of educational control, the State examination system, was still disparaging girls and the intellectual skills of women while they ran the country for their men at war. Post-war education was left with the gender-differentiated legacy and the traditional polarities between their subjects of study.

Textbooks for teachers continued to bang the same old gongs. 'The value of needlework as educative handwork for girls cannot be too strongly emphasised' carolled one in the 1930s. 'The ordinary needlework course need not be discarded, but the handwork side of the subject should be worked along with it so as to prove a valuable aid in making Ruskin's 'queenly art' a useful and economic help in the home, a pleasurable pastime and an important function in developing refinement of thought and habit.' (Carter undated: 216). Like Dodd's suggestions of nearly half a century before, the recommendations that follow the exhortation again consist of what in a boys' woodwork class would by then be recognised as mathematical, or at least pre-mathematical skills, but for girls are rendered in babyfied language that eschews any intellectual effort. Carter tells teachers that 'their children can make 'figures of animals with funny angular outlines' on canvas 'or simple geometrical patterns, stripes and squares': the children are to make notes of their measurements: to be taught to use rulers, cut oblongs and ensures that their stitches are more than 1/8th of an inch in length' (Carter undated :216-223).

Even after the Sex Discrimination Act of the mid 1970s needlework remained a female subject with commensurate academic status, and continuing biological associations. Writing of the first major survey after the Act, Searle (1985:29), a mere ten years from the time of writing of this text, noted a remark made by a Home Economics teacher that it is 'an inescapable biological fact that girls have a more natural aptitude for needlework' than boys. The strongest maintainers of hegemonies are those brainwashed by them, and many educated women seem happy to remain in an unquestioning state of needlework-induced submissive ignorance, that the early Church would have appreciated. In April 1995 the Independent Newspaper published an article by a teacher noting the passing of needlework as a separate school subject under the new National Curriculum. Is this the end of era, she asked,

> for women have plied the needle since the dawn of time. 'When Adam delved and Eve span...' It would seem the female role was fixed at creation.

> So does it matter that this long tradition of the spinster and her needle may be drawing to a close? That a generation of girls is emerging that is unable to sew on a button, let alone recognise a flat-fell seam? Are we depriving them of an essential skill?

> ... it is as a leisure pursuit that sewing will surely survive. There are many young women who now turn to tapestry kits and needlecraft magazines to satisfy that instinct for home-making that they have inherited. (Leeson, 1995)

A few days later, in the same newspaper, another article by another advocate of feminine helplessness, bewailed the passing of the sewing on of buttons as a female curriculum item.

> I belong to a generation of women who have to call the AA every time a tyre goes flat. Nor have I mastered the black art of changing a plug. But my daughters are extremely handy, thanks to their schools' technology lessons ... My only quibble is that their schools seem to have abandoned lessons in needlework and cooking, while knitting and crocheting are unknown skills. I suppose that it is down to me to pass on these homely practices. Just as my father was lumbered with putting on all those plugs, I don't want to be the only one, in a household of six, able to sew on a button. (Brown, 1985)

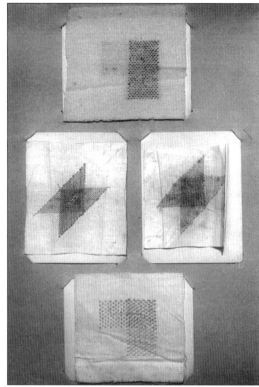

Figure 4: Pages from the needlework sample book required by every student teacher, worked by the author's grandmother in 1900.

Ruling Girls Out

As girls were defined by their needlework, so were they defined by absence of mathematics. When the national education system slowly ground into action, there had long been strongly-held arguments against teaching the poor any arithmetic at all. 'It is doubtless desirable that the poor should be generally instructed in reading' wrote a Justice of the Peace in 1806 'if it were only for the best of purposes – that they may read the scriptures. As to writing and arithmetic, it may be apprehended that such a degree of knowledge would produce in them a disrelish for the laborious occupations of life.' (Williams, 1965:156). However grudgingly offered to the poor, arithmetic was more grudgingly offered to girls. The Annual Report of the National Society of 1840 argued that if it be said that a knowledge of arithmetic is of little importance to poor children and especially to girls, surely then, time need not be wasted on it' (Gomersall, 1988:47).

Already by 1846 an Inspector could write, 'for many years the complaint was to be heard that the girls' arithmetic lagged behind the boys' because of the daily needlework lesson' (Sutton, 1967:74). But such a situation was already accepted and ten years later an Inspector noted 'With respect to acquirement, boys are ordinarily a little in advance of girls, because they have more time for it. The girls compensate by a somewhat livelier intelligence, by prettier reading, by better discipline and by needlework, on which two fifths of their time is spent. (Board of Education, 1912:5). Livelier intelligence, even prettier reading however, were no criteria for education in a social class whose girls were seen as having less need, less time and less ability even than their brothers. Inspectorate reports soon added the inevitable fourth negative, with evidence of less in achievement. One HMI report of 1847 declared figures in his district: 13.5% of boys studied compound arithmetic against 8% of girls and while 0.6% of boys were learning fractions, no girls at all were (Gomersall, 1988:47). Such a situation would have been acceptable to Mr Anderson who reported on the British and Wesleyan schools twenty years later, and who 'found the arithmetic of girls to be unsatisfactory in character and limited in extent' and 'that in this branch of instruction they should display an inferior capacity to the generality of boys, is to be expected' (Gomersall, 1988:47).

If the result of low achievement was inevitable, then the corresponding lack of confidence, if not intentional, was at least predictable. It was certainly reproduced in teacher training in a cycle that maintained a self-fulfilling prophecy. Female pupil teachers were permitted a lower standard of achievement in arithmetic and female teachers in training were not taught to the same level as their male counterpart (Gomersall, 1988: 47). What was taken as both inevitable and acceptable, soon achieved formality in the requirements of administration. As teacher training developed, female pupil teachers were excused from Euclid and algebra, but examined in domestic economy if they wished to sit for a Queen's Scholarship and entry to training college. The downward spiral gathered momentum and it is hardly surprising that from lower expectations, less time, lower achievement and less concern, assumptions of lower ability and more limited teacher training, arithmetic in girls' schools was constantly said to be less well taught.

By 1878 Inspectors were advised to treat girls more leniently in arithmetic 'in consideration of the obligation ... to learn needlework while boys have no corresponding obligatory claim upon their school hours' nor were they to apply to girls exactly the same standards of proficiency as to boys in examination. Even in subjects with a mathematical content, syllabus developments worked against a mathematical education for girls. By 1886 when the argument for practical training and technical literacy had finally broken through the much modified 'literary' curriculum model, drawing for boys was made compulsory in schools for boys, but in schools for both boys and girls, both took the subject. As drawing became more technical, girls dropped out, but they took it up again when the spherical geometry content was dropped from the examination (Davin, 1966:147). In 1895, the Code decreed that in the VIth standard, tables of square and cubic measures and mensuration of the rectangle and rectangular solids were for boys only.

None of this relentless negative pressure of mathematics on girls passed without protest. The Inspectorate itself had long had evidence of girls' ability in arithmetic, but ideology was the stronger force. The report of 1847 (above) that compared the performance rates of boys and girls in various pieces of arithmetic, also showed that girls reached a higher standard in arithmetic to compound level when taught by a woman: the same finding was made in research into village schools in Derbyshire, cited by Gomersall (1988: 49). Girls also did better in the mixed schools which discouraged the practice of favouring domestic economy over other subjects. In spite of the pressure of domestic subjects on girls, many schools did expect and demonstrate high standards in their academic subjects. Inspector Fitch's report of 1870 on the King Edward foundation school in Birmingham is almost irritated in his affirmation:

> I know of no other schools which so completely refute the popular fallacy as to the incapacity of girls for the advanced study of arithmetic, and the inappropriateness for them of many of the intellectual exercises generally confined to the best boys' schools. The teaching of needlework is not neglected, but fortunately neither the governesses nor the parents seem to

think that the mental improvement of girls should be sacrificed to that art. (Gomersall, 1988:50)

Inspector Marshall was equally impressed by schools in Nottingham, Wolverhampton, St Leonards and elsewhere, though these were unlikely to be typical. 'I can by no means admit that female teachers are necessarily inferior to males in teaching this subject' he declared (Gomersall, 1988:50).

The post-war tripartite system of grammar, technical and secondary modern schools had little effect on the curriculum for working-class girls, most of whom were to be found in the latter. Domestic subjects were compulsory and in the comprehensive schools of the 1960s, often unintended gender restrictions in combinations of option subjects still nudged girls into domestic subjects under assumptions that had hardly changed for centuries. Boardspeak continued to expect lack of interest of girls in mathematics, and to deny the potential of mathematical content in what they were forced to do. In the increasing load of domestic subjects that had joined needlework since the end of the previous century, and with their steadily improving teaching and teacher training, it could no longer be rationally denied that the domestic subjects themselves did contain certain amounts of arithmetic and mathematical thinking, but again the discourse on girls' education trivialised or ignored it. The Board's Educational Pamphlet 101, *Senior School Mathematics* of 1934, notes as usual that girls spend less time on mathematics than boys, both because of time spent on domestic subjects and because girls' practical subjects 'have less connection with mathematics than those of boys' (Board of Education, 1934:58). 'The occupations of girls and women in and out of school, make generally speaking, less specific demand on mathematics than do those of boys and men.' Since so little time was available for it, it was important to ask 'what mathematics is essential for girls ... and how far it is desirable or possible to go beyond a utilitarian minimum.' What girls needed was 'domestic arithmetic' by which was meant mainly shopping sums. The task of making curtains was chosen as one 'not affording much basis for further mathematical discussion and practice'. It did include the 'power to visualise a situation involving simple spatial relations' upon which geometry depends, but such a problem, the report argues, calls for estimation and judgment rather than calculation and exactitude, which was what was required. Nonetheless, furthering the mathematical education of girls is argued, firstly because 'too rigid a limitation to utility defeats its own end' and because 'the girl as a person and citizen deserves attention in so far as time permits. But then, the interests and opportunities of girls lead them rather less naturally than boys into many of the [academic] subjects discussed in these pages, but

Figure 5: 'Much of girls' work had ben
mathematical all along'. Pinafore geometry on the
blackboard of an elementary school,
Liverpool c 1914.

where the boy is following his bent, the girl may be widening her horizon and both have duties as citizens' (Board of Education, 1934:60). Thus is the mathematical ability and potential of girls rubbed out again. When their prescribed work contains it, it is the wrong sort of mathematics for girls.

Yet much of girls' work had been mathematical all along. Every medieval embroidery required attention to symmetry and structure. Every spun and woven fleece was part of calculated effort in someone's economy. Every garment structured from flat cloth of particular dimensions to fit the three dimensional form a particular body, is an exercise in practical geometry. Every eighteenth century embroidered sampler contains rows of symmetrical patterns worked on the square grid of canvas by constructing symmetries, through counting and the use of mirror images (see Figure 1 page 2). Every garment knitted to fit a particular body depends on the principle of ratio. Every pinafore pattern copied from a blackboard requires visual interpretation of scaling and the ability to draw a smooth curve. All the fine stitching that the early Inspectors were unable to tell from machine stitching depended on the ability to judge equal distances by eye and maintain them in a straight row.

It is clear that at the time the close relationship between the doing of needlework, and the arithmetic skills and mathematical thinking involved in it were recognised and were occasionally developed. But it is also clear that such things did not count when in the context of the work of women and girls. The whole discourse of mathematics and its junior partner arithmetic, remained masculine. The working of needlework, however geometrically planned and constructed, or numerically measured and calculated, was feminine, and any conflation of the two represented a confrontation of opposites almost as threatening as bud-nipping.

References

Ball Nancy (1979) Practical Subjects in Mid-Victorian Schools. *History of Education* Vol 18 No 2 p 109-12.

Board of Education (1912) *Suggestions for the Consideration of Teachers and Others Concerned with the Work of the Public Elementary Schools*. London: His Majesty's Stationery Office.

Board of Education (1934) *Senior School Mathematics Board of Education Educational Pamphlets 101*. London: His Majesty's Stationery Office.

Brown Maggie ((1995) Diary May 24th.London: *The Independent* Newspaper.

Carter Ethel (undated but c 1930) Handwork and Plain Needlework. In H Holman (Ed) *Handwork for Infant Schools*. London: Caxton Publishing.

Davin Anna (1996) *Growing Up Poor: Home, School and Street in London 1870-1914*. London: Rivers Oram Press.

Dodd C I (1895) Needlework as Manual Training. *Journal of Education* No 313 August p 460-462.

Dyhouse Carol (1976) Social Darwinistic ideas and the Development of Women's Education in England 1880-1920. *History of Education* Vol 5 No 1 p 41-58.

Dyhouse Carol (1981) *Girls Growing Up in Late Victorian and Edwardian England.* London: Routledge and Kegan Paul.

Gomersall Meg (1988) Ideals and Realities: The equation of working class girls 1800-1870. *History of Education* Vol 17 No 1 p 37-57.

Horn Pamela (1988) The Education and Employment of Working Class Girls 1870-1914. *History of Education* Vol 17 No 1 p 71-82.

Hunt Felicity (1986) Divided Aims: the Educational Implications of Opposing Ideologies in Girls' Secondary Schooling, 1850-1940. In Felicity Hunt (Ed) *Lessons for Life: The Schooling of Girls and Women 1850-1950.* Oxford: Basil Backwell.

Hunt Felicity (1991) *Gender and Policy in English Education: Schooling for girls 1902-1944.* Hemel Hempstead: Harvester Wheatsheaf.

Leeson Margaret (1995) The Bias is No Longer on Sewing. April 13th. London: *The Independent* Newspaper.

Purvis June (1984) The Experience of Schooling for Working Class Boys and girls in the Nineteenth Century. In Ivor F Goodson and Stephen Bell (Eds) *Defining the Curriculum: Histories and Ethnographies.* London and Philadelphia: Falmer Press.

Purvis June (1989) *Hard Lessons: The Lives and Education of Working Class Women in Nineteenth Century England.* Cambridge: Polity Press.

Purvis June (1991) *A History of Women's Education in England 1800-1914.* Milton Keynes: Open University Press.

Searle Clive (1985) Sugar and Spice and Needlework: *Liberal Education* Issue 54. Autumn.

Sutton Gordon (1976) *Artisan or Artist? A History of the Teaching of Art and Crafts in English Schools.* Oxford: Pergamon Press.

Turnbull Annemarie (1987) Learning Her Womanly Work. In Felicity Hunt (Ed) *Lessons for Life: The Schooling of Girls and Women 1850-1950.* Oxford: Basil Blackwell.

Williams Raymond (1965) *The Long Revolution.* Harmondsworth: Penguin

Chapter 4

Educating Ladies

Introduction

By the beginning of the twentieth century, mathematics had been firmly established as a middle-class boys' study while needlework was that of girls. Both subjects emphasised exclusive differences in school experience, intellectual content and social expectation, and both were firmly entrenched in schooling, society's most potent way of socialising its young.

So complete was the separation, that the gender effect in mathematics education did not really become an issue until the 1970s when comprehensive schooling was well established, the Sex Discrimination Act was on the statute book, and the work of feminist researchers began to explore its many manifestations. Until then it was as difficult for a working-class girls to obtain an education in mathematics as it was to escape from one in domestic subjects. There was some traffic from the elementary to the secondary system through scholarships and the increasing range of post elementary provision, but by far the greater number of the small proportion who made the cultural and economic crossing, and obtained a passport to further and higher education were boys. By the 1960s the Robbins Report noted that working-class girls still only had a 1:600 chance of achieving further education beyond schooling.

By mid-nineteenth century, the decorative needlework of a middle-class man's wife and daughters that covered every surface of his drawing room, was the measure of the number of women he could keep in idleness, a clear indicator of his social status (Bryant, 1979: 29). The aim of education for the daughters of such households was to capture a suitable husband; the content often a dolly mixture of accomplishments and social graces suitable for a not too developed mind in a modestly enticing body. The showiness of the superficiality was matched only by the expense of obtaining it. By mid-century in one often quoted and far from unique case, it was more pretentious, costly and shallow than it had ever been.

> Even the accomplishments in which it took pride were unreal; the pupils could neither paint, draw, play nor sing properly; nor had they the least desire to pursue these occupations except for display... Girls were excluded from classics and mathematics, the only subjects of which the educational value had been in the least thought out, and were brought up on catechisms and epitomes, designed to give an appearance of familiarity with names and events which it would be considered a mark of ignorance not to know, but leaving the pupils utterly unaware of the facts which these names represented. (Cobbe quoted by Archer, 1966: 231)

Such an education was aimed of course at an ideal of femininity: the idle middle-class woman often related more to it in aspiration than reality. There is plenty of evidence that middle-class women engaged in varied and purposeful domestic activity (Bryant, 1979:30) as there is of charitable ladies setting up organisations to alleviate the less than animal conditions under which their labour-intensive garments were made (Neff, 1966:137). Nor were all small private schools as bad as Cobbe's. The alternative to schools was the employment of a governess, usually the impoverished daughter or sister of a middle class home, forced by circumstances to fend for herself in the one respectable job available to her. Many such women were ill-paid and ill-treated and had little to offer from their own trivial education and it was their plight that was the reason for the foundation of the Governesses Benevolent Institution in 1843. That such a radical move should focus on comparatively few women is a measure of the importance placed on maintaining society's structure in a time of threatening change, for in 1851 there were 25,000 governesses compared with 750,000 domestic servants and their sufferings were incomparably less than those of textile workers and dressmakers. Neither were they themselves politically active but, in a highly class-conscious society, their status was incongruous. The spectacle of a lady 'reared to ornament her father's drawing room [yet having] to sell herself to display her employer's prestige' threatened the Victorian romantic ideal of womanhood' (Delamont, 1978a:137).

The educational arm of the Governesses Benevolent Institution was Queen's College in London, founded five years after its parent foundation, for the purpose of educating girls over 12 years of age. Two of its pupils were the well-known reform figures, Frances Mary Buss, who with her mother founded the North London Collegiate School for Ladies in 1850, and Dorothea Beale who became second Principal of Cheltenham Ladies College in 1858. Between them they established a form of school curriculum for middle-class girls which gave them access to the same high status curriculum, including mathematics, that was available to middle-class boys, while maintaining their femininity notably through skill with a needle.

The assumption that their achievement was the work of feminists however, in even the lightest sense of the word, cannot be maintained (Dyhouse, 1981:57. Initially the reformers had to work from a position of powerlessness for at the time women were entirely dependent on men socially, politically and legally. If they had not worked from within the existing conventions of society regarding the deportment of ladies, they could not have succeeded, for there was no platform from which they could have spoken. Two particular taboos still worked towards keeping middle-class women at home, their dual 'protection' from dealings with money (until the Married Women's Property Acts of 1870 and 1882) and from public exposure generally. By the Victorian era it would have been as unladylike to know how to finance and manage a school as it was to canvass support for one by appearing at a meeting, by writing signed articles or letters to the press, or by speaking in public. Emily Davies, who was used to the necessity of having her papers on education read publicly by a sympathetic male, had to support Buss, already recognised in 1865 as formidable, but whose nervousness in the unprecedented giving of female evidence to the Taunton Inquiry, reduced her to tears. The idea of women even being included on the governing body of a school was radical, and Davies' argument for it to the same Commission of Inquiry was treated with some scepticism (Dyhouse, 1987:33).

The male motivation to support reform was not entirely without self-interest. Pederson (quoted by Dyhouse, 1981:58) argues that necessary support for the new schools came from 'professional groups and wealthy businessmen who aspired towards a new standard of gentility which would differentiate them from the bulk of the middle-class.' Such a class and time still needed the dependent wife to maintain status, but required a more responsible and cultivated one. In an increasingly harsh and competitive world of male employment outside the home, the wife within it was to be the civilising force against the rough world outside, the moral guardian of the hearth and curator of the cultural heritage.

The reforms made in the size, structure, management, curriculum and status of middle-class girls' education thus began within an institution set up, governed and run almost completely by men.

> Women played an altogether subordinate role as junior 'tutors' and 'Lady Visitors'. The 'Lady Visitors' were older women who chaperoned pupils on a rota basis when they attended lectures. They had little formal power. They were allowed to 'make suggestions' in a locked suggestion book. (Dyhouse, 1981:60)

By the time she came to Cheltenham, Beale had already had problems with gender politics of all-male committees. She had resigned from her teaching post at Queen's College over the position of women in the male-run establishment, and had been dismissed by another school managed by reactionary churchmen. Both she and Buss had severe problems in securing professional authority in the schools of which they were heads. The success of their campaigns depended heavily on their own personal conduct in maintaining the social conventions for ladies, for they knew that any woman who took on the financial and administrative management of a school ran the grave danger of de-feminising herself. Not only did they fight for better education for middle-class girls, but they had to negotiate roles for themselves as professional women and authorities on education (Dyhouse, 1987:36). They achieved both through subtle re-definitions of the concepts of both liberal education and femininity. The former resulted in a compromise curriculum that necessarily led directly to overload, the latter in a new category of lady, that of the professional, independent but celibate woman.

Negotiating a Curriculum

The maintenance of social class was still the prime concern of education. A true liberal education was still equated with both the highest intellect and the greatest social prestige. Since it was a liberal education that made a boy a gentleman, it was the obvious education for making a girl a lady for, as Beale herself was to point out later 'it cannot be seriously maintained that those studies which tend to make a man nobler or better, have the opposite effect on a woman' (Hunt, 1987:8).

At the time, the liberal curriculum for upper class boys was still dominated by the classics, the importance of which was 'symbolic – a form of consumption – rather than pragmatic' valued as an acquaintance with culture, of no vocational relevance (Delamont, 1978b:167). Nevertheless the ideal itself was goal-directed: it was intended to send high-flying, or socially superior boys to university from whence the young men would enter the exclusively male professions, the Church, medicine, law or academic teaching (Hunt, 1991:118). The destination of middle-class girls however was not an occupation but a role, and the liberal ideal itself was at last under serious challenge, notably in mathematics and science. There were thus strong reasons of both principle and practice for not adopting it wholesale. The women reformers saw no conflict between femininity and its maintenance through education, and the training of the intellect and emotions which produced the gentleman and scholar. Their aim 'was to take those elements of a male liberal education which seemed most effective and worthwhile and discard the rest' while remaining well aware that too much pruning would lead to accusations of inferiority.' (Hunt, 1987:6). Neither could they compromise their pupils (and lose the support of fee-paying parents) by removing the pedestal on which stood the social ideal of wife- and mother-hood. Within the complexity of the arguments, Delamont (1978a:154) classifies the women campaigners into two groups 'the uncompromising – who were determined that women should do what men did, warts and all – and the separatists – who favoured modified courses for women. At times they worked in opposition and at times together in their efforts to maintain the principles of the liberal ideal while realising that much curriculum practice would sabotage it.

An obvious practical reality was that for large numbers of educated girls, the marriage target was not achievable. The British Empire had taken many men abroad and the 1851 census showed that one third of British women would not be able to find husbands: there were 870,000 more women than men' (Delamont, 1978:139). Among those men of the right age and class that were available, there were large numbers who could not afford to support a dependent wife, brought up to idle and conspicuous consumption, particularly if they had to support unmarried sisters as well. The plight of such women totally dependent on their brothers was a main concern of Buss in setting up the sort of education that would enable them to earn their own living. Whether in teaching, nursing or the newly available clerical work, a new sort of lady, without a husband but without compromising her femininity, was required. Such respectable celibacy did not compromise what both Beale and Buss always saw as the higher calling of the educated wife and mother. Nearly thirty years after Beale became Principal she still found it necessary to defend the teaching of classics and mathematics on the grounds that it would help a mother 'to take an interest in her schoolboy sons: [for] 'it was [still] scarcely possible to defend the right of even a middle-class girl's intellectual education in terms of her own interests' (Attar, 1990:88). 'Ultimately the dilemma [of the reformers] was that of the perceived incompatibility of paid work and the domestic role, and how schools deal with it' (Hunt, 1987:xx). It was not resolved in the days of Beale and Buss and is still not resolved.

From the beginning, the curriculum had to be negotiated against parental expectation and the current theories of female biology. The type of education for capturing husbands was useless for spinsters, but no parent would want to condemn their daughters to spinsterhood by educating them specifically for it. Neither did they want an education for their girls that would masculinise them: in the view of the day, a genuine risk. In the late 1880s the *Saturday Review*, with time-honoured invective that would have done credit to the early Church, called educated women, amongst other things, 'defeminated' 'hermaphrodite' 'mongrel' 'a species of vermin' and 'one of the most intolerable monsters in creation' (Delamont, 1978b:179).

Such gross vituperation from educated gentlemen, had a considerable audience and arguments against educating women were receiving considerable 'scientific' support. These reached a crescendo in the first decades of the twentieth century, but in the latter half of the nineteenth, they became focussed on the publication of Spencer's *Principles of Biology* in 1867 and *Principles of Sociology* in 1876. A trace of them remains today in small pockets of research, still looking for sex differences in brain function in mathematics (Leder, 1992:614). The arguments caused considerable impact on the education of girls, focussing again on the extreme contrast of the intellectually taxing nature of masculine mathematics, and the trivialised manual skill of feminine needlework. Spencer's belief was that the society in which he wrote was the peak of civilisation. For him, the mental inferiority of women was a mark of that civilisation, for it was only in 'primitive' societies, like those being discovered in the colonies, or already visible in the uncivilised working classes at home, that women did hard physical work on a level with men. The arguments took two directions, the first that secondary and higher education made women physiologically unfit for motherhood and the second that a bookish education at even the elementary level, disinclined them for it. In either case, the moral decline of the family, indeed of the race and empire, was seen as the inevitable consequence of educating girls away from the prospect of motherhood alone (Dyhouse, 1976:44). Various physiological disasters were confidently forecast, ranging from a distorted pelvis to flat chestedness, accompanied by brain fever, the inevitable result of mental overstrain.

The notion of overstrain, particularly during adolescence, proved harder to overthrow than the belief in the grosser physical distortions. Medical opinion regarded physiological strength as a fixed entity, and unmentionable menstruation as a drain on resources: extra expenditure of brain energy on book learning would debilitate females physically. The subject universally agreed to be the most mentally strenuous was of course mathematics. The bad effects on the brain of both males and females of too much mathematics was accepted even among those highly educated in it. James Wilson, one of the first curriculum developers in mathematics education and co-founder of the AIGT had a nervous collapse soon after being named Senior Wrangler at Cambridge in 1856. So complete was his breakdown that he 'could not differentiate or integrate; I had forgotten ... all Lunar Theory and Dynamics; nearly the whole of Trigonometry and Conic Sections was a blank . . Happily algebra and Euclid were safe' (Howson, 1982: 126). Ada Lovelace's illness of 1843 (in which her mother had treated her with blood-letting, laudanum, morphine and alcohol) stated that 'one ingredient (but only one among many) has been too much mathematics'. Professor Augustus De Morgan concurred. Referring to Lovelace's very great mathematical ability De Morgan advised the mother against her daughter's 'obvious determination to try not only to reach, but to go beyond, the present bounds of knowledge . . the very great tension of mind which they [mathematical studies] require is beyond the strength of a woman's physical power of application' (Alic, 1986:162).

That the pioneers of middle-class girls' education showed that girls could study some mathematics without succumbing to brain fever was a major achievement. The first generations of the new headmistresses went some way along the path of the physical strain theory however, though they supplied increasing amounts of evidence to refute the predicted anatomical effects. All paid particular attention to the health of their pupils, indeed the reforms that Buss were to introduce included proper medical supervision and medical certificates. But their first curricula advertised the teaching of needlework and mathematics was not mentioned.

Mathematics 1850-1900

It was as necessary for the new middle-class schools to want to teach mathematics as it was to have to teach needlework, but to launch straight into a subject as unfeminine and endangering as mathematics, was both tactically and practically impossible. Beale 'dared not introduce Euclid at first, for 'had I done so, it might have been the death of the College' (Howson, 1982:73). In the early days of Cheltenham Ladies College even arithmetic was suspect to some parents. 'My dear lady,' a father grumbled, 'if my daughters were going to be bankers, it would be very well to teach arithmetic as you do, but really there is no need!' (Kamm, 1958:56).

Beale herself was already an experienced teacher of mathematics. Her love of the subject and her 'passionate desire' to know more of it, had been inspired by public lectures on astronomy when she was 16. Her experience of learning was not untypical, for most women who had learned any mathematics had done so with their brothers, or brothers' tutors, or had been taught by their fathers. Mary Somerville's experience of formal educational was as unstructured as any. She had followed mathematical puzzles in journals, and borrowed copies of Euclid's elements and Bonnycastle's algebra from her younger brother's tutor. When her parents removed the candles to prevent her from reading them at night, she memorised the books and worked out the problems in her head (Alic, 1986:183).

Beale had taught mathematics at Queen's College for seven years. At a time when there was virtually no training for secondary teaching, women who could teach mathematics in the new schools were almost impossible to find: even arithmetic teachers were a grave problem. As Buss told the Taunton Commission in 1865, although she could recruit teachers who knew arithmetic she was not allowed to employ teachers who had been trained in Government training colleges. Part of the pioneers' reforms were to expand teacher education but in the meantime they sent their teachers to lectures as and when they could: the minutes of the early staff meetings of the North London Collegiate contain notes of such lectures. Buss's immediate successor, Sophie Bryant, was herself a mathematician. As a beautiful young widow, with a notable absence of brain fevers, she filled all possible criteria for a lady principal.

A particular problem was the low base line from which the new schools had to start. Evidence of it was given by both Beale and Buss to the Taunton Commission. Buss pointed out that she had large numbers of girls aged thirteen, fourteen and fifteen who 'can scarcely do the simplest sum in arithmetic'. Beale produced an analysis of a hundred entrance examinations to Cheltenham, based on each girl's estimate of her own knowledge:

Number of Pupils over fifteen years of age who professed to have learned

Fractions	8	each sum set was wrong
Rule of Three, or Practice	18	each sum set was wrong
Compound Long Division	14	of these 13 were wrong
Compound Short Division	1	it was wrong
Compound Multiplication	5	all were wrong
Simple Multiplication	3	2 were right.

(Kamm, 1958:80)

Low base was to remain a problem which well illustrated the lack of access that all girls had to mathematics education. In 1912 the Head-mistress of Queen Mary High School Liverpool, E R Gwatkin, noted that girls sent to boarding schools had often been under the charge of governesses who knew no mathematics themselves and that the mathematical experience of girls coming from elementary schools was usually confined to 'an extraordinarily over-elaborated arithmetic' (Board of Education, 1912: 573).

By the time of the Taunton Commission, Buss's initial difficulties in teaching arithmetic had been more publicly exposed. In 1862, twelve years after the founding of North London Collegiate, Emily Davies joined battle with London University, who had refused Elizabeth Garrett permission to take their matriculation examination. Davies' response was to set up a committee to persuade the universities to admit women to their local examinations. Since these were public written papers with no vivas, girls could take them without impropriety. Six weeks before the examination date, Cambridge replied with a willingness to examine girls at their London centre, under the same regulations and simultaneously with boys. For most girls at the time the standard was far too high, but Buss responded to Davies' request with twenty-five candidates out of the final ninety-one whom it was possible to find. In spite of the short notice, no girl suffered brain-fever and on the whole all acquitted themselves well, except in the arithmetic paper, where the results were disastrous. Of the fifty seven who failed, ten were Buss's pupils. The reason given by the Board was poor teaching: the girls had been taught by rote and had not understood the rules that they had tried to use. From that date arithmetic teaching became a priority at North London Collegiate and the 1863 paper heads the School's curriculum archive. Unlike the elementary schools whose curricula were controlled by the Code, the new secondary schools worked out the detail of their curricula as they went along. At North London Collegiate they are recorded in Buss's neat copperplate in the minutes of Monday staff meetings as arithmetic results continued to improve.

In 1862 the girls had done well enough generally for the Cambridge Examinations Board to continue the experiment for a trial period of three years: girls would take the same subjects and follow the same syllabuses as boys but no girls' names were to be published on the class lists. Davies immediately set about making the trial period a permanent one achieving success two years later. It was a triumph for the uncompromising group of reformers and ensured equal rating of boys' and girls' results, even without publication of their names. Disagreement came from a separatist point of view which Beale represented. She disliked competitiveness, preferring a quiet, ladylike 'general testing of work done.' (Kamm, 1958:70). Neither did she think it expedient for girls to take the same exams as boys, not because she thought that their abilities were inferior but because she believed that men's and women's roles were different. She was also acutely class conscious, as was demanded by her school, which catered for a higher class of gentry than Buss's. The examinations at that time were known as 'middle-class examinations' because they were to test standards in middle-class schools, but

> There seems to be some difficulty in applying them to the higher middle-classes... The brothers of our pupils go to the Universities. Now, generally speaking, those who go in for the Local Examinations occupy a much lower place in the social scale, and our pupils would not like to be classed with them, but regarded as equal rank to those who pass to University. (Beale quoted by Dyhouse, 1978b:177)

Figure 6: Cambridge Local Examination Paper in Arithmetic, taken by North London Collegiate girls in 1863.

UNIVERSITY OF CAMBRIDGE.

LOCAL EXAMINATIONS.

JUNIOR CANDIDATES.

Tuesday, *Dec.* 15, 1863. 11 A.M. to 12½ P.M.

Preliminary Arithmetic.

[N.B. All Candidates are required to satisfy the Examiners in this paper. The working of the sums is to be sent up, and the answer clearly written under each.]

1. Express in figures

    (*a*) One thousand and one.

    (*b*) Fifty thousand and fifty.

    (*c*) One hundred million forty thousand seven hundred and six.

2. The populations of the different parishes and districts of a large town are 16640, 321, 3750, 3906, 5144, 2684, 13360, 391, and 5797, respectively; by how many does the whole town's population fall short of a million?

3. Multiply 1863 by 365, and the product by 24.

Also multiply 18603 by 365, and 1863 by 3650.

4. Multiply £45. 19s. 9½d. by 8, and by 80.

Hence find what the sum total distributed is, when of 88 persons each receives £45. 19s. 9½d.

5. Divide 7227 by 9, and 2239605 by 317.

803

[*Turn over.*

2

6. Four bills of the following amounts £27. 10s. 3¾d., £13. 4s. 7½d., £43. 0s. 6d., and £5, are paid out of £100, what money is left?

7. Divide £15942. 16s. 6d. by 108.

If you had to distribute this sum of money equally amongst 216 persons, what sum would each receive?

8. Add together $\frac{7}{16}$, $\frac{2}{3}$, $\frac{5}{48}$, and $3\frac{19}{24}$.

9. How much is $12\frac{2}{9}$ less than 14?

10. Divide $\frac{4}{7}$ of $9\frac{1}{3}$ by 7 times one-fifth of 30.

11. If the price of 3000 copies of a book be £4725, what sum will the sale of 1937 copies produce?

12. By Practice, find the rent of 69 ac. 3 ro. 27 po. at 30s. an acre.

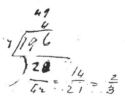

The whole business of mathematics examinations was already controversial for boys' mathematics education. The girls' rapidly improving performance, and their schools' improvement of teaching did not however ensure that women educators had an equal share in the development of the examination and courses, for the business of mathematics education was still virtually a gentleman's club. In 1875 the one hundred members of the AIGT included only one women, Beale herself (Howson, 1982: 135). Its Mathematics Teaching Committee, set up in 1902 to pursue reforms, contained no women. The middle-class girls' schools continued battling with tradition, stereotype, low expectation, prejudice, a low starting-point and very few qualified teachers, taking the examinations of which there were now two. Like many boys' schools, the girls of Notting Hill High School in London took the 'AIGT syllabus first for the sake of their intelligence' then Euclid for the sake of the Cambridge examination' (Howson, 1982:136).

As soon as Beale had felt that her Management Committee were confident enough in her for her not to have to apply for special permission, she had introduced the necessary Euclid into her top class, together with her own teaching methods: she would not allow textbooks in case pupils should try to learn propositions off by heart. By 1884 it was possible to write 'the days when parents threatened to remove their daughters if set to study such masculine subjects as mathematics were in the distant past' (Delamont, 1978b:180). Beale's personal commitment to mathematics continued with a single-mindedness that eventually gained her admission to the anecdotal category of eccentric mathematics teachers. A teacher who was leaving to be married, came to her to say how sorry she was that she could not finish correcting a batch of geometry papers before she left. 'Take them on your honeymoon, dear' said Miss Beale, 'they will give you something to do.' And to a teacher who came to say good-bye at the end of one term, Miss Beale said, 'You had better read *Differential Calculus* in the summer holidays. It will give you a new view of life' (Kamm, 1958:232).

That it was possible for such remarks to have been recorded, is some measure of the progress that a remarkable generation of women teachers had made in mathematics education for middle-class girls, for above all subjects, success in mathematics was an indicator of intellect. The Taunton Commissioners noted the fact already remarked by some of the Inspectors of elementary schools that 'there is mighty evidence to the effect that the essential capacity for learning is the same or nearly the same in the two sexes' (Kamm, 1958:89). Forty years after the Busses, mother and daughter, founded North London Collegiate came the announcement at Cambridge that, although she could not as a woman qualify for a degree, Philippa Fawcett's performance in mathematics was above that of the Senior Wrangler, and Buss rejoiced that 'we have abolished sex in education' (Kamm, 1958:97). The achievement was indeed remarkable but the rejoicing was premature.

Needlework 1850-1900

From the beginning of reform, the liberal ideal had always been compromised by the demand of femininity. Buss's first curriculum reassured potential parents that their daughters would receive 'a liberal education and the accomplishments necessary for ladies' (Kamm, 1958:45) and the first School Prospectus of 1850 listed Plain and Ornamental Needlework in The Course of Education (Scrimgeour, 1950:208). The founders of Cheltenham Ladies College stated that 'they considered that it was possible to give sound instruction without sacrificing accomplishments' (Kamm, 1958:52).

By now there was hard pressure for an educational, in contrast to a utilitarian, vocational or social justification for teaching needlework. Buss, who had herself hand-made a shirt for her father by the age of ten, encouraged its teaching both as social service and as a domestic and liberal art. Sewing as social service was the aim of the School's Dorcas Society which met monthly on Wednesday afternoons. As in the elementary schools, the differential status of academic subjects was maintained by teaching them in the morning. The minutes of the staff meetings show clearly that plain needlework was from the beginning, the top non-academic priority. The 1877 syllabus for 'High Schools, Public Day School Scholars, also for Children under Private Home Tuition' that had been devised by the London Institute for the Advancement of Plain Needlework, was discussed. Rising standards were noted, items for holiday tasks carefully considered, and the Dorcas Committee reported regularly. A millinery class came and went. No response is recorded to a letter of 1890 from a Miss Falkend, a professional dressmaker applying to Miss Buss for apprentices, but one three years later from Mrs Peile inviting pupils to join the Needlework Guild for West St Pancras in making garments for the poor is seriously considered, and the decision taken to ask the girls if they themselves would like to make things, perhaps as a marked holiday task, with an exhibition in school.

The new century saw a continued interest in sewing with mending as priority and a continued concern with clothing for the poor. Kamm (1958:46) reports that soon after it began the Dorcas Society was turning out between five and six hundred such garments a year. A pupil of the 1880s remembers it:

For two hours we sewed horribly coarse cotton, of a dull biscuit colour and queer smell, with little blackish threads poking out of it here and there. It was to become in time chemises for the poor. We were not taught how to cut them out, for our mistakes would have been wasteful. Our duty was to join long stretches of stuff together ... Even here marks pursued us. Since they were not to be taken off for talking in this blessed instance, ten or less were allotted for the amount of sewing we had achieved. ... But ... the Dorcas marks never 'counted'. (Purvis, 1985:157)

The tedious manipulations of sewing seem to be more often recorded than pupil's reaction to the tedious manipulation of the sort of fractions of the 1863 examination paper that would have formed a major part of arithmetic lessons. It can be argued with considerable justification that much of such sewing is rather more of a mathematical activity, and certainly of much more obvious use, than the ability to 'divide $4/7$ of $9^4/5$, by 7 times one-fifth of 30' that features on the 1863 examination paper. The acceptance of the chores and purposes of arithmetic was not questioned in the same vein as the low status but equally useful sewing.

The Dorcas Society remained active until just before the beginning of the Second World War and it is interesting to note that the first intimation of its demise in the Staff Meeting Minutes comes not from any matter of principle but because of a time table clash with games. Those of January 15th 1937 record both the time table clash and Dorcas' redundancy to the schools' formal teaching of domestic subjects. On March 8th 1937 'it was agreed that the time had come to bring the Dorcas Society to an end. When it was started it was almost the only form of social service open to the girls, but for years now it has tried to serve the double purpose of giving the girls useful training in needlework and of providing articles which will be useful to their poorer neighbours – and these two ends are often incompatible. The Dorcas classes will cease.'

From the 1880s, all girls' schools had come under pressure to teach additional domestic subjects. Needlework always had an ambiguous relationship with these, 'its acceptability as a genteel lady's occupation compensating for its status as a domestic subject' (Attar, 1990:88). Domestic subjects were a continuing cause of conflict from the 1870s as more girls' schools, notably the High Schools of the Girls Public Day School Company (later Trust) were founded. In their version of the liberal education such subjects should follow a sound intellectual, general education, not replace it, and a clear distinction was made between education and instruction. The idea of domestic training in school was dismissed with contempt. School Inspectors who visited the small number of High Schools which did claim to do some domestic training found that 'the provision was likely to be limited to a few rather apologetic classes in needlework, mainly confined to the lower forms' (Dyhouse, 1976:53).

With changes in public opinion however, the strength of the arguments for an intellectual education over a practical one wavered and the views of the new generation of headmistresses began to diverge. Lilian Faithfull, new Principal of Cheltenham Ladies College, regressed:

> In recent years there has been a widespread movement to bring the education of our girls into relation with their work as home-makers. The old 'blue-stocking' type, who prided herself on not knowing how to sew or mend, and who thought cooking menial and beneath her, no longer appeals to anyone ... we want our girls to grow up into sensible, methodical, practical women, able to direct intelligently and practically the manifold duties of the home. (quoted by Dyhouse, 1976:54)

With the resurgence of domestic ideals, came a resurgence of doubts about girls and mathematics. Sara Burstall, who had obtained high marks in domestic economy as a pupil at the North London Collegiate, and was now Headmistress of Manchester High School, argued against the line her predecessors had taken, insisting that the need for domestic training was now clear:

> Greater emphasis is now placed on the special duties of women as such to the community, on the basic value of the social organism of the family and the home, on the reality and importance of biological and sociological differences between men and women.

Mathematics, she argued,

> should be kept at a minimum for girls, it does not underlie their activities as it does so many of the activities of men ... it is needed for training only; an excess of it, the subject being useless to them, and disconnected with their life, has a hardening effect on the nature of women. (quoted in Dyhouse, 1976:54)

The Chief Woman Advisor to the Board of Education concurred:

> Lessons requiring much concentration and therefore using up a great deal of brain energy, Mathematics for instance, should not be pushed ... such subjects as cookery, embroidery or the handicrafts may well be introduced into the curriculum as they cause comparatively little mental strain. (Campbell quoted by Dyhouse, 1981:134)

The Board of Education's Special Report on the Teaching of Mathematics in the United Kingdom, published in 1912 published both views. Gwatkin summarised the case against the Burstall view, before demolishing it. It was simply not true that girls found the subject uninteresting. When it did appear to be true it was debatable how much was due to the inherent nature of the subject and how much to teaching: Gwatkin believed that it was mainly the latter. Teachers still rarely received any training, there were not enough of them to go round and mathematics teaching did not have the tradition of years of experience that lay behind the teaching of literature and history for example. Like many since, Gwatkin argued strongly that relating mathematics exercises to the girls' own experience stimulates a personal interest in the subject and reduces the chances of the sort of nonsensical answers that are too often given to abstract and unrealistic arithmetic problems. And if, as they were often accused, women argued off the point, mathematics was the best way of teaching them not to. Mathematics encouraged independent thought, something that girls brought up to be dependent needed greatly. Many girls who seemed to be good workers were really mentally lazy, 'they reproduced but they did not produce'. Good mathematics teaching would help them assert their own thinking (Gwatkin, 1912).

As for the notion of strain and the desire to return to the age of accomplishments, Gwatkin was scathing. Most people find mathematics hard, but that is no reason for not teaching it. The question of health was a difficult one, care was needed but there was still no argument for not teaching mathematics.

> We have made mistakes in the past, and it is to be feared that many girls have suffered in health through their zeal for higher education: we need not therefore, return to the days of our great-grandmothers, when the domestic and fine arts, together with a little French, were considered to make sufficient demands upon what intellect a girl had, and when it was correct for a woman to swoon on occasions which would appear to us to call for instant action. Let a girl work, and work hard while she is at it, ... and we shall have fewer idle discontented women who live in enervating ease, and breed weaklings for the nation. (Board of Education, 1912:569)

The mathematics to which Gwatkin and Burstall referred, consisted at that time of following textbooks in algebra and geometry. Through the books and the examinations towards which they aimed, the subject was confined to a closed circuit of rote and regurgitation, enlightened by the occasional abstract arguments of propositions. (It will be remembered that Beale would not allow textbooks at Cheltenham when she first introduced Euclid, for fear that the girls would learn the propositions by rote.) The Cambridge, pre-university view of mathematics still dominated the examinations. Any practical orientation of examples in the textbooks were geared towards industrial and engineering examples from the closed world of male employment. Thus, although some schools recognised the mathematics content and potential of some at least of the activities of the feminised subject of needlework, there was little possibility of their being taken seriously both in a subject and controlling profession that was exclusively masculine. To study mathematics at all, to become a teacher of it, a girl had to work within prescribed content, competitive method and control, that were entirely separate from the way in which she was expected to live and work in every other sphere.

Though small in proportion to the schoolgirl population as a whole, numbers of women mathematicians and scientists who mainly went into teaching, continued to be produced by the girls' secondary schools. During the world wars, many emerged from school to do essential war work and returned to the more feminine pursuit of teaching when it was over. Even then, involvement in mathematics education for middle-class grammar school girls was not on a par with that of their brothers, and a female mathematician as a university lecturer was a rare object of comment, and sexist insinuation. The first female professor of mathematics education in England was appointed only in 1984 and, at the time of writing there are only six woman professors of mathematics.

Domestic subjects remained perforce on the curriculum of middle-class girls schools in receipt of Government grant, and continued to be treated with the intellectual contempt at which academic institutions excel. They were taught in the lower classes and to girls regarded as academic failures, a phenomenon that had been noted by Inspectors from the beginning of the century. Needlework also continued to be taught in middle-class girls' school where its status too remained low. Evans (1991) writing of her experiences as a grammar school girl in the late 1950s, contrasts its status with that of mathematics. The legacy of the nineteenth century boys' curriculum remained in the competitiveness of the curriculum, both pupils and subjects. Mathematics was one of the serious subjects with pupils graded into A, B and C divisions for its study. Domestic Science was not a serious subject, was badly taught and only required for the academic pupils for their first year. At a time when the under-representation of women in science and mathematics was not considered significant, being good at them at this particular girls' school had no great appeal. At the same time, Evans and her peers half-recognised that making clothes and cooking puddings were not skills that had a great deal of either social or economic value. 'Very plainly, we recognised and endorsed the cash nexus and the limited social value of the traditional work of women'(Evans, 1991:12). She, like all her predecessors since the age of Beale and Buss, still had to take on conflicting identities,' first that of the androgynous middle-class person who is academically successful in an academic world that is apparently gender blind' and 'second, that of the well-behaved middle-class woman who knows how to defer to and respect the authority of men.' In the context and time, the needlework she was taught was a social education in 'the thankless task' of the elementary school girls of the previous century, through which all girls learned their place.

The position of needlework in the schools for middle-class girls and its dethroning as a curriculum subject lies in a much more complex collection of causes than straight competition with academic subjects. The justification for teaching it varied from practical utility, as feminine accomplishment, vocational skill, social control and instrumental grant-earner, occasionally as art but never as having any serious content. Although from the beginning it was separated in status from the academic subjects, its status as a curriculum subject was maintained at least at North London Collegiate. The final justification for ending Dorcas still maintained the value of teaching needlework.

The Buss compromise of devoting time in a liberally-oriented school to the teaching of needlework was a clever way of dealing with both the stereotype of femininity and the practical realities of being a middle class woman. By teaching plain sewing to young ladies she equipped them with an essential skill in home-making, a means of clothing themselves economically on a tight budget, a potential fall-back for earning money, however little, vocational skills, and an appropriate accomplishment of an educated, socially responsible lady. In the circumstances of the day, the angry rejection of the stereotype of femininity by the next generation of High School Heads, itself rejected by the Burstall camp, can be understood. But by rejecting the symbol of femininity, the second wave of reformers maintained the under-valuing of the content, which in turn re-inforced the stereotype. This middle-class attitude had a devastating effects on the education of working-class girls, the vast majority of the schoolgirl population.

None of the developments in mathematics education that affected the education of middle-class girls had any effect on working-class girls. Even in the 1970s the feminist movements in mathematics education that brought world-wide recognition of the forces that act against girls, were mainly middle-class in orientation, showing scant interest in the lives of working-class girls whose school careers ended before academic,

Opposite: **Figure 7**: Even the arrival of the sewing machine did little to reduce the demand on the curriculum of girls for hand sewing. *Punch* cartoon February 3rd 1866.

46   PUNCH, OR THE LONDON CHARIVARI.   [February 3, 1866.

THE SEWING-MACHINE.

Draper. "A most Wonderful Invention, indeed, Mum, and it really Executes the Work so Efficiently and Quickly, that, 'pon my Word, I think there's nothing left for the Ladies to do now but to *Improve their Intellects!*"

BUMBLE'S COUNTERBLAST AGAINST CENTRA-LISATION.

Did you ever! Well I never! Here's a turning topsy-turvy
Of the good old British principles, for the sake o' paupers scurvy;
Paternal Government's put down (now the rule of Daddy ceases)
By despotism and Mayne-force, which I take it them police is!

What becomes of our self-government, if the coals we're thus hauled
    over
By your Farnalls, and such fellows, as lives on the rates in clover?
Chaps as has their salaries paid 'em out o' *pour* pocket, and mine, Sir,
And yet comes to cheek the guardians, all along o' paupers' whine, Sir.

"Mustn't do this," "Mustn't do that," and "Must do as you're
    told," 'tis—
Change the water in the casuals' baths, and try how hot and cold 'tis!
Mustn't shut paupers up at night, without bells, gas, or fuel!
Cocker up with beef-tea and wine them that fights shy o' gruel!

Find Union doctors in quinine, cod-liver oil, *et cetera*—
The expensive things we takes ourselves, when we're ill and would be
    betterer;
Change sick-ward sheets, and dress bed-sores, not trust to pauper
    nurses:
Bless me! Do they think ratepayers has no bottoms to their purses!

And now they're kickin' up a row about the casual wards, Sir;
As if casuals had a right to more than dry bread and bare boards, Sir!
As if Boards had any business to be payin' a night warder,
For the sake of keepin' wagabonds like them in peace and order!

As for them as says misfortin' has druv 'em to sich places,
Boards can't be making rules to meet exceptionable cases:
All casuals is bad 'uns, and them as ain't, to start with,
Is certain, in sich company, to ketch more than they can part with.

Wot's the use o' spendin' money to improve what's past improvin'?
The police have got enough to do to keep sich varmint movin':
As for lettin' 'em inside the House, at Villiers's dictation,
It's the small end of that horful wedge—*you* know—Centralisation!

And where that comes it's all U. P. with the British Constitootion,
Magna Charta, Habeas Corpus, and our glorious Revoolootion:
Our Westries all go to the wall, Police and Press grow stronger:
Englishmen's houses cease to be their castles any longer!

LORDS HIGH MENIAL.

By one of Reuter's telegrams we are informed that the King of Prussia has charged Prince Biron von Courland, Lord High Cup-bearer, with the mission of proceeding to Brussels to congratulate Leopold the Second on his accession to the throne. A Lord High Cupbearer is a very proper officer to attend on a monarch who may be described as the Landlord of the Spread Eagle, but, when he is sent out, those to whom he is accredited would rather perhaps be disposed to welcome him as Lord High Pothoy, particularly if he came convey-ing an acceptable plenty of pots from Potsdam. He might be accom-panied by the Lord High Post-boy, leaving the Lord High Waiter at home to preside over the Lords in Waiting, whilst the Lord High Ostler directed the affairs of the stalls, and the blacking department was administered by the Lord High Boots. Employment suitable for such High Lords as these might be found at the new grand English joint-stock hotels whose landlords are among the chiefs of the landed aristocracy.

A Pilgrim in Progress.

The significant intimation following appears in the *Morning Post :*—

"Dr. Pusey.—The French clerical journals announce that Dr. Pusey, on leaving Bordeaux, proceeded to Orleans on a visit to Bishop Dupanloup."

It is expected that Dr. Pusey will proceed from Orleans to Rome.

university-oriented qualifications in mathematics, in any meaningful sense of the word, become the measure of intellectual achievement.

Neither of the two new female roles that emerged from the reform, the celibate career woman nor the intellectual wife was of use to working-class women as role models. Rather, the earlier reformers in particular 'needed a houseful of servants to live out their new life styles' (Delamont, 1978.b: 184). In their own way the reformers maintained the Victorian domestic ideal while creating a new élite in terms of class, gender and intellect. By maintaining the Victorian domestic ideal they condemned their working-class sisters to an education burdened even more by domestic chores, with even less access to the intellectual pleasures and employment possibilities which they themselves enjoyed. The 'uncompromisers' victory was a Pyrrhic one.

> Although they won access to male subjects for clever middle-class and upper-class girls, the inevitable narrowness of the social ideas prevented them from stopping separatist ideas dominating working-class education. By the time this mass system was emerging the pioneers were unable, or unwilling to stop thinking in class terms and so [working-class education] was built along sex-specific lines. (Delamont, 1978b:164)

Since working-class education was kept geared towards gendered jobs, the education of working-class girls was geared towards future work as housewife, servant, or worker in the developing clothing, textiles and food industries. Again there was a reason for the needle (and spoon) to dominate the girls' curriculum at the expense of the rest of their education. They continued their diet of sums and sewing.

References

Alic, Margaret (1986) *Hypatia's Heritage. A History of Women in Science from Antiquity to the Late Nineteenth Century*. London: The Women's Press

Archer R L (1966 reprinted from 1921) *Secondary Education in the Nineteenth Century*. London: Frank Cass

Attar Dena (1990) *Wasting Girls' Time*. London: Virago Press.

Board of Education (1912) *Special Reports on Educational Subjects Volume 26. The teaching of Mathematics in The United Kingdom. Vol 1*. London: His Majesty's Stationery Office.

Bryant, Margaret. (1979) *The Unexpected Revolution: A Study of the History of the Education of Women and Girls in the Nineteenth Century*. London: University of London Institute of Education (New Series) Number 10.

Delamont, Sara (1978a) The Contradictions in Ladies' Education. In Sara Delamont and Lorna Duffin (Eds) *The Nineteenth Century Woman: Her Cultural and Physical World*. London: Croom Helm

Delamont, Sara (1978b) The Domestic Ideology and Women's Education. In Sara Delamont and Lorna Duffin (Eds) *The Nineteenth Century Woman: Her Cultural and Physical World*. London: Croom Helm

Dyhouse Carol (1976) Social Darwinistic ideas and the Development of women's education in England 1880-1920. *History of Education*, Vol 5 No 1 p 41-58

Dyhouse Carol (1981) *Girls Growing up in Late Victorian and Edwardian England*. London: Routledge and Kegan Paul.

Dyhouse Carol (1987) Miss Buss and Miss Beale: Gender and Authority in the History of Education. In Felicity Hunt (Ed) 1987. *Lessons for Life. The Schooling of Girls and Women 1850-1950*. Oxford: Blackwell.

Evans Mary (1991) *A Good School. Life at a Girls' Grammar School in the 1950s*. London: The Women's Press.

Gwatkin E R (1912) The Value of the Study of Mathematics in Public Secondary Schools for Girls. In Board of Education, The Teaching of Mathematics in the United Kingdom Part I: Being a Series of Papers prepared for the International Commission on the Teaching of Mathematics. *Special Reports on Educational Subjects* Vol 26. London: His Majesty's Stationery Office.

Howson Geoffrey. (1982) *A History of Mathematics Education in England*. Cambridge: Cambridge University Press.

Hunt Felicity (Ed) (1987) *Lessons for Life. The Schooling of Girls and Women 1850-1950*. Oxford: Blackwell.

Hunt Felicity (1991) *Gender and Policy in English Education: Schooling for Girls 1902-1944*. Hemel Hempstead: Harvester Wheatsheaf

Kamm J (1958) *How Different from Us. A Biography of Miss Buss and Miss Beale*. London: The Bodley Head.

Lawson John and Silver Harold (1973) *A Social History of Education in England*. London: Methuen.

Leder Gilah (1991) Mathematics and Gender: Changing Perspectives. In D A Grouws (Ed) *Handbook of Research on Mathematics Teaching and Learning*. New York: Macmillan.

Neff Wanda F (1966) *Victorian Working Women. An Historical and Literary Study of Women in British Industries and Professions 1832-1850*. London: Frank Cass. First published in 1929.

North London Collegiate (1894) *Extracts from Minutes of Staff Meetings*. London: North London Collegiate Archive (unpublished)

Purvis June (1985) Domestic Subjects Since 1870. In Ivor E Goodson (Ed) *Social Histories of the Secondary Curriculum. Subjects for Study*. London and Philadelphia: Falmer Press.

Scrimgeour R M (1950) *The North London Collegiate School 1850-1950. A Hundred Years of Girls Education. Essays in honour of the Centenary of Frances Mary Buss Foundation*. Oxford: Oxford University Press.

Chapter 5

Girls, Mathematics and Work

Introduction

Mathematics in education has had some remarkable effects for a neutral discipline, theoretically detached from the daily affairs of life. In the world to which education directs people, mathematics is immensely powerful. It supports, controls and communicates political and economic messages and policies: it grades, labels and classifies individuals: it analyses, summarises and condemns whole cultures. Within education, mathematics also has high prestige and power. It is the subject more than any other that labels differences in perceived overall abilities between students, that separates the 'bright' child who moves on to more mathematics and more education, and the child who 'cannot even add', who leaves school at the earliest opportunity for ill or unrewarded manual labour. In public perception, mathematics has a daunting press: for most people it exemplifies something way over their heads that only a few egg-heads are capable of. In many individuals it can arouse feelings of distaste, inadequacy, fear or even panic (Buxton, 1981). Such a record is a strange one indeed for an emotionally, intellectually and culturally neutral field of study.

Exclusion from, or limitation of the study of mathematics can have devastating effects, economically, socially and psychologically. It can leave people vulnerable to manipulation by misuse of statistics: it prevents their access to status jobs and career advancement; it can leave them scarred with feelings of inadequacy, even an implied moral failure through being marked 'wrong' (Buxton, 1981). The conscious exclusion from mathematics of a selected group of people, can leave them with all these scars. Girls barred from mathematics by expectation, convoluted theory, or the habits of long history, are deprived of input to and status in one of the most powerful parts of their own heritage and culture.

Mathematics in Contexts

But in the 1970s and 80s, mathematics education as the pursuit of a masculine, middle-class, white pastime was assailed on all fronts. Much of the early work on gender and mathematics focused on the girls themselves for the long years of conditioning had pathologised them, not the content or the pedagogy of mathematics. In the 1960s, the 'common sense' acceptance about girls and mathematics was that of their history: girls 'could not, need not and would not want to do advanced mathematics – or at least not to the same extent as boys.' (Willis, 1989:2). Research began in America and took the poor participation of girls as a fact of life, setting out to try and explain the phenomenon under the general research question of 'why *can't* girls do as well as boys?' (Willis's emphasis). Genetic factors were still pursued, now with emphasis on possible differences in spatial abilities: there was still an acceptance of some biological 'deficit' in girls. By the 1970s political, social and psychological arguments in the nature versus nurture debates on the concept of intelligence, and the reemergence of feminism as an analytical force, changed the focus of the debate from the question of why can't girls do as well as boys, to why don't they. Affective factors were investigated: did girls dislike maths: did they fear success: how could they be motivated to succeed? By the late 1980s the question had shifted again to why won't girls do as well as boys, why did they choose to participate less. By this time an enormous amount of research data on girls' mathematical performance had accumulated, which has been well summarised elsewhere (for example by Leder, 1992). The problems does not lie with girls, but with mathematics education, the way it is defined and the uses to which it is put (Willis, 1989:2).

Analyses of learning materials showed a universal acceptance of masculinity in mathematics, in the delivery of the subject to even the youngest children. As Northam (1981:11) points out, mathematics texts do not have a narrative story line, but for young children in particular, they are lavishly illustrated and offer many glimpses of social life which can present a very potent 'hidden curriculum'. She reviewed school texts for the 3-13 age group published between 1970 and 1978, all of which reflected gender stereotypes. She draws a summary from one scheme:

> The visual material contains a number of adult figures, cowboys, soldiers, sportsmen, clowns, pedestrians and tractor drivers; they are tall, short, fat, thin, they climb ladders, they mend roofs, and they are almost all men. Two examples only depict women. Mr and Mrs Smith are seen walking to church and two female heads are seen in relation to three hair ribbons. The men are highly individualised ... Whereas women appear bland, expressionless, and lacking in individuality, the men have ages, personalities, distinguishing features, occupations, tasks and intentions. Men are not depicted staring

vacantly out of the picture, in sharp contrast to the portrayal of women and children. (Northam, 1981:13)

Teaching materials in mathematics deliver a much more potent message than a merely mathematical one.

But not only were girls absent from any positive presence in the texts, their whole approach to learning appeared to be wrong. In another piece of theory building, girls were wrong-footed again, this time in the way they learned mathematics. Theories of learning had changed considerably during the years in which mathematics was developing as a school subject. By the time the child-centred pedagogies of the second half of the twentieth century were featuring in schools, mathematics had already become the science of reason and reasoning and, as we have seen, females were socially and politically situated outside rationality itself (Wakerdine, 1989:22). By the time mathematics as reasoning had became a primary school subject, very much influenced by the epistemologist Jean Piaget, this whole issue had become hidden. Piagetian theories redefined the nature of learning as an individual's construction of concepts, from which followed particular ideas about what constituted proper learning and proper pedagogy. The role of both pupils and teachers changed, the pupils' from that of passive recipients of knowledge to that of active learners through practical activity for whom the teacher now provided appropriate activities and appropriate assessment. No longer was the teacher a marker of pages of sums in checks of accurate performance, but one who had to look for evidence, not only of success in stages of learning, but that learning had been achieved through the right activity in the right way (Walden and Walkerdine, 1985:11).

But the ideal learning child, the inquiring, discovering, creative and playful young person, has just the characteristics of masculinity of the ideal boy (Walden and Walkerdine, 1985:12). Feminine girls are not expected to behave like this, but to be responsible and hardworking. Girls are successful in mathematics, but their very success is judged in a different way from that of boys: it is attributed to hard work, rule-following and lack of confidence in the 'correct' behaviours. The results are that girls are protected, not pushed, so as not to jeopardise their already weak confidence, to give them work in which they feel safe, to enter them for low-level examinations which do not threaten them. The 'common sense' of girls' inability to do real mathematics is again confirmed, and the new, universal mathematics and its learning turns out to be as deeply gendered in both conception and practice as its antecedents.

A similar depth of bias in other theories was also revealed by other research. Two fields in particular, those of psychological development and those of occupational choices are particularly relevant to women, mathematics and work. While teaching a course in moral development to her Harvard students Gilligan (1982) followed Kohlberg's (Piagetian) theory in which particular stages of moral development are marked by the type of response made to particular social dilemmas. In her work with both male and female students, Gilligan noted a consistency in the alternative responses to moral problems to those on which the stages were based. She set out to explore this 'different voice', the title of her book, pursuing the theme rather than its empirical association with women. Her thesis thus presents a distinction between two modes of thought, rather than generalities about either sex. Her aim was to 'expand the under-standing of human development by using the group left out in the construction of the theory, to call attention to what is missing in the account' (Gilligan, 1982:2). Seen in this light, the discrepant data on women's experience which had had the effect of pathologising women's moral development in relations to men's, provided a base upon which to generate a new theory, potentially yielding a more encompassing view of the lives of both the sexes.' (Gilligan, 1982:4) Gilligan distinguished two modes of psychological development, 'separated' and 'connected'. The former is characterised by a focus on rules and principles: it objectifies areas of concern and objects of knowledge: it sees moral reasoning as the impartial application of rules of justice without concern for human issues: it values reason and reviles feeling. It is an ethic of rights, consistent with a view of the world as us and them, right and wrong, good and bad, and it is part of the cultural definition of masculinity. The different voice is the 'connected' perspective. It is concerned with human connections, with relationships, with empathy and caring, with the human dimensions of situations. It is an ethic of responsibility, and part of the cultural defini-tion of femininity. Kohlberg places justice as the highest value; Gilligan argues that human connectedness should be placed no lower.

Kohlberg's values are in accord with the propositional view of mathe-matics, with its rigour, logic, proof, structure, abstraction, elegance and pursuit of a higher truth. But in Gilligan's analysis these are cultural values, in particular those ascribed to masculinity. The polarity of Kohlberg and Gilligan is analogous to the subject-centredness or person-centredness of learning and teaching mathematics (Ernest, 1991:168). Gilligan's distinctions were taken up in a mathematics education by now sensitised to its two cultures and the values they bring with them into the education of young people in what was at last recognised as a pluralistic, democratic society. Stephen Brown (1984) in particular took up

Gilligan's argument that the 'different' category does not suggest simply a different dynamic, or a logically inferior mind-set, but a category that urgently needs to be incorporated into the existent and deficient one. Brown's particular interest was teaching mathematical problem-solving in school and he was concerned that the existing perspective was too 'Kohlbergian'. The 'propositional-type' curriculum is 'de-peopled': 'contexts and concepts are for the most part presented ahistorically and unproblematically' and 'as it is presently constituted, the curriculum offers little encouragement for students to move beyond merely accepting ... non-purposeful tasks' (Brown, 1984:12). It concentrates on seeking similarities between situations, in ignoring extraneous variables instead of exploring differences. In Brown's view, 'mathematics is not only a search for what is essentially common among ostensibly different structures, but is as much an effort to reveal essential differences among structures that appear to be similar'.

A Gilliganish perspective on the other hand is characterised by a concern for the context of a problem, by a disinclination to set up general principles for future use, and by a concern for interconnectedness. 'As a profession' Brown argues 'we correctly appreciate that we need to do more to prepare students to operate in an uncertain world', wherein 'one's fate is not sown with the kind of exactitude that much of the earlier curriculum has implied' (Brown, 1984:13). The responsibility of educators transcends passing on only mathematical thought, for it does not adequately provide for the large percentage of pupils who do not intend to become mathematicians. The task is not to 'soften' an otherwise rigorous curriculum, but the rather more intellectually demanding one in which mathematics is 'embedded in a web of concerns that are more 'real world' oriented than any of us have begun to imagine' (Brown, 1984:14). In other words Brown is suggesting a curriculum more along the lines of the sort of mathematics that Davis and Hersh (1983) described as often more difficult than pure mathematics alone.

The Kohlberg-Gilligan confrontation serves two purposes for the mathematics educator. Behind the Gilligan perspective are dimensions of purpose, situation and people-connectedness, for which very little of the mathematics curriculum caters. Secondly both Kohlberg and Gilligan are concerned with morality 'a field of inquiry that it may be as important to integrate with mathematical thinking as are the more standard disciplines that form the backbone of more conventional application' (Brown, 1984:15). School mathematics does have context.

As Maxwell (1991) points out, it is often easier to recognise this in mathematics texts from outside our own culture. She took examples from different school texts.

> Twenty-three peasants are working in a field. At midday six guerrilla fighters arrive to help them from a military base near their village. How many people are working in the field? (Mozambique)

> One upon a time a ship was caught in a storm. In order to save it and its crew the captain decided that half of the passengers would have to be thrown overboard. There were fifteen Christians and fifteen Turks aboard the ship and the captain was a Christian. He announced that he would count the passengers and that every ninth one would be thrown overboard. How could the passengers be placed in a circle so that all the Turks would be thrown overboard and all the Christians saved? (USA) (Maxwell, 1991:67)

The existing social context of mathematics in English classrooms was brought home by the Commission on Racial Equality in 1985 when it published the Swann Report, and its evidence of under-achievement of pupils of some ethnic groups, many of whose parents had arrived in waves of immigration from the 1950s onwards. Institutionalised racism was revealed in school organisation, biased textbooks, content and processes of assessment, in the unconscious behaviour of teachers and the cultural content of the curriculum of mathematics itself. The traditional absolutist, de-contextualised, abstract and formal mathematics, was shown to alienate pupils, erect linguistic and cultural barriers and devalue other cultural heritages (Ernest, 1991:267). The education authorities, particularly those in large conurbations with proportionately high immigrant populations, responded with policies and initiatives to counteract the racism through 'anti-racist' mathematics that consciously valued the cultures from which both immigrants and much mathematics came. Valuing cultural origins and contexts became a leading issue: the Inner London Education Authority published the book *Everyone Counts* which helped teachers identify the sort of cultural insensitivity that Northam (above) revealed in the case of gendering (ILEA, 1985).

Another field biased in theory was revealed in relation to work, which had long been gendered. The analysis of theories of girls' occupational choice were shown, like Kohlberg's, to have been based on middle-class, white, male samples and therefore tending to pathologise those who are not of the same category (Chisholm, 1987). From the 1970s social theories had emphasised social class as a variable, and there was only a little work that concerned itself directly with gendered transition from education to work. Feminist analysis insisted on the distinctiveness of the female experience while it pursued the more traditional feminist plea for valuing women's work in the home. Such pleas are not simply political statements or a search of ways of raising self-esteem, but like Gilligan's analysis, ways of developing less biased, theoretical frameworks for research itself.

Crucial to theorising about occupational choice and destination, is the concept of skill itself and again the pathologising of girls is accepted as the norm. In social analysis, Chisholm suggests (1987:36) it is more appropriate to speak of skills as points in a network of practices, than as particular objective competencies of individuals. How else, she asks, can we understand the rating of the US Federal Government's *Dictionary of Occupational Titles* that has influenced so much skills research, that gives the lowest possible rating to the occupation of foster-mother in the general category of 'Domestic Servants'. Even the occupation of horse-pusher (one who tends horses en route by train) is rated more highly. The stark reality is that women cannot choose skilled work because they cannot possess skills in the traditional androcentric ideology, neither can occupations practised by women be skilful. This leaves them with un-skilled manual labour or the traditional caring jobs which are seen to depend on women's 'natural' self-dedication. We are back in sacrificial, domestic femininity again.

From the mid-1970s, in a fresh wave of industrial interest in the curri-culum, employers concerned themselves with the skills of school leavers in what was to become by the late 1980s, a minor industry in itself. The concern was mainly with the traditionally arithmetic end of the mathe-matics curriculum, still apparently perceived by employers in the un-challenged equation of arithmetic with low level mathematics, with low ability and with low social class. The industry lobby became a powerful one in government policy-making, and a powerful force in maintaining what the profession of mathematics education had already long regarded as archaic and socially divisive views of mathematics education (Margaret Brown, 1993). Industry's concerns stimulated a number of research pro-jects across the country, set up to investigate the mathematics used in work. This research has been reviewed elsewhere (Harris, 1991a), suffice it to note here that because of its continuing assumption of the traditional equation, it concerned itself with the identification of mainly arithmetic skill, thereby maintaining the status quo. It did not question whether in the late twentieth century, traditional arithmetic was the best or indeed the only foundation for learning mathematics, neither did it consult the profession of mathematics education itself, for it was interested in its own perception of what was required in work, and assumed traditional pedagogy as the only way of achieving it.

Meanwhile mathematics itself was undergoing its own revolution: the absolutist paradigm of mathematics as a body of infallible, objective truth above the affairs and values of mankind, was itself under challenge; mathematics was increasingly recognised as a product of human inventiveness and therefore, like any other body of knowledge, both fallible and changing (Ernest, 1991:xi). The consequences of this change, inside and outside mathematics education, are well analysed by Ernest (1991). He argues that school mathematics can be reshaped

> to give all groups more access to its concepts, and to the wealth and power its knowledge brings; the social contexts of the uses and practices of mathematics can no longer be legitimately pushed aside, the implicit values of mathematics need to be squarely faced. When mathematics is seen in this way it needs to be studied in living contexts which are meaningful and relevant to the learners, including their languages, cultures and everyday lives, as well as their school-based experiences. (Ernest, 1991: xii)

Maths in Work

By the 1980s, anyone in mathematics education working at the interface between schools and workplaces was thus working in a field where all the paradigms were shifting. It was within this complex field of multiple change that a project called *Maths in Work* devised and set up some work that confronted the stereotypes of mathematics and of women's work with each other, weaving them together in a way that demonstrated mathematical richness in the very field that was supposed to define women by its absence. And from this point some of the conventions of academic writing are abandoned as I discuss my own work and some of its consequences.

My job was to use data from a skills' survey in a large sample of work-places, as a resource for informing mathematics curriculum development in schools, and as an inspiration for the design and production of learning materials (Harris, 1991a). The data generated by the survey consisted mainly of the counts of skills traditionally expected by employers of young people in their first 'unskilled' jobs. In other words the questionnaires that elicited the data probed only those skills that maintain the status quo of traditional educational thinking about low level employment. The struc-ture of the questionnaires however made it possible to probe behind the skills counts into the contexts that generated them, and this revealed much more mathematically rich activity than it was possible to detect by asking about the frequency of use of skills alone. My role in handling the research data became one in which I challenged the traditional relation-ships in so-called low-level skills of low-ability school leavers for low-level work. Since I was also a member of the Inner London Education Authority's Mathematics Advisory Team, I also had a role in INSET, the in-service education of practising teachers. The learning materials I was to devise therefore had to have a dual role; that of supporting the teaching of mathematics in class, and that of alerting teachers to research results which they would want to use in practice. My target pupil group was those whose school experience of mathematics had often consisted of repetitions of arithmetic at which they had already repeatedly failed.

I was unhappy about available texts for linking school and workplace mathematics. My criticisms were two-fold. Firstly, in a recognisable descent from the nineteenth century, they tended to limit the pupils' mathematical experience to arithmetic. Secondly, the examples used in such texts were frequently devised ostensibly to illustrate the realities of the 'unskilled' workplaces into which students were expected to go, but in reality giving practice examples for school-learned, arithmetic skills in quasi-realistic contexts. Some of them are clearly invented for that purpose, for example giving people names that begin with A, B, C and D (X and Y presumably thought to be too difficult), an unreality which is often immediately detected first by the pupils themselves. An additional characteristic of their unreality is that the rogue variables that can make a job interesting (and which make the mathematics more difficult to access) and from which a worker in real life has to select before deciding what to calculate and how, are edited out, so as to clarify the problem, and reduce it to a routine. All too often, the result is materials that provide no challenge, but rather confirm the pupil in the depressing, self-fulfilling cycle of low expectation, low performance and low self-esteem.

The language in which such teaching materials was written also caused me concern. I had already had experience of designing and using teaching materials for pupils in special schools, who could not read or who had other language difficulties, but who demonstrated their ability to operate conceptually by manipulating pictures or objects (Harris, 1980, 1981a and 1981b). I was thus aware of at least some of the ways in which dependence on certain aspects of language can restrict mathematical development. I aimed therefore to produce materials that used as little language as possible in presenting practical tasks. Many commercially published materials seemed to be unaware of the results of available research in this area, for example that of Shuard and Rothery (1984) on the range of problems generated for learners by inadequately considered language in textbook instruction. Materials tended to be verbose in instruction and explanation, often with a distracting and patronising jokiness, as if consciously addressing a limited understanding. Recently Dowling (1991) has made a closer, theoretical analysis of the way in which text books still maintain social class differences in mathematics education. He analysed some texts from the SMP 11-16 scheme (Cambridge University Press) which markets four series of books for mathematics, differentiated on the ground of 'ability'. Many of the books in the G series for the less able, relate to manual work. His analysis of the language, illustrations, layout and content of the books reveals the banality of the series in contrast with the erudition of the Y series, for the most able (Dowling, 1991:145). He is particularly critical of the inadequacy of defining 'manual' in terms of 'using the hands' and 'intellectual' as 'using the brain'. In his example writing demands both as does fixing a car engine.

> The two are to be understood in a more dialectical manner. Thus, the Y series *intellectualises* the manual through the use of highly technical language and trivialises necessary manual activity by providing the briefest of instructions. The mundane inevitably enters the domains of both series, but whereas, in the Y books, the everyday world is sacrificed on the altar of mathematics, in the G series, the everyday appears as an effusive apology for the tentative intrusion of the academic. (Dowling, 1991:146, his emphasis)

Dowling concludes that the structure of the series continues in the tradition of equating 'ability' with social class and thus makes use of and reproduces the social structure. The liberal – mechanical distinction is still with us and once again the workers' children are told their place.

I viewed workplaces not as destinations for students drilled in arithmetic, but as resources that would tax and develop mathematical processes that pupils already had, but which they may not have recognised in contexts outside the classroom. I did not want to provide materials that would be used to supplement a particular published scheme nor to preach the vocational message that particular jobs might use particular skills. Neither was I suggesting an approach that should abolish syllabi or the judicious use of textbooks. Rather I wanted to offer a collection of problems that would mediate between school and daily activity in a way that recognised mathematics as an ordinary daily activity already present in the lives of most people, and that both teachers and students could use heuristically. My aim was to produce learning materials that would take practical, open-ended problems from workplaces and put them, with the minimum of instruction, into the hands of teachers to use and develop as they willed. The tasks themselves would be creative, not routine and to which there was no single, correct answer. I preferred to express my confidence in the professional ability of teachers to interpret the materials in the ways most appropriate to their uses, rather than provide more patronising and detailed 'teacher proof' instructions. I needed a format and content that would present a more genuine reality than existing texts, that would offer opportunities for access to a wider range and greater depth of mathematics than current skills-based materials.

I had also learned that the traditional method of developing learning materials, of writing drafts and testing them in school until they were 'right', often had the reverse effect to the one that I wanted. Such a process nearly always leads eventually to the 'safe', 'teacher proof' and unchallenging materials I was determined to avoid. The format I finally produced was of a collection of single, loose-leaf, photocopiable sheets, each one offering a different practical problem, all presented in a plastic folder along with a collection of cards and papers and some relevant examples that teachers might find useful. In this format, mistakes or lapses of clarity, or suggested improvements could still be responded to but immediately and cheaply without having to reproduce the whole pack. The fact that the first run of the pack sold out within a few days was encouraging.

The origin of the problems in my first pack was my experience as a temporary warehouse worker as I checked the skills data on which I worked. Working with cardboard boxes all day, I could not fail to notice the ingenuity in the design of the packs which contained the products in economically made constructions that were easy both to handle and store. Many cartons were made to fold flat for easy assembly at point of sale or for space-saving storage before eventual recycling, once empty. Designing such cartons clearly required spatial and numerical thinking of a high order: in some cases the geometry invited immediate exploration. My conviction, that there was plenty of mathematics in the daily handling of such materials, seemed to contrast sharply with that of the Cockcroft Report on teaching mathematics in schools, published while I was working on the materials. As the brief of Cockcroft Committee required, it presented in its chapter on the mathematics of employment, a traditional, utilitarian view. But the whole tone of the chapter seemed to be regressive and one of its specific examples seemed to continue to disqualify the mathematics I was trying to develop, by reducing it, once more, to stereotype. The report declared that it was often possible when watching work in progress to describe it in geometrical terms. Even if pupils had come across such concepts in class, the Report argued, the employee would 'probably not consciously analyse in such terms the operations which are being performed; nor, if he were to do so, would he necessarily be able to do his job any better.'

On the other hand, many jobs require the employee to make explicit use of mathematics – for instance, to measure, to calculate dimensions from a drawing, to work out costs and discounts. In these cases the job cannot be carried out without recourse to the necessary mathematics and it is this latter use of mathematics to which we refer ... (Cockcroft, 1982:18)

In other words, although the geometry was there, it was to be discounted, since the purpose of mathematics education for pupils entering work (in contrast to those likely to enter further or higher education) was to concentrate on the traditional numerical skills for menial jobs. The opinion that a pupil's interest in geometry might not help 'him' do 'his' job better is an opinion based on an attitude and a prejudgment, no more. It did not permit the thought that workers might be sufficiently interested by some intriguing solutions of the geometrical designs of the boxes they handled every day, to think up some of their own. It confined workers to the routines, closing the door to any recognition that they could be active problem solvers. It confirmed the opinion that many employers had given me, that problem solving was a management skill. Although they clearly wanted the under-educated 'bright lad' of the Industrial Revolution, who would today be attending university, they evidently did not want their workers to be too bright.

My response to the 'Cockcroft' attitude maintained my own stance, that a warehouse worker may not do many sums, but would still have to have the ability to judge weights of boxes by looking at their volume, and the vertical distances between shelves. Such skills are as explicit as you choose to make them. The ability of warehouse workers to deal with things that go wrong, was not regarded.

Many people in industry and far too many in education share the very narrow view of mathematics that I am complaining about. But by asking questions about where the gremlins usually strike you can get not only a truer picture of what life is like but many examples of the problematical situations which demand the real thought, rather than the routine calculations which don't. A firm survives by the way it deals with its problems, not by the way it does its routine calculations, unless they themselves constitute a problem. (Harris, 1985:45)

The richness of the materials of the pack *Wrap it Up!* with its cartoon on the cover and relaxed title and look, was as different from standard texts for low attainers in mathematics as I could make it. Its potential for school use was tested by a conference of mathematics teachers who devise and follow the scheme known as SMILE (Secondary Mathematics Individualised Learning Experience). About 240 teachers were given an activity in the form of an internal memo from the managing director of an up-market design company to his visualisation team, requesting them to produce some models for a pack for wrapping a sports ball, for a client he wanted to impress. The teachers were asked to work in groups and to write down any mathematics they found themselves doing as they worked. The list of mathematics skills and processes was lengthy. Remarkable too was the behaviour of the groups. One small collection of senior people distanced themselves from the working groups, analysing the task by the mathematics they assumed would be involved and thereby confining themselves to the theoretical models they had chosen. Containers for sports' balls are not however theoretical constructions, but boxes that have to be stacked, with lids, joints and enough space left for labels, bar codes and manufacturers' names.

> Those who set about the task in a practical way however, continually came up with further problems both of construction and design which in turn generated more problems and more mathematics. In short it was the theoreticians who limited themselves by their 'theory and applications' approach. The practitioners found themselves involved not only with wider but with deeper mathematics as it emerged from the task itself. Of course, the practitioners were mathematics teachers who knew what to look for, but there is no doubt that they surprised themselves. (Harris:1987:27)

There was also little doubt that the approach I had taken had been vindicated. A further measure of the success of the format was the extent to which it was copied, both as intended by teachers, but also by other projects. Both *Wrap it Up* and another pack *Cardboard Engineering* which, being a one-person project, I had had no time to develop, were acknowledged inspirations behind the pack *Be a Paper Engineer* published by a much larger and much more substantially funded project (Shell Centre JMB, 1988). The ultimate statement of the usefulness of the pack came in the form of an only half-humourous request from the Chief Inspector for Mathematics to produce another pack about something else, because everywhere she went she found classes designing cardboard boxes.

Thus an effective way of revealing and developing some mathematics in work was established, and it was possible to move on to challenge other stereotypes. Cardboard, at least in its design function, is neutral in culture and gender. Symbolically it represents the ordinariness of daily working life, but as a material for entering high status mathematics as well a practising low status arithmetic, it crossed the cultural divide in mathematics education. For my next pack I crossed the cultural divide of gender. For cardboard I substituted cloth, for through cloth I could demonstrate some of the mathematics that women were already doing in textiles work, that has always been invisible to the masculine subjects of mathematics.

A woman making a dress from a commercial paper pattern* will do a number of mathematical things. If she does not already know the size of pattern to buy, she will measure herself appropriately and refer to a table of standard measurements in the pattern catalogue. Having bought the correct size she then refers to the two-way entry table on the back of the packet, which will advise her on how much cloth, in a range of widths, she will need to buy. This information is usually given in both metric and imperial units, since much cloth is still made on looms built before metrication. Having bought her pattern and cloth, she next identifies the particular pattern pieces, made of tissue paper, that she will need from the total supplied, for several modifications of one design are often included in one pattern. She may want to make some adjustments to some of the pattern pieces to fit her own measurements, by reducing or increasing the area in crucial places. Her next task is to place the pieces on the cloth in preparation for cutting them out. This requires careful attention to the symmetries of the pattern pieces, and those of the grain and designs of the cloth. For a particular draped effect, she may cut some pieces on the bias, that is by placing the grain line on the pattern at 45° to the grain of the cloth. At the same time she will place the pattern pieces so as to use the minimum amount of cloth.

Having laid out the pattern pieces and cut her cloth to her satisfaction, she then temporarily joins the pieces with long 'tacking' threads or pins. Next she sews the various parts together in a particular order, using appropriate sized needles and gauge of thread for the cloth, keeping the needle of the sewing machine an exact and regular distance from the edge of the cloth, by practised eye or by following her temporary fixings or markings. The order of sewing the pieces together is important, since the places where seams cross is significant in the construction of the whole garment. To complete the garment she will probably attach some sort of fastening: a slide fastener will need careful placing in the correct-sized opening, buttons will need buttonholes that are precisely placed, accurately cut and regularly sewn. Finally a hem will be marked and sewn, the length usually decided by repeat accurate measurements from the floor or from the waist, at approximately equal spacing along its full length.

Thus, while she is working, the needleworker uses two-way entry tables to obtain information, calculates allowances and distributes measurements, manipulates shapes on a surface using parallel lines, analyses symmetries, uses minimising strategies, maintains parallel lines, systematically orders operations, and makes accurate repeat measurements. Such skills have always been part of dressmaking, embedded in the feminising tasks of elementary and secondary modern schoolgirls.

A similar analysis can be made of knitting. The most important single factor in knitting a garment that fits a particular person, is tension, another ambiguous term which in the context of knitting means the ratio of the number of stitches per unit length, the convenient inch now giving way to groupings of centimetres. This ratio depends on the thickness of the knitting needles, the composition of the yarn and the individual style of the knitter. Forces of equilibrium in a piece of knitting, will, in the absence of any obstruction, eventually relax it to a state of even tension, which is why so much old knitting looks so regular. By the time it reaches equilibrium, the tension is determined solely by the length of the loop (Rutt, 1987:16).

Knitted garments are usually made from separate pieces of knitted fabric, sewn together. The individual pieces are shaped by increasing or reducing the particular numbers of stitches in a row, derived by calculation from the tension ratio. Any garment that carries a design in colour, as in Fair Isle style, or in construction, as in Aran style, requires further mathematical skills. The designs on a Fair Isle, contain unbroken runs of up to seven stitches of one colour of a row, and are worked with a strong diagonal emphasis. Although a Fair Isle garment can contain any number of colours, yarns would become tangled if more than two colours were used in one row. While one colour of the current pair is being used, the other lies at the back of the work, to be brought to the front when needed, and leaving a loop along the back of the work behind the stitches that have just been worked. If this loop is more than seven stitches long, it can hang down at the back of the work, interrupting the double, insulating layer of fabric that make these sweaters so warm, and forming traps for fingers as the garment is put on. The diagonal emphasis in individual designs prevents columns of stitches of one colour forming, with the potential for a tight column of loops behind them.

A further constructional feature of a well-made Fair Isle sweater is its helical form. If two pieces of knitting are sewn together at the sides to form a garment, there will be an in-built potential weakness at the seams. If the garment is made continuously on a single, flexible, double-ended needle however, the fabric will emerge as a cylinder, strictly speaking a helix, with no weak joints. Garments are made to fit people, so the number of stitches in a coil of the helix will be specific. It is arrived at by way of the body measurement, the appropriate tension calculation, and an allowance for movement known as the 'ease'. Any design worked into a specific number of stitches must be a factor of the number of stitches if it is to appear continuous round the whole garment.

The design and making of most cloth and most garments requires such embedded mathematical skills, and it was their exposure and development that formed the contents of the next pack of teaching materials. Many garments are made in workshops to which a pattern and the correct amount of cloth for the required number of garments are supplied. If by skilful manipulation of the pattern on the cloth, a garment maker could make more than the specified number, then the extras can be disposed of for cash. Historically, this was sometimes their only income. The extras came to be known as *cabbage* from the old French word *coupage*. The practice of cabbage was widespread in the garment industry until the arrival of computer technology eliminated the hand and eye skill of placing pattern pieces, but remains disreputable because it can result in paring down seam allowances that weaken a garment. I decided to name the pack *Cabbage* however, in honour of the broad range of unsung and time-honoured skills of street-wise needle-workers.

Cabbage finally contained twenty two activities for mathematics classes starting from textile activities both domestic and industrial. Initial discussions with teachers, in which it was confirmed that all of the men interviewed but only a few women could not knit or sew, suggested that I would have to extend the teachers' notes to explain how both knitting and weaving are constructed. Since in England at least, all people of all cultures wear clothes, I had chosen *Cabbage* items from a range of nationalities and ethnic groups so I also provided notes of the context of many of the activities.

Most of the activities involved analysis of design or construction, and one used the scale reductions that are used in the garment industry. By reducing a pattern to one fifth normal size, I was able to introduce an activity in which pupils could lay out and cut out garment pieces on reproductions of cloth on A3 paper. Eight of the activities had identified ethnic origins, an activity investigating the symmetry of Adinkra designs from Ghana, one exploring spirals in baskets from Botswana, one exploring ways of using rectangles of cloth to make a 'Buba' blouse (Nigeria), an investigation of symmetry in the design of Turkish kilim rugs, an investigation of tessellations in Sylhet fans (Bangladesh), an exploration of the geometry of circular designs in Naksha embroidery (Bangladesh), an invitation to design an Aran sweater using appropriate number groups for the individual designs, and one exploring the different ways of making ponchos. The others involved strip patterns in cross-stitch embroidery, the costing of manufactured jeans, the tessellation geometry of patchwork, invitations to design a sweater, T shirt and a dress, and explorations of the two-dimensional geometry of neckties and the three-dimensional geometry of umbrellas and socks.

By the time *Cabbage* was published, photocopies of *Wrap it Up* activities were in use in schools as far apart as Australia, southern Africa and South America. The impact of *Cabbage* was as widespread but more challenging. Feedback from teachers' workshops in England where I began to use items from *Cabbage* instead of from *Wrap it Up*, gave some indication of the extent to which the pack had come up against some of the traditional gender stereotypes. At a conference of the Association of Teachers of Mathematics, I introduced some textiles activities into a workshop on the mathematics of workplaces for practising mathematics teachers, where all the teachers relished a fresh challenge. These teachers would not have been at the conference if they had not been professional enough to want to develop their own practice. I offered one teacher a shirt pattern and a piece of cloth to explore mathematically. After an hour's work he announced in exasperation that it was all mathematics but a more realistic mathematics than, for example, the manipulation of small diagrams in textbooks.

> The whole thing was maths from reading the 2-way entry table on the back of the pattern, through laying out the pattern pieces in parallel with the grain of the cloth, to ensuring that the two sleeves are a right and left sleeve and not a pair of one. Between these necessary examples are plenty of other interesting questions to pursue; like why does some of the curve of the neck of the larger size lie inside the curve of the neck of the smaller size. The intrepid needle-man had no time to finish cutting out my shirt and when the session ended was seen to go out muttering angrily about all the time-wasting nonsense of fiddling around with tiddley little hexagons. (Harris, 1987a:43)

On another occasion, teachers were less responsive to the challenge. To the majority of male teachers who had never sewn or knitted, the task was clearly as daunting as the presentation of equally unfamiliar contexts to girls, and they reacted in the same way.

> they 'backed off' allowing more 'technically literate' colleagues to proceed with the task; they found a range of excuses for not doing the task or did an alternative task from within their own range of interests; on some occasions they announced that the activity was 'not mathematics' or 'this is silly', a well-known pupil response meaning 'I don't understand this.' A not infrequent response was to enter the activity with alacrity with remarks of relief such as 'I was afraid that you were going to give us something difficult' only to find that the activity was rather more difficult than it was assumed to be and that assistance was required. (Harris, 1991:288)

There were occasionally some extreme reactions. On one occasion a teacher refused to do the task at all on the grounds that in his culture this was women's work and a degrading thing for a man to be seen doing.

Cabbage items were obviously less immediately accessible than *Wrap it Up* to teachers unfamiliar with needlework or the cultures from which I had taken the activities, and therefore required more preparation. When teachers undertook the preparation, the results were rich indeed. Some *Cabbage* materials spoke directly to the home cultures of some recently arrived immigrant children, placing 'home' on a level with the one in which they newly found themselves. Two activities, *Naksha* and *Fans* were derived from an exhibition of Crafts of Bangladesh that I had visited, knowing there would be much mathematics in the weaving and embroidery exhibited there. In the preparation of the activities, there had been no problem in London in finding a Bengali translator and typesetter so that the instructions were published in both languages. That alone was enough to stimulate the interest of many pupils. One teacher reported on his use of *Cabbage*:

> For a while we had been been planning a project on the role of symmetry in Islamic culture – we saw connections between this work and *Cabbage* materials that were too strong to ignore and thus the *Naksha* and *Fans* sheets formed the main component of the second phase of this project – the first phase concentrating on the role of symmetry in Islamic art and religion. (Jones, 1987)

The activity *Bags* caused the most lively response from teachers that was available to me through feedback, possibly because it was one that was most easily assimilable to a mathematics classroom without further pre-paration. The activity presented two pictures of square patchwork bags made of nine and sixteen squares respectively. It asked pupils to find ways of making one bigger square bag from two smaller ones, with the least amount of unpicking.

One teacher, in reviewing the pack reported that:

> *Bags* provided a lovely starter recently for Pythagoras with a class of second year pupils. Having demonstrated that my 3x3 and 4x4 (paper!) patchworks could be unpicked and reassembled to make a 5x5 patchwork, I then asked the class to find some other patchworks for which this is possible. The activity took off – indeed, it was even more enjoyable than I had imagined because my question left it open as to the number of bags you can unpick to reform into the larger one so some children were immediately able to extend the work in this way. (Morris, 1989)

During the debate as to whether or not it should be included in the SMILE network of materials, another wrote:

Opposite: **Figure 8**: Mathematics from traditional girls' work. From the *Cabbage* pack

Bags

You have made two squares of patchwork because you were going to make two bags.

Then you decide that the bags will be too small.

So you decide to make a bigger bag from your smaller bags so that your new big one is still square.

What size will your new bag be?

Where can you unpick the old bags so you have to do the least amount of unpicking?

For what other sizes can you make one big square bag from two small square bags?

Investigate!

MiW Cabbage
Drawing by Juliet Breese
© Maths in Work

Firstly, *Bags* is one of the few tasks on the network which acts genuinely in anti-sexist mathematics learning and teaching. Secondly, it has always proved for me, a wonderful task for generating some stimulating group work with surprising outcomes across the ability range. Thirdly, students are expected to make links across artificial mathematical boundaries. Fourthly, it has provided a means of dialogue with colleagues in cross-curricular work beyond the often forced attempts at linking Year 7 and Year 8 courses. And lastly, but far from least, *Bags* generates confidence in below average ability Year 11 students who begin to view their perception of algebra very differently when they *discover for themselves* on their way through the task that $(x+1)^2 = x^2 + 2x + 1$! (Edwards, 1992: 22 her emphasis)

This particular review encompassed all that I had hoped to achieve in the pack. Though a challenge for many people, *Cabbage* held its own as a mathematical resource, with no dilution of mathematics on the grounds that it was a supposedly female set of activities. It has been used throughout the world and I have translations of some of its items in Danish, Norwegian, Turkish, Thai and Malay. It was also the origin for the exhibition called *Common Threads* that sent this productive (and indeed positively destructive) clash of stereotypes first on a tour of England, then to twenty-three other countries.

Note

* The words 'pattern' and 'design' can cause considerable confusion when discussing textiles, since both can refer to form, structure and placement of motifs on a garment or piece of cloth. For consistency I have used the word 'pattern' for commercially published instructions on how to construct a piece of sewing or knitting and 'design' for an arrangement of motifs on a piece of cloth, or the planning of a particular effect.

References

Brown Margaret (1993) Clashing Epistemologies: the Battle for Control of the National Curriculum and its Assessment. Inaugural lecture given by Margaret Brown, Professor of Mathematics Education at King's College, London, 20th October 1993. Teaching Mathematics and its Applications Vol 12 No 3 p 97-112

Brown Stephen (1984) The Logic of Problem Generation from Morality and Solving to Deposing and Rebellion. *For the Learning of Mathematics* Vol 4 No 1 February p 9-20

Burton Leone (1986) *Girls into Maths Can Go.* London: Holt, Rinehart and Winston.

Buxton Laurie (1981) *Do You Panic About Maths? Coping with Maths Anxiety.* London: Heinemann Educational.

Chisholm Lynne (1987) *Gender and Vocation. Working Paper No 1 New Series.* London: University of London Institute of Education Post 16 Centre.

Davis Philip J and Hersch Reuben. (1983) *The Mathematical Experience.* London: Penguin Books.

Dowling Paul (1991) A Touch of Class: ability, social class and intertext in SMP 11-16. In David Pimm and Eric Love (editors) *Teaching and Learning School Mathematics.* London: Hodder and Stoughton in association with the Open University.

Edwards Julie-Ann. (1993) Dear Splash. In *Splash* Volume 11100110, January. London: Smile Centre.

Ernest Paul (1991) *The Philosophy of Mathematics Education.* London: The Falmer Press.

Gilligan Carol (1982) *In a Different Voice. Psychological Theory and Women's Development.* Cambridge Mass. and London: Harvard University Press.

Harris Mary (1980) *Dice Games for Slow Learners.* ILEA Struggle. Vol 3

Harris Mary (1981a) Getting it Sorted, or What Shall I Do Next. ILEA *Struggle* Vol 4.

Harris Mary (1981b) Concept Snap. ILEA *Struggle.* Vol 5.

Harris Mary (1985) Wrapping it Up. *Mathematics Teaching* Vol 113. December)

Harris Mary (1987) An example of Traditional Women's Work as a Mathematics Resource. *For the Learning of Mathematics.* Vol 7 Number 3.

Harris Mary (1987a) Mathematics and Fabrics. *Mathematics Teaching* Vol 120.

Harris Mary (1988) *Common Threads: Catalogue of an Exhibition of Mathematics and Textiles.* London: University of London Institute of Education, Maths in Work Project. [now out of print]

Harris Mary (1991) Postscript: The Maths in Work Project. In Mary Harris (Ed) *Schools, Mathematics and Work.* Basingstoke: The Falmer Press and Bristol PA: Taylor and Francis.

Harris Mary (1991a) *Schools, Mathematics and Work.* Basingstoke: Falmer Press.

ILEA (Inner London Education Authority) (1985) *Everyone Counts: Looking for Bias and Insensitivity in Primary Mathematics Materials.* London: ILEA Learning Resources Branch.

Jones Keith (1987) Private communication on *Cabbage* Evaluation.

Leder Gilah C (1992) Mathematics and Gender: Changing Perspectives. In D A Grouws (Ed) *Handbook of Research on Mathematics Teaching and Learning.* New York: Macmillan.

Maxwell Jenny (1991) Hidden Messages. In Mary Harris (Ed) *Schools Mathematics and Work.* London: Falmer Press.

Morris Greg (1989) Social Fabric. *Mathematics Teaching* Vol 127.

Northam Jean (1981) Girls and Boys in Primary Mathematics Books. *Education* Vol 10 No 1 Spring pp 11-14.

Open University (1986) *PM645 Girls Into Mathematics.* Cambridge: Cambridge University Press.

Rutt Richard, Bishop of Leicester (1987) *A History of Hand Knitting.* London: Batsford.

Shell Centre JMB (1988) *Be a Paper Engineer. Module of the Joint Project on the Assessment of Numeracy by Shell Centre Nottingham University and the Joint Matriculation Board.* Harlow: Longman.

Shuard Hilary and Rothery Andrew (1984) *Children Reading Mathematics.* London: John Murray

Walden Rosie and Walkerdine Valerie (1985) *Girls and Mathematics. From Primary to Secondary Schooling.* Bedford Way Papers 24. London: University of London Institute of Education.

Walkerdine Valerie (compiler) and the Girls and Mathematics Unit (1989) *Counting Girls Out.* London: Virago Press.

Willis Sue (1989) *'Real Girls Don't do Maths.' Gender and the Construction of Privilege.* Victoria: Deakin University Press.

Chapter 6

Common Threads

Introduction

An exhibition is an unusual but effective resource in mathematics education. I had previously been involved with two. In one, reported by Hart (1978), learning materials I had designed and made for teaching mathematics in special schools were displayed, alongside an extended theoretical model which demonstrated their purpose. Such a display, in a situation where visitors can handle the materials and evaluate the model for themselves, was clearly a much more accessible way of demonstrating materials than a written article containing descriptions and photographs of the materials could be. Visitors can choose their own point of entry with a particular object or practical activity that attracts their attention and they can spend as long as they like exploring it and perhaps suggesting an improvement. Such an exhibition was entirely within the philosophy of the *Maths in Work* project and its learning materials. Indeed the idea, suggested by Ann Taylor, a member of its steering committee, was so fertile that the limitations of lack of time, a complete absence of a budget, and no idea of a title, took second place to its pursuit.

Research

An exhibition's more public and extensive format than materials addressed to colleagues in the same line of work, required formal justification and explanation. During research for *Cabbage* I had become aware of at least some of the published work that already linked mathematics and textiles, but it was nearly all of the 'disconnected' sort, in a Gilligan sense. Work emanating from the textiles industry itself would naturally be more 'connected' since the production of textiles was the object of the industry, and mathematics one of the necessary tools for achieving it. In other words, there was no particularly high status attached to it whatever its conceptual difficulty; in this context it was a means to an end, a thoroughly mechanical art. Other users, like the various textile crafts organisations also had their own literatures, with a rather more cautious view of mathematics. In addition to the familiar library of the University of London Institute of Education where I worked, I also drew on the libraries of the London College of Fashion, the Textiles Institute in Manchester, the Crafts Council and a number of craft organisations including The Lace Guild, the Quilters Guild, and the Knitting and Crochet Guild. The latter produces an excellent publication called *Slip-knot*, which regularly contains articles on historical, structural and social aspects of the craft.

From what I gleaned from this disparate field, papers seemed to fall into five categories, those of the professionals in the textiles industry, those of professional mathematicians enjoying themselves, those which use textiles to make pedagogic points in mathematics, those which show mathematics that can be done with textiles, and finally those that show people doing mathematical things with cloth but without noticing or focusing on the mathematics. All categories had different implications for the content of an exhibition, though none shared its spirit or made its main point, that of the interdependence of textiles work and mathematical concepts.

Professionals within the textiles industry

Engineers designing machinery for textiles factories, and textiles technologists setting up such machinery, necessarily use mathematics of university level. A modern loom is complex machinery that can manipulate differential performance of warp and weft threads simultaneously at very high speeds through mechanical and computer controls. The inclusion of designs in the weave adds to the complexity, indeed the jacquard mechanism for dealing with just this problem is often cited as the earliest computer. Publications from within the textiles industry also explore the mathematics of woven cloth itself, in contrast to the machines that generate it. The Journal of the Textiles Institute in Manchester has a long tradition of publishing articles on textile geometry and in 1978 republished two classic papers which provided the basis for most of the numerous studies of woven-fabric geometry that followed it. (Peirce and Womersley, 1978). From a university department of Clothing and Textiles I found an article (Hoskins, 1983) which also explored the mathematics of weaving, again at university level. It was clear from this literature and from advice I had sought from industrial and amateur weavers, that something of this richness and range of mathematics in weaving should go into the exhibition, though I would need to be selective.

The arrival of computerised design and production was and is having a radical effect on the textiles industry. At the time of my research, technology was advancing so fast that new looms of higher speeds were being announced almost by the month and anything that I put into the exhibition about computer-aided design and computer-aided manufacture (CAD/CAM) was likely to be out of date by the time the captions had come back from the printers. Nevertheless, it was necessary to include something of it, if the exhibition was to reflect accurately the range of mathematical activity within some parts of the textiles industry.

Mathematicians enjoying themselves

In this category I included people who may not be mathematicians by profession, but whose work nevertheless showed that they were enjoying mathematics in the context of textiles. Such people circulate instructions for knitting Klein bottles round university departments, or may enjoy making themselves a Möbius hat in crochet (Ross, 1985). Their purpose is recreational, though sometimes a professional mathematician will use such activity to make pedagogic points in passing. An example is an article by Zeeman (1982) who in one of his lesser-known works described how he made a dress from a length of cloth he had brought back from Bangkok, but which had been decreed too short for the purpose by professional dressmakers. He interpreted the main problem as one of fitting a flexible flat surface round a curved surface, particularly the negative curve of the small of the back – a quadric in cloth. He also had problems with dressmaking terminology, but he did produce a topological proof of why it is impossible to turn a dress inside out once a lining has been attached at both neck and armholes. A similar approach is taken by Gordon (1978) who describes a 1926 bias cut dress by the couturier Vionnet, as one which 'exploits the low shear modulus and high Poisson's ratio of certain square weave fabrics in the 45° direction.' (Gordon, 1978: Plate 17). Some articles in this genre tend to be gendered, indeed the humour of Zeeman's article and Gordon's illustration lies in their conscious crossing of the gendered divide. Such articles also tend to be rather esoteric, written as jokes between colleagues working at a conceptual mathematical level rather higher than the entry points I was intending to illustrate. I did however include one example from this category, a photograph of an Aran sweater knitted by Griffin (1987) while commuting to her work as a polymer chemist, in which she had used random number tables instead of traditional Aran designs. My justification was that Griffin could provide both a professional role model for schoolgirls and an inspiration to knitters.

Textiles as Examples of Mathematics

At the same high mathematical level were some members of my third category, articles which make pedagogical points in mathematics using textile activities as examples. Such works investigate the relationship between the structure and use of fabric as mathematical phenomena, giving respect to both. Two such articles were a pair written for university level students of crystallography and symmetry, using traditional Hungarian cross-stitch designs as examples (Hargittai and Lengyel, 1984, Hargittai and Lengyel, 1985). A series of three others (Knight, 1984a, 1984b and 1985) also explored symmetry, this time through Maori weaving and carving, and a further example of strip patterns in Kuba weaving is given by Zaslavsky (1973:179). All three examples demonstrate how textile workers untrained in western mathematics, cover all theoretically possible patterns in their work. Little of this work suggests that the embroiderers or weavers were consciously doing mathematics in the traditional liberal sense: group theory is in any case a more recent piece of mathematics than some of the textiles. But neither does it consider that all the textiles work is highly systematic, that it is not the random work of entirely thoughtless people.

Also at university level Grünbaum and Shephard (1980), explored the geometry of fabrics in a mathematical investigation into patterns of weaving which revealed subtle problems in combinatorics and geometry. Another article on weaving and matrices (Clapham, 1980) develops mathematical points made by Grünbaum and Shephard (1980).

A mathematical problem more accessible to school students, on the relationship between a patchwork quilt and its border, is offered by DeTemple (1986) whose opening remark is that the problem comes from the 'unexpectedly fertile area' of textiles. Nevertheless the problem 'is easily stated and understood ... the solution is elusive but elegantly simple ... and involves the concepts of least common multiple and greatest common divisor, even though the problem itself is essentially a geometric one'. Other textile-based resources appear occasionally in the mathematics education journals, but in the form of enticingly geometric pictures offered to a readership of mathematics educators who would know how to exploit the mathematics suggested by them. Such for example was a collection of pictures of baskets from Botswana showing some of the symmetries worked into the coils of three-dimensionally symmetrical constructions as they are made. (Lea, 1987).

In the same journal, Walter (1980:60) reviewed a book for trianglepoint needlework after she happened to see it in a bookshop while looking for something else. Immediately following it is the review of a book for beginner weavers, also by Walter. The reviews appear in an issue of the journal that features the first of two articles on Weaving Tessellations by a mathematics educator working at school level (Fielker, 1980).

Mathematics being done with textiles

Textiles sometimes appear as an applied context for examples of particular mathematics activity, in a spurious reality. For example the well-known 'rug-cutting problem' involves cutting a square with carefully prepared dimensions so that when reassembled as a rectangle, it appears to have acquired a difference in total area (Lamb, 1987). The problem is to find out why. Here the use of a rug as context is irrelevant to the mathematics of the problem: it is difficult to imagine anyone actually cutting up a rug in the way suggested.

Also in this category are occasional publications which appear to aim to link textiles and mathematics. They fail because they maintain the stereotype of textiles work as something without intellect, upon which mathematics can be imposed thereby giving it value it did not previously have. Such work contains no recognition of any inherent mathematics in the making or the use of the textiles and the message that mathematics is something separate and superior to the textiles activity is usually clear. Such publications often sell themselves as 'girl-friendly' with the gendered and patronising message along the lines of 'Look girls, here is something serious you can do with your pretty stuff.' One such publication is that called *Mathematics and Craft*, published by ILEA in 1983 (Roake, 1983) and aimed at primary level children. The booklet is concerned with the application of mathematics to textile activity, but gives no recognition to the mathematics already there. For example it tells children how to make spirals with coloured threads but does not suggest that they look at the spiral within the thread itself, without which it could not hold together. Suggestions for using gingham for counting squares, buttons for sequencing and cloth for making a tangram reinforce its message and raise the question as to why cloth was chosen, when more traditional classroom materials could have done the mathematical job just as well.

In summary, articles in this category tend to reinforce stereotypes of both mathematics and needlework. Clearly it would be inappropriate to include their activities which ran counter to the message of the exhibition.

Doing mathematical things with cloth without noting the mathematics

The fifth category also reinforces the stereotypes, but by default. It includes the vast literature of the craft magazines that publish instructions for decorating or making things with cloth. Mathematics is involved, in that cloth usually has to be measured, often cut quite specifically, or traced from squared paper; threads are counted and grouped; or particular shapes are made and joined together. In general, such mathematical activity is embedded within the practical activity, but words like 'simple' or phrases like 'easy to do' sprinkle the text as authors reassure their readers that they need not fear that their brains will be taxed. Mathematics is there but at the best trivialised or rendered invisible, at the worst treated as a threat.

An example of this genre from within education is *In the Pattern* (ILEA, 1979), a pack written for the purposes of linking literacy and fashion skills with creative crafts. From its illustrations it is assumed that it was aimed at girls since all the illustrations are of girls, women or small children. The main objective was to enable students who were not native speakers of English to follow instructions unaided, with the short-term objective of introducing them to both the language and the basic processes of three needlework crafts, knitting, sewing and patchwork. The pack contained four sets of cards with clear and detailed instructions on how to knit a top, how to design and make a pattern for a skirt and then make it, and how to make patchwork from hexagons. A fourth set of cards on the subject of measurement is included. Because part of the aim of the pack was literacy, the language is controlled and instructions are assisted by the use of graph papers and tables, in fact something numerical or geometrical appears on practically every page. Given that the pack was meant for literacy and craft teachers, it was not to have been expected that any particular piece of mathematics would have been developed, but the word 'mathematics' is not mentioned once. The hidden curriculum of the pack is that mathematics is just not there, or that if it is, it must not be mentioned as such, that it is inappropriate in a home-economics and literacy-oriented resource for girls. It is hard to visualise a parallel pack for carpentry that would not make a feature of the equally necessary mathematics of measurement, calculation and drawing.

In addition to looking at existing publications, I talked with textile workers who clearly used mathematics in their work, three of them with the confidence of high qualifications in mathematics, and one with no confidence but obvious ability. Montse Stanley, an architect turned knitting designer and teacher, had recently published ratio graph paper which I was able to use as a resource in the exhibition (Stanley, 1982). The stitches (or loops) of knitting, though often represented on squared paper are rarely square in practice. A knitter using squared paper to draft a design of footballs on a child's sweater for example, would have to draw ellipses of the correctly proportioned axes. The ratio of stitch width to height depends on the size of the needles, the characteristics and tension of the yarn in use, and the structure of the stitch. A knitter wishing to work a pictorial design into some fabric has two options, one of which is to draw a grid (on which to plot the design) to fit the particular rectangle of the stitch she will be using. The other, more empirical approach is to knit a square, count the number of rows and stitches to say 10cm, calculate the width:height ratio and apply the appropriate distortion to the plot (Cochrane, 1988). Most knitters work empirically by knitting a square and then calculating or estimating the width to height ratio. Experienced knitters can judge this by eye but the advent of domestic knitting machines whose fabric comes off the machine stretched and distorted, makes this impossible. The answer is Stanley's ratio graph paper with grids consisting of rectangles with sides in the ratio of 1:1.3, 1:1.5 and 1:1.7. As I noted at the time these 'are a resource just waiting for mathematics teachers to get hold of' (Harris, 1988a:16).

Margaret Clark, mathematician and lace maker, had also devised her own papers. She uses her diagonally ruled paper so that two sheets can be glued together to produce the consistently correct angle needed for a particular piece of lace. Scientific graph paper, first offered for sale in 1795 had a significant effect on lace making but was not generally available until the middle of the nineteenth century (Harris, 1988:c). The availability of relatively cheap squared paper in the mid-nineteenth century had a significant effect on mathematics education (Brock and Price, 1980), by which time lace makers were already exploiting its accuracy for their particular mathematical activity.

The third mathematician to be consulted was Bridgid Sewell who had carried out some of the research for the Cockcroft Report. Sewell is also a weaver and she prepared display examples in both woven cloth and paper symbolism, of the compact way in which weavers record instructions for even their most complex designs.

The less confident textile worker is an experienced knitting machine operator and at the time I was setting up the exhibition, was experimenting with a new, programmable machine. Having explained to me that if she programmed a motif, her machine could reflect and translate but not rotate it, and having volunteered to knit me some samples of her machine's transformations for my display, she asked what the exhibition was about.

Her response was that she could not possibly make me something for a mathematics exhibition, since she knew nothing about mathematics.

An Exhibition in the Making

Preparing an exhibition is a very different job from preparing paper learning materials for use at a desk. The value in mathematics education is now well enough recognised for exhibitions to be more widely pursued (Harris, in press). The exhibition was to be aimed at the general public as well as at schools and to mathematics education generally. To schools I wanted to show the mathematical nature of a very familiar substance. For the general public I aimed to show that there is more to mathematics than arithmetic, and that mathematics is embedded in a great deal of ordinary daily activity, including domestic activity. For mathematics education I wanted to devise at least part of the exhibition in enough depth for traditional mathematicians in the educational hierarchies to take it seriously, while displaying it in a developmental way, so as to suggest a full range of activities for schools. And finally I wanted to demand respect for the large number of women throughout the world who clothe their families with inventive, beautiful and often unremarked geometries.

I thus needed a theme that would run horizontally through a range of concepts, processes and networks of mathematics and daily life, and vertically through mathematics itself. The theme of symmetry did not come as blinding illumination, neither did the title *Common Threads*, but they emerged together as themes that would weave the double meaning together, for 'common' can mean both 'ordinary' and 'widely distributed' and threads can form a line, or weave a mesh, or represent the abstract idea of connectedness.

I decided that the exhibits of Common Threads would consist entirely of textiles but that I would caption them in the language of mathematics. This unfamiliar juxtaposition would sometimes jar, and sometimes be deliberately provocative, but would certainly demand a response. It would be simple for example to put a T shirt into Common Threads and label it in textiles language with the tautology 'Cotton T shirt, size 14, made in Erewhon'. A mathematical caption such as 'Intersection of three cylinders' however, with no other wording, would draw attention to its structure and might immediately trigger a school investigation along the lines of 'what is the minimum diameter of the sleeve intersection that would provide the most comfortable freedom of arm movement, whilst permitting the best fit of the garment as a whole?' By extending the caption from its mathematical description to the shirt's origin, I could invite a different sort of mathematical investigation. For example ' T shirt made in Erewhon and bought in Oxford Street for £2.99. Assuming that three stages of middlemen each make a 15% profit on their buying price, how many T shirts will the factory worker have to sew before she can buy a loaf of bread for her family?' Eventually I settled on less politically provocative contexts and devised labels for a range of artifacts that would offer the widest and deepest mathematics. The opening and largest section was called Symmetry with the following four sections illustrating mathematical themes beneath it: number as a tool of mathematics and of everyday life: creativity as a neglected aspect of mathematical thinking: and information handling and problem-solving as two processes in mathematical thinking.

The Symmetry section itself began with a piece of cross-stitch embroidery bought in a tourist market in Split, in former Yugoslavia, and I placed metal mirrors on elastic beside it with which visitors could explore the symmetries in its designs. I re-embroidered its central motif, stopping it at several stages to show how an embroiderer might build up the design. Such workers use the cloth as graph paper, counting along, and up or down, to map the symmetries of the design to a new position. On one of the samples I embroidered x and y axes in a contrasting colour to illustrate how the embroiderer could have worked. The captions consisted of an imaginary conversation between two women using mathematical language as part of the conversation. The Yugoslavian embroidery had been worked from the front and I followed it with some examples of cross-stitch worked from the back, by Mien refugees in Thailand, and lent to Common Threads by Oxfam.

The next two panels of Common Threads contained an explanation of some of the different ways in which mathematicians have coded relationships in space by co-ordinates, mappings, transformations, functions and graphs, followed by some of their definitions and notations for handling basic concepts in symmetry. In mathematics text books it is usual to illustrate the ways in which a motif can be combined along a line to form what are usually known as frieze or strip patterns*, by means of right-angled triangles of unequal sides, though any other asymmetric motif would do. Since the exhibition was about cloth and since I had been exploring the mathematical nature of knitted socks, I decided to use the rather more familiar and less threatening motif of socks to demonstrate the strip patterns. For the space I had, this would have required thirty-four identical sock images which

Overleaf: **Figure 9(i)** and **Figure 9(ii)**

Figure 9(i): The seven strip of frieze patterns demonstrated with baby socks.
Original Common Threads exhibition.

Figure 9(ii): Frieze patterns from a haberdashery counter.
Original Common Threads exhibition.

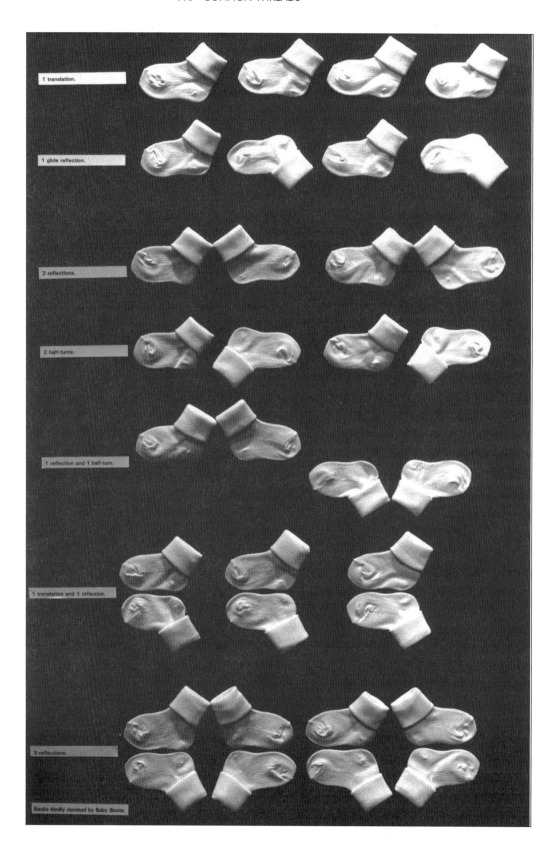

1 translation.

1 glide reflection.

2 reflections.

2 half-turns.

1 reflection and 1 half-turn.

1 translation and 1 reflection.

3 reflections.

Socks kindly donated by Baby Boots.

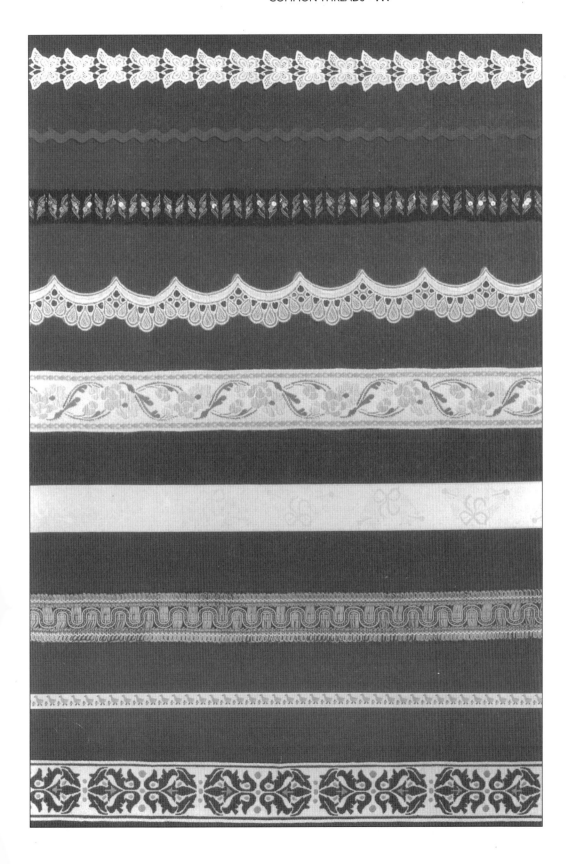

would have been difficult to handle with the office equipment I had and within the small budget I had managed to raise. A generous donation of Boots' baby socks provided the solution and some of the most affirmative reaction to the exhibition. Viewers, like me, found it easier to follow the designs with an object everyone is familiar with in different orientations.

The two panels of mathematical explanation were the minimum I felt I should provide to make mathematical sense. That they were more substantial than is usual in exhibitions became a point of some difficulty when Common Threads came to be redesigned later by professional exhibition designers for overseas touring, but since my original design was as a resource for learning mathematics, I felt they were justified, and I used fairly substantial explanatory panels throughout the exhibition. I received no complaints about the demands they made on reading, in fact many visitors referred to them repeatedly as they followed their explanations in the textiles.

Different aspects of symmetry were further explored in hair ribbons, furniture trimmings, and a Fair Isle Sweater and I used a piece of weaving from Bangladesh to demonstrate the strip patterns* worked as part of the construction of the textile. I was fortunate enough to interview the weaver Sarat Mala Chakma, who explained how she worked the designs on her back-strap loom, raising the warps with short lengths of well-polished sticks to allow for her shuttle to pass underneath. Each of the seventy five strip patterns is a picture from her life: literally as flowers, animals, footprints or fish, or pieces of jewellery, or the border pattern on her sarong: or symbolically in representations of a snail trail, the flight of a bird, moonlight, or ancient symbols in complex designs traditional in her family. This weaver, who had had no schooling, used different groups of numbers of threads in building her designs: she usually worked with pairs of warps, but liked exploring the patterns that odd numbers made.

Plane symmetry, designs worked over a flat surface, were introduced by the reflected and translated motif worked by the knitter with the new programmable machine, and were followed by a Turkish kilim, a veritable symphony of symmetries (Harris, 1987). The section ended with rotational symmetry, shown in a Fair Isle tam o' shanter, some appliqué work by Hmong people in Thailand, and baskets from Botswana.

The Number section, that followed Symmetry consisted mainly of knitted textiles. It began with a 'scarf for Dr. Who', knitted in strips each made by a unique combination from three different sized needles, three different thicknesses of yarn and three different styles of stitch, all on the same number of stitches. The scarf, a cartesian product of three sets, was accompanied by a collection of twenty-seven clothes pegs hanging in a bag, each marked in code as a particular combination of needle size, thread size and stitch style. Visitors were invited to identify for each strip, the size of needle, yarn and style, by clipping the appropriate clothes peg to it. The activity proved difficult though many visitors tried. Its main impact was the visual illustration of the effect of a triple multiplication. Most visitors were perfectly well aware that in the abstract $3 \times 3 \times 3 = 27$ but many commented on their own surprise at how different the visual growth was from 3 and 9. A similar elaboration was clear in the Aran sweater that followed. The structure of knitting is binary, plain and purl. All the complex designs worked into Arans derive from it whether work with traditional symmetries or with Griffin's (1987) random numbers. The section ended with an exhibit on lace, and one on crochet, topologically a single loop worked on one hook.

For the Creativity section I was fortunate enough to be able to borrow an entire exhibition of quilts that had recently appeared at Greens Mill and Science Centre in Nottingham (Turner, 1987). The exhibition had been called 'Mathematical Magic in Textiles' and, as well as presenting some most beautiful needlework, showed some of the pleasure that the quilt-makers had taken in the mathematics that had inspired them. The exhibits made a positive antidote to many female attitudes to mathematics. One patchworker, Louise Briggs, who commented that she was 'often intrigued by the way numbers relate to each other' systematically combined colours with numbers, to work a 10 x 10 panel called *Primary Factors*, in which 'primary' referred to both colours and prime numbers. Another who clearly enjoyed mathematics, was Linda Maltman who began her comments with the words 'I have always found it fascinating that if you take a solid cone and slice it in various ways, the cut sections will give you 'conic sections' and thus they are all related'. Sheila Scawen wrote of her Pythagoras in Black and White patchwork that 'Maths had been my favourite subject at school ... Pythagoras theorem was one of the 'high lights' of those days and the proof of the theorem is still indelibly fixed in my mind.' Two more patch workers took their inspiration from their children's mathematics homework: others from designs from books or gardens (Turner, 1987). Characteristically of work that relates women to mathematics however, Turner's article about the exhibition begins with a caution, warning readers that the title Mathematical Magic in Textiles might seem daunting. When Common Threads closed, Mathematical Magic had to be returned to its makers, but the Creativity section was kept in Common Threads as it went on tour, to encourage people to put in their own view of mathematical creativity.

The two process sections of the exhibition, Information Handling and Problem solving were represented through weaving and garment making respectively. With great difficulty I eventually found a working model of a jacquard mechanism, and an owner, Middlesex Polytechnic, generous enough to lend it. It formed the bridge between the explanation of weaving and its symbolism prepared by Bridgid Sewell and some state of the art textile manufacture donated by Courtaulds. Part of the section was an exploration of some of the mathematics involved in making neckties and the cloth from which they are made. Ties are made from three pieces of cloth, all cut at 45° to its grain so that the completed tie fits the curve of the neck without wrinkling. If a tie is to carry a motif, a club badge for example, then the motif will have to be woven at 45° to the grain if it is to appear horizontally on the tie. If it is required to appear only once, on the front of the tie, then further ingenuity is needed in designing the cloth and in cutting out the ties, because constraints of the jacquard mechanism require that the motif is repeated at particular intervals as the cloth is woven. In addition, ties are cut from cloth with great economy. Their orientation and three piece construction means that there is practically no wastage of material, unless a motif has to appear in a particular place. The motifs can of course appear on the tie in places where the tie itself would not show when it was worn.

The Problem-Solving Section was in two parts, dealing mainly with clothing problems. The first part took rectangles of cloth and showed how garment makers exploit the uncut rectangle itself or cut it so that it can be sewn together again to make garments. A garment made from an uncut rectangle can display a woven design to particular advantage. The border pattern on a sari shows the symmetries of a repeat design in graceful movement. A kilt is made by pleating the chequered patterns of a tartan cloth in such a way that the pattern is continuous on the completed garment.

The second part of the problem-solving section, and the final part of the exhibition itself was concerned with textiles in three dimensions. The problem of turning the heel of a sock, that of making a right-angled bend in the fabric while maintaining an even surface, is one which has exercised many minds over many centuries. The sculptor and knitter Paul Cochrane has researched different solutions to the problem and in Europe alone had already found 30 by the time I was setting up Common Threads. He had time to knit and graph twelve of them while I knitted one of the solutions in several stages to demonstrate the construction.

Design and Making

Having assembled all the artifacts, drafted captions and taken the advice of the art technician at the Institute of Education, I made simple wood frames from timber of about 2 or 3 cm cross section, depending on what was available at a local timber merchant. I chose a neutral base colour for the whole exhibition, one that would show both cloth and captions to advantage, and one that was available in both hessian and card. For displaying textile items, I stretched hessian over the frames, stapled it to the back and sewed the textiles to the hessian. For mounting captions, I cut the base card to the right dimensions, glued it to the frames and glued the captions to it. Since the gallery space was only available for ten days, this relatively flimsy construction was perfectly adequate. It was less so however when the exhibition went on tour, something for which I had not planned. Although I protected each frame with its own travelling bubble pack, there was nothing I could do to prevent some of the frames from warping: bracing across the corners proved inadequate for the timber was not seasoned. When it came to displaying the frames in the exhibition gallery, I drove nails into the existing horizontal batons on the wall already fixed at the appropriate height, and slipped the frames over the nails at intervals that I judged as I went along.

Immediate Effects

The impact of the exhibition can be gauged in several ways. A straight count of the number of people who came was not an adequate measure, for the gallery was small and for safety's sake I had to limit the number of school groups that applied to come. Many schools came long distances and teachers had arranged for their children to develop the work in Common Threads in another museum or gallery on the same day. One asked the Tate to lay on a lecture on mathematics and art for half their party while the other half was at Common Threads, and changed the groups half way through the day. Another, a boys' school, brought the whole of one year in four batches, and one school returned with the same small group several times, using the exhibition in depth. So far as gallery space allowed, it was used to capacity.

Secondly many visitors, teachers, children and members of the public stated their enthusiasm clearly and often. Teachers commented on how pleasant it was to be able to come on a *mathematics* outing at all. There was a consistent response from craft workers, several of whom were also mathematicians, that such an exhibition was long overdue. Thirdly, so many requests were made to borrow the exhibition that I had no choice but to set up and organise a national tour, one that lasted for two years until my original flimsy frames finally wore out.

The exhibition's achievement can be summarised through its impact in schools and outside. The repeat visits of several groups and the enthusiasm of single ones was a clear demonstration that classrooms are not the only places where mathematics can be learned. Outside school mathematics classrooms, mathematics *is* a cross-curriculum subject. Common Threads certainly challenged the normal range of textbook examples and drew attention to a rich mathematical resource literally under people's noses. It even presented the possibility of teaching an entire secondary course starting from cloth and running the risk of following a course just as unbalanced, but in a different direction, as many were already. Common Threads inspired confidence and motivation. A common response from pupils both to Common Threads and to Cabbage was something along the lines of 'My mother does that at home' often with the implication that she did it rather better. Whether or not this had the effect of increasing appreciation of mothers, there is no doubt that it drew attention to their talents. Common Threads inspired interactiveness, not least because visitors were expected to explore how articles were made, to argue about their construction and whether or not they involved mathematical thinking.

Reports from various locations of the subsequent tour showed enthusiasm and inventiveness in its use. Roger Brown from Newcastle Polytechnic wrote of 'golden moments of insight, joy, wonder, awe, inspiration and challenge.' In Sunderland, a series of workshops was laid on for visiting schools. 'We invited a person to work with computers and knitting machines and the children made their own punch cards. We borrowed saris and kimonos from people in the community (Nissan being pervasive here). We also had a patchwork quilt maker, a weaver and a lace maker, who got them to take decisions on types of knot, using probability.' In Bedfordshire, a traditional lace-making district, local lace makers were invited to work in Common Threads during children's visits. On one occasion they left their work untended and were warned by the exhibition organisers that if they did so, children would touch the bobbins and possibly move them. The lace makers' response was a typical one of attitudes to Common Threads: 'Of course they will. How else will they learn?' In some locations, learning was deliberately extended beyond textiles themselves. In Buckinghamshire, children worked on the designs on some of the textiles before being given the architectural problem of fitting houses into a given area. Feedback from all the locations reported not only unusually enthusiastic use of an exhibition, but demonstrated unusual care, indeed affection for its fabric. No doubt it is something to do with the nature of fabrics and the traditional skills of its carers, but it is unusual to have a exhibition returned to base not just with nothing lost or broken, but sometimes with something added, accompanied by a note along the lines: 'We found this a useful addition to the Symmetry Section.' (Harris, 1990).

Common Threads also spoke clearly to members of the public whatever their attitude to, or experience of mathematics. It made something, usually seen as specialist, comfortably and immediately available, something both ordinary and extraordinary. It spoke to all ages, classes, cultures and genders. Whether or not people wanted to take the message, it showed that 'women's' work could be as mathematical as 'men's'. Finally it was beautiful: it connected in a Gilliganish way with feelings, with social circumstances, with all the daily domestic activities that are associated with cloth, from putting on a shirt in the morning to pairing socks out of the tumbler dryer.

Press reports confirmed its impact. In its review of Common Threads, the *Morning Star* remarked 'At a time when study after study reveals our innumeracy as a nation, and argument rages in academic circles about the apparent mathematical under-achievement of girls, perhaps it is time to shift the goal posts and start by analysing the maths inherent in what many of us have been doing all along' (Coben, 1988). The *Times Educational Supplement* summed up its review thus 'Adding up, it shows what ... thousands of women have known all the time: that what they do with their hands is a very intellectual thing.' (Hofkins, 1988).

Common Threads did not completely satisfy everyone however. There remained, and still remain, those who argue that 'this is not mathematics', an argument that addresses the interface problem between the practicalities and processes that are considered to constitute the learning of mathematics in schools, and the understanding, development and use of its abstractions. This I tried to address in one of my own articles on Common Threads

> If mathematics really is the specialist abstract and symbolic system they claim, then much of school mathematics is not maths either but a collection of steps on the way to a goal many never reach. And if maths is the wholly abstract system it is, why is it necessary to have so many text-book examples of practical maths from the environment? And having chosen practical examples, why are they so often limited to mechanical ones? By choosing to ignore or disparage half our environment we are blinding ourselves to a very rich mathematical resource, one that is common and natural to all cultures and both sexes. The reasons for this choice are not mathematical. (Harris, 1988a:28)

The seamless robe is no mean metaphor for textiles in mathematics education. Our first garment is a wrapping cloth, our last a shroud. The hands that knit the shawl and weave the shroud are the hands that rear the children, make the home and provide the protective care without which independent thinking, and the experience of knowing cannot grow. One of the activities in the *Cabbage* pack came from Ghana and concerned the symmetries of adinkra stamps, small pieces of carved calabash which are used to print symmetrical designs on cloth. Each design has a name, a symbolism and a symmetry. *Dwennimen* represents a ram's head, has two axes and rotational symmetry, and it combines four ideas in a refreshingly un-European but nevertheless closed form: strength and wisdom, learning and humility. *Duafe* represents a wooden comb and is the symbol of the wisdom, patience and concern of women. It has simple bilateral symmetry, but its arms are infinitely extensible.

Figure 10: Dwennimen and Duafe. Traditional symbols on Adinkra cloth. Ghana.

Notes

* Here I have broken my self-imposed consistency of use of the words 'design' and 'pattern' in accordance with the established convention of the name 'strip patterns'.

References

Brock William H and Price Michael H. (1980) Squared Paper in the Nineteenth Century: Instrument of Science and Engineering, and Symbol of Reform in Mathematical Education. *Educational Studies in Mathematics* Vol II p 365-381.

Clapham C R J (1980) When a Fabric Hangs Together. *Bulletin of the London Mathematical Society.* Vol 12 p 161-164.

Cochrane Paul (1988) Knitting Maths. *Mathematics Teaching* Vol 124 September p 26-28.

Coben Diana (1988) Adding to Everyday Skills. In *The Morning Star.* Women's Page. January 1st 1988.

DeTemple Duane (1986) Reflection Borders for Patchwork Quilts. *Mathematics Teacher,* February p 138-143.

Fielker David. (1980) Weaving Tessellations. *Mathematics Teaching* Vol 91 June p 34-39

Gordon J E (1978) *Structures, or Why Things Don't Fall Down.* Harmondsworth: Penguin Books.

Griffin Mary (1987) Wear Your Own theory: A Beginners Guide to Random Knitting. *New Scientist* March 26th 1987.

Grünbaum Branko and Shephard Geoffrey C (1980) Satins and Twills: An Introduction to the Geometry of Fabrics. *Mathematical Magazine* Vol 53 No 3 May.

Hargittai Istvan and Lengyel György (1984) The Seven One-Dimensional Space Group Symmetries Illustrated by Hungarian Folk Needlework. *Journal of Chemical Education* Vol 61 12 December p 1033-4.

Hargittai Istvan and Lengyel György (1985) The Seventeen Two-Dimensional Space-Group Symmetries in Hungarian Needlework. *Journal of Chemical Education* Vol 61 No 1 January p 35-36

Harris Mary (1987) An Example of Traditional Womens' Work as a Mathematics Resource. In *For the Learning of Mathematics* Vol 7 No 3 p 26-28

Harris Mary (1988a) Common Threads. *Mathematics Teaching* Vol June p 15-16

Harris Mary (1988b) Common Threads: Mathematics and Textiles. *Mathematics in Schools* Vol No 4 September p 24-28

Harris Mary (1988c) *Common Threads Catalogue.* London: Maths in Work Project, University of London Institute of Education.

Harris Mary (1990) Common Threads Feedback MSS. Unpublished.

Harris Mary (in press) Travelling Mathematics Exhibitions. In Andy Begg (Ed) *Popularising Mathematics: A Resource Guide.*

Hart John, (1978) No Longer Forgotten. ILEA *Contact* No 7 June 9th. London: Inner London Education Authority.

Hofkins Diane (1988) Common Threads. *The Times Educational Supplement.* March 4th 1988.

Hoskins J A (1983) *Factoring Binary Matrices: A Weaver's Approach. Lecture Notes in Math* 952 pps 300-326. Winnipeg: University of Manitoba Department of Clothing and Textiles.

ILEA Inner London Education Authority (1979). *In the Pattern.* London: ILEA Resources Centre.

Knight G H (1984) The Geometry of Maori Art: Rafter Patterns. *New Zealand Mathematics Magazine* Vol 21 No 2 p 36-40.

Knight G H (1984) The Geometry of Maori Art: Weaving Patterns. *New Zealand Mathematics Magazine* Vol 21 No 3 p 80-86.

Knight G H (1985) The Geometry of Maori Art: Spirals. *New Zealand Mathematics Magazine* Vol 22 No 1 p 4-7.

Lamb John F Jr (1987) The Rug Cutting Puzzle. *Mathematics Teacher* January.

Lea Hilda (1987) Botswana Baskets. *Mathematics Teaching* Vol 118 March p 57-58.

Peirce F T and Womersley J R (1978) *Cloth Geometry.* Manchester: The Textiles Institute.

Roake Dorothy (1983) *Mathematics and Fabric.* London: Inner London Education Authority.

Ross Joan (1985) How to Make a Möbius Hat. *Mathematics Teacher.* April.

Stanley Monste (1982) *Knitting: Your Own Design for a Perfect Fit.* London: David and Charles.

Turner Gill (1987) Mathematical Magic in Textiles. In *Patchwork and Quilting* Summer Issue No 7 p 9-11

Walter Marion (1980) Reviews of Trianglepoint by Sherlee Lanz and Spiders' Games by Phyllis Morgan. *Mathematics Teaching.* Vol 91 June p 60-62

Zaslavsky Claudia (1973) *Africa Counts. Number and Pattern in African Culture.* Westport: Lawrence Hill and Co.

Zeeman E C (1982) The Mathematics of Dressmaking. *Manifold* No 2 Spring. Warwick: Mathematics Institute, Warwick University.

Chapter 7

Cloth in the Classroom

Introduction

Common Threads and *Cabbage* were not the first attempts to use such a feminine activity as needlework in such a masculine activity as mathematics. The exhibition in particular acted as a focus for teachers already thinking and working along similar lines. It also came at a time when research was confirming the significance of the context on learning mathematics, and when gender and culture issues were high priorities. The time was exactly right for Common Threads and many teachers responded either by taking up its ideas for the first time or by coming forward to offer their own. The project was fortunate in being able to act as a centre of communication in a fine example of connectedness, and the impact was in both teaching and research. The effects of conscientisation – in Freirean terms – (Mellin-Olsen, 1986:103) have been wide, deep and lasting.

Teachers using Textiles

In March 1989 a group of teachers met at the Easter Course of the Association of Teachers of Mathematics, with the purpose of recording and pooling their experiences of using textiles for teaching mathematics, for the benefit of other teachers who would like to use textiles in this way (Harris, 1990). By chance the work of the eleven teachers who formed the group, (Hawkin, Hepburn, Mayle, McDevitt, Paechter, Thomas, Lolley, Ross, Benson, Bloomfield and Mardell) included infant, primary, secondary and tertiary levels. Their aims had been varied and included, to cover a particular piece of mathematical learning, to cover a particular area of the mathematics curriculum, to teach to a particular requirement of the mathematics curriculum, to help work a piece of software. into a current teaching scheme, and informally to introduce a topic that would be taught more formally later. But more social aims were also considered directly, for example one teacher's aim was to raise the low expectations on pupils' time-tabled needlecraft lessons, by introducing an extended, mathematically-oriented project derived from it. None of these aims alone was gendered. The main concern was with widening the traditional concerns of the mathematics curriculum. As Hawkin (1990a:7) stressed,

> Within the conjunction of maths and textiles there are two conceptually different types of activity. First, the textile activities which have mathematics embedded in them: where the particular activity, such as patchwork or weaving, relies on mathematics for its success even if this is not usually made explicit. Secondly, there are the ways in which certain mathematical concepts can be illustrated using the particular qualities of textiles. Both of these aspects are stimulating, motivating and endlessly absorbing for boys as well as girls.

Three of the teachers however had chosen textiles with the aim of raising confidence or awareness in girls of their own mathematical ability. One chose:

> to make explicit the mathematical processes and content of traditional women's crafts, work that girls may have seen their mothers and grand-mothers doing or that can be clearly seen as something that many ordinary women did or do at other times or places. I want to show girls that even while doing culturally stereotyped work, they can be doing mathematics; that women traditionally have been mathematicians. At the same time I aim to make some areas of mathematics more 'real' by putting them into an accessible context. (Paechter, 1990:14)

One of two teachers working together, wrote:

> I wanted them to be in a position of wanting and/or needing to learn to 'make maths their own' so that they could keep it with them and not leave it behind in the classroom. (Lolley and Ross, 1990:18)

Hawkin (1990a), who is both an artist and a mathematics educator, is experienced in using textiles as a mathematics resource in both the senses she describes above. In Harris (1990) she describes work she did with an infant class (Hawkin, 1990a:7) and with a group of able mathematicians at the top of a junior school (Hawkin, 1990b:10). In the infant class, she had set the task of making felt mice. The children were involved with some mathematics as soon as they began:

> How much fabric? How many needles (matching one-to-one with the children)? How many pins (matching three-to-one)? How long should the thread be? (Hawkin, 1990a:7)

Once the mice were finished the real mathematics began. Hawkin's planning had included a number of differences in the materials she had provided: eyes (stuck on or sewn), two different sizes of mouse template, three different colours of felt, two different-shaped ears, and three different sorts of tail, including an unplanned category of no tails at all, because some children in their excitement at finishing their mice had forgotten to put them on. Instead of investing in abstract and expensive bought sorting blocks for teaching basics in logic, Hawkin asked the children to sort their own mice whose characteristics they knew intimately, and with which they were anxious to 'play'. They

> sorted for all the different attributes, and for two or three different attributes at a time. They used Venn, Carrol and Tree diagrams to represent their results. They played the 'one difference' game where you start with one object (mouse) and have to follow it with another which only differs by one attribute, for example colour, then by another differing by another attribute, for example shape of the ears, and so on, and they extended it. They discovered the properties of the 'missing mice' – the ones that could have been made but were not and they drew some simple block graphs to illustrate some of the information they had discovered about their mice.
>
> Thus inherent in what the children were doing anyway, with familiar materials and context, the mathematics is made explicit so that children can begin to develop the discrimination skills, the logic skills, and the concepts of 'same' and 'difference', the ability to handle and classify data, indeed all those things that appear in the early levels of the National Curriculum. (Hawkin, 1990a:7)

For her class of eleven-year-old able mathematicians, Hawkin had set individual investigations. One child, Susan, was exploring which shapes will tessellate. Hawkin's suggestion that she conduct the investigation in cloth 'turned a dry, abstract experience into an exciting, creative adventure'.

> She discovered that if the angles at a point added up to 360° then the shapes would tessellate and she had a wonderful collection of different triangles and quadrilaterals which all 'worked'. Then she went on to explore more complicated polygons and those which would only make a semi-regular tessellation (ie: which left regular shapes of background cloth showing between them). Finally at the end of the investigation, Susan ... sewed all the samples together. This resulted in a patchwork bedcover of which she was justly proud – and through which she had achieved National Curriculum Target 10: Shape and Space, Level 6. (Hawkin, 1990:10)

Thomas' concern with her six-year-olds was with teaching fractions, starting with the different ways in which halves of a square can be represented. The children drew their halves on squared paper before cutting them out in fabric. Help was given in sewing the fabric together on the school sewing machine and Thomas herself sewed all the children's work together to make a quilt. More mathematical work followed from this as the children worked out different areas of different fabrics that would be needed for different sized beds (Thomas, 1990).

Paechter (1990) reported that she used patchwork a good deal in teaching tessellation.

> In its traditional form, as a means of making a larger piece of cloth out of scraps, patchwork gives a clear reason for tessellating shapes. The process also introduces additional constraints which extend and enrich the activity... The patches themselves have to be cut along the grain of the fabric so that they sit properly when the piece is made up; this necessitates a further tessellation on the material from which they are to be cut, to get the maximum number of patches from a particular piece of cloth. (Paechter, 1990:14)

As she points out, it is essential to be very accurate when cutting templates, otherwise the pieces do not fit properly. 'For once there is a transparent reason to insist on really precise drawing'. Mathematical extension that arises when using cloth in this way is additional experience of handling shapes in space.

> The sewing itself is straightforward, but when working from a plan it is actually very difficult to see exactly which piece fits where, especially if you have a design in which rectangles fit half way along each other. Because you are working from the back of the patchwork, what you would see if the templates were not in the way would be a reflection of the original design. Thus, in order to sew the design together, students have to reflect the design in their heads while at the same time being aware of which bit of it they are working on. Meanwhile they cannot always see the front of the design, as it is folded together for sewing. (Paechter, 1990:15)

Patchwork was used by Lolley and Ross (1990) both for teaching geometric concepts and in developing teaching strategies. Already a successful mathematics teacher, Lolley had enlisted the help of Ross, an Advisory Teacher appointed to develop anti-racist curricula and strategies. Lolley was nervous of changing her formal teaching methods but felt that it had not been giving the girls enough experience in active learning. By undertaking a class patchwork quilt she felt that she could involve the girls in a more interactive style of learning while covering the syllabus areas of the rectangle, angles, the triangle and rhombus, and symmetry. Her preparation provided definitions of polygons and regularity and some prompt sheets containing investigations into the geometry of polygons. The project was launched with a story about patchwork quilts and an illustrative poster, and immediately it had a life of its own.

We explored

- Which polygons will tessellate
- How many triangles are in a polygon
- What happens when you rip off the corners of polygons and stick them together
- Drawing polygons by dividing circles
- Using Logo to construct polygons
- Measuring interior angles of polygons and adding them up
- Symmetry of polygons.

(Lolley in Lolley and Ross, 1990:18)

In other words, the project extended well beyond the syllabus items that Lolley had intended to cover.

Benson (1990) had not used textiles in class before, indeed he had never made a garment, but the publication of *Cabbage*, the arrival of a new textiles teacher in the school where he was Head of Mathematics, and the requirement of the examination syllabus for extended coursework, suggested the idea of making a garment as a practical mathematics exercise with a valued end product. His prime concern was to enable pupils to generate extensions themselves from a task which was their own: he wanted the coursework to be a context for the practical use of mathematics rather than an applied mathematics problem. Like Lolley, Benson was nervous about the possibility of losing necessary syllabus items in a radical idea, but after discussion with his colleagues, including the textiles teacher, a concise instruction for coursework was agreed. Pupils were asked to design and make a garment to their own measurements, and given further details of specified outcomes that would be expected of them at each design stage, on which assessment would be based. Specifically pupils were asked to

- Identify a number of different patterns
- Use a scale diagram to produce layout plans for each fabric width which will minimise waste
- Produce scale mockups
- Make a full size pattern drawing
- Make a plan of production requirements including an estimate of time and costs
- Produce a log book.

(Benson, 1990:21)

The assignment was presented to the students in the last period before half term, to allow the time for the immediately sceptical to think about it. This strategy proved effective: at the first period after half term, a girl brought a scale drawing and mockups of a skirt she wanted to make, and a boy brought scale drawings of a shirt he had dismembered. After that the tasks established themselves very quickly.

The assessment scheme was founded on examination criteria, but enhanced by written comments from both mathematics and textiles teachers on students' work at a particular stage of the project. The final assessment was based on the guidelines which they added to the examination board's requirements.

Mathematical content	Process
Measuring	Design Development
Conversion	Rethinking of design
imperial, metric	
Approximation	
Scale drawing	Planning
Layout plans:	
minimisation of waste/area	Communicating mathematical ideas
Organisation	
Costing – best buy	Embodiment and realisation
Time planning	

(Benson, 1990:22)

Mardell (1990) also chose to set garment making as an assessment task. Her teaching group were Post-Graduate Certificate of Education (PGCE) students training to teach mathematics. They were not mathematics graduates but their degree subjects, geology, politics or economics, all contained it. The course aimed to cover 'the usual PGCE material' and to develop the students' own mathematical knowledge and understanding.

> Alongside calculus, number systems, geometry and such like, the students have an 'Introduction to Mathematics' unit which reviews some school mathematics and offers some alternative approaches to them. It was as part of this unit that I did some work on clothing and textiles with the group. (Mardell, 1990:26)

With ideas from *Cabbage*, and the work of Watson (1988) and Burnham (1973), Mardell's aim was to develop the idea of the economic use of cloth in garments making, using examples from other cultures, past and present. The culmination of the classwork was an assessment task wherein the students were asked to design and make a garment, with sleeves, to fit themselves. They were required to submit any measurements they took, a scale drawing of the pattern layout, cutting and sewing instructions, and comments on the mathematics they had used in the whole process, as well as the garment itself. The quality of sewing would not be assessed.

Learning Effects

All the teachers reported that they had more than covered the syllabus items they intended to cover. All also reported the positive effects of high motivation and involvement, sometimes after initial reluctance, if not actual disbelief on the part of students. Benson for example reported an immediate chorus of 'what has this got to do with maths?' and Mardell reported 'some good-natured groaning'. But since a number of her students were politically active or interested – 'on the left' – they could not present serious opposition and maintain their political credibility. Hepburn's school students also did not see sewing as school work, 'and when I suggested that they were engaged in a mathematical activity, they seemed to doubt my sanity'. The difficulty children, particularly young children have, in seeing the 'fun' work of textiles as mathematical is also reported by Partridge (1992) and discussed in more detail below.

The extended involvement of students of all ages, once engaged, was undeniable. Hawkin wrote of the 'enthusiasm' of her infants and the 'creative adventure' of her able top juniors. Hepburn explained that her project remained uncompleted because the children wanted to take their work home with them. Paechter took advantage of the personal commitment of her secondary girls in developing their mathematics. Thomas remarked on the satisfaction her children showed when working with fabrics and the 'great excitement' of the boy who finished the first square of the project. Mayle and McDevitt reported that their hearing- impaired children 'thoroughly enjoyed' their activity. Lolley and Ross reported 'satisfaction'. Benson, like many others realised that he had 'underestimated the interest of boys, many of whom are more fashion conscious than their 1970s forebears'. Mardell recorded that 'The written material conveyed a real sense of involvement, with descriptions of struggle, frustration, inspiration and triumph in varying proportions.'

The context of all this activity with textiles was practical activity, selected by teachers to reveal or generate mathematical activity. This was in contrast to the more traditional method of teaching a piece of mathematics first, then trying to find a realistic situation in which to demonstrate an application. Teachers are sometimes sceptical about the former way of proceeding, but as Benson noted:

We had provided an environment which was mathematically rich and we were able to observe a variety of individual applications as students coped with necessary design changes suggested by mock ups, and embodied them in the patterns which were continually referred to in the manner of working drawings. In short, we felt that the process of making a garment allowed us to witness the application of maths as well as teach it. It is clearly an area which we would need to refine and develop in future courseworks of this kind. (Benson, 1990:22)

In life outside school, such practical work is often done in the context of social interaction. Textiles work, with its images of women chatting as they sew, is no exception and it is merely a pursuit of the stereotype to assume that the chat is 'idle gossip'. Informal research discussed in Chapter 10 below, suggests that much of the talk is task-centred, particularly when the activity is non-routine, and that in these circumstances, task-centred talk contains a great deal of mathematical language, which in turn implies mathematical conceptualisation.

Gorman (1990) for example, noted some of the content of the 'chat' while a group of her class of top juniors worked together without teacher intervention. The children were making Temari, the 'hand balls' of an ancient Japanese craft in which coloured threads are interwoven on the surface of a ball, to form systematic designs. In this classroom context, polystyrene balls were randomly wrapped in thread to form a working surface and lines of 'latitude and longitude' were marked on the surface with paper and pins. Gorman listed some of the words the children themselves chose to use as they worked at this craft work. These were:

division	angles	estimate
surface	sphere	circumference
equator	segment	halving
dividing	sixteenths	quartering
eighths	bisecting	doubling
opposite	adjacent	alternate
spaces between	points	shapes
centre	intersect	square
anti-clockwise	plane of symmetry	symmetrical
point of symmetry	equal	axis
balanced	curved sides	tri-star
radiating from	hexagonal	approximate
measure		

(Gorman, 1990:28)

Such absorbed group-work was also responsible for the relaxed but focussed atmosphere reported by Hepburn. It provided her with an unexpected bonus: she was able to relax, and spend more time in deeper discussion with individuals and groups on a wide range of topics which otherwise might not have been raised. Many of the teachers commented on these productive aspects of co-operative group work, the self-generation of further problems, the elective use of mathematical conceptualisation and language, the meaningful contexts, and the freeing of the teacher to devote more time to dealing with individual or group problems in depth.

Benson also noted how the co-operative behaviour of the students moved outside the classroom.

> A collaborative effort produced a new suit for a girl who didn't own one. Log books revealed extensive local shopping expeditions to establish the best buy...

> We discovered that many parents were involved in the textiles trade either as suppliers or producers. The coursework reflected not only the multicultural realities of Southall in pupils' designs, but also in its links with the local economic reality. This not only gives us teachers food for thought, but has presented the students themselves with unfinished business – one boy now has an order book for five waistcoats just like the one he made in maths. (Benson, 1990:22)

The two teachers who had been particularly nervous about losing sight of the syllabus, had been particularly impressed. As they had hoped, the students had indeed 'made their learning their own' but they had pursued further questions that had arisen in the process. Lolley and Ross (1990: 20) summarise what their students got from their patchwork project.

- The work was fun for them
- They felt satisfied with their work
- They directed their own learning to a great extent, for example they learned new mathematical terminology because they wanted to
- Their learning was generalised, for example they developed a fascination with and an understanding for patterns, both in creating them and appreciating them
- They were able to explain their learning in everyday language
- They understood that traditional 'woman's work' has a complex mathematical content
- They wanted to learn more about patchwork.

(Lolley and Ross, 1990:20)

Gender effects

Of the teachers who recorded their experiences in Harris (1990), three had actively directed their work at raising the self-confidence of secondary-aged girls in their ability to do mathematics, and in stressing the mathematical heritage in traditional feminine activity. Lolley and Ross had deliberately set up their patchwork project with this aim. For the girls, the project was a success:

- because it shows us, as well as other people, how good we are at mathematics already; us as individual students in the classroom and us as women from all over the world

- because we enjoy it and it helps us to destroy the fear of maths which so many of us suffer from

- because it helps us to understand about lots of other things in our experience

- because it develops our ability to explain our experiences and our world

- So that we can see that the teacher doesn't know all the answers

- So we can feel stronger and have more power to control our lives and our world.

(Lolley and Ross, 1990:20)

In the same publication the rest of the teachers note how boys were as enthused as girls by the work, and all the teachers welcomed this. Paechter (1990:32) however cautioned that at secondary level, peer group pressure on boys not to be seen conforming, can be extreme. One 'macho' boy who got very involved in embroidery was hounded out of his tutor group by threatening 'friends'.

Implications

Appropriate preparation for classroom activity, and evaluation of the effects of a particular activity are routine practice in all good teaching, particularly when there is a change in pedagogy. All the teachers stressed the importance of making the mathematics in these practical tasks explicit: students do not see the mathematics in what they are doing unless it is made plain to them. There could be a number of reasons for this, not least, in the particular case of textiles, the centuries of social conditioning that textiles work is both feminine and unmathematical. There seems to be less evidence in carpentry for example, of the necessity for stressing mathematics when it appears, because it is assumed, or is at least accepted to be present in a stereotypical masculine activity. Dowling (1991) offers a more detailed theoretical analysis of the different contexts in which mathematics in perceived as being produced, reproduced and recognised. He analyses contexts of mathematical activity according to the social organisation within the contexts, distinguishing four fields of activity orthogonal to four 'career' or social locations of mathematical practice. The crossing of the fields of Production (creation of mathematics), Recontextualisation (teacher language and pedagogy), Reproduction (class or lecture room practice) and Operationalisation (use of mathematical knowledge) with Academic, School, Work and Popular careers thus produces sixteen cells. Dowling argues that discourses and activities within the cells, some of which would be empirically empty, are highly specific. We would not expect the primary school career to produce original mathematics for example, but neither should we expect that school mathematics, recontextualised for the purpose of learning mathematics produced in the academic career, should be identical with work or popular mathematics in the operationalisation field. Dowling's model offers a challenge to the highly simplistic view that school mathematics simply transfers to, or is instantly recognisable in a vast array of different practices. It could perhaps be extended to admit the quite different social expectations of mathematics in gendered work. Meanwhile, it was the experience of all the teachers who taught mathematics in the context of textiles work, that it was necessary to be explicit about mathematical activity in this unexpected context.

Hawkin's skill in making explicit the mathematics of mouse-making and sorting has already been noted. There are implications too for the place of mathematics in compartmentalised curricula.

> [Children] should be able to identify the mathematics they are working with and have the confidence to discuss it with others. We should not try to conceal the mathematics in some other area of the curriculum. It should be explicit in what they are doing and they should value the mathematics they are engaged in. (Hepburn, 1990:9)

Paechter makes a similar point: if mathematics is not made explicit its devaluation in the context can be perpetuated. She also adds some practical warning notes for those who might feel tempted to link, or jump across Dowling's cells without adequate experience of the appropriate work career:

> Begin with a craft you know and practice yourself... Without this you will not only find yourself in a muddle in class when something happens that you had not allowed for, but you will also find it harder to appreciate the mathematics involved ... Teachers who jump on the bandwagon without understanding the processes involved, trivialise the work itself and hence the mathematics as well... (Paechter, 1990:32)

There are also some pedagogic implications in presenting over-simplified 'real life' problems for classroom investigation or simulation.

> Problems which crop up in the real situations can be avoided in a simulation, lessening the complexity of the task and therefore the process of learning. Beware also of simplification of reality because it makes for a 'good investigation'. You must be explicit about what you are doing if you simplify. The main problem with simulations is that children don't understand the constraints and simply ignore them. It is a problem with simulation that what would be [real] constraints, can be seen as being imposed by the teacher. (Paechter, 1990:32)

In emphasising the need to be explicit, these teachers are also recognising the need to justify textiles activity as mathematical. In more traditional classroom activities there is a long history of recognising particular activities as mathematical tasks. The strange activity of attempting to fill a bath with no plug is an example. But with or without a teacher's careful use of mathematical language in analysing such a classroom problem, the context of children's total lives, that includes classrooms, is also associated with their *mathematical* learning. All pupils learn gender roles both from peer groups (as noted by Paechter above) and from the traditional social pressures of the classroom in particular. The bath tub problem might be thought to be gender-neutral, but even a Gilliganish perspective might suggest that the feminine response to being asked to do it is likely to be to look at the context and ask why.

Social factors and their effects on mathematics learning were the subject of much of the work of Walkerdine and her colleagues, discussed in Chapter 5 above. The imposition of needlework as a mathematical activity adds a further and particular gender pressure. It would seem doubly necessary in the case of needlework as a mathematical activity to be explicit about the mathematics. For teachers who have both the background understanding and the will to make the mathematics explicit, the results can be intensely productive and professionally rewarding.

> This approach was so dynamic, so self-perpetuating that ordinary teaching now lacks flavour. I am used to a very structured approach and very used to girls not understanding and so repeating my explanations. The only thing they did not seem to understand now were my worksheets! ... I could see and hear girls building up their own conceptual structures. These were 100 times more meaningful than anything that I could impose. (Lolley and Ross, 1990:19)

Another detailed study of students' reactions, and one also inspired by Common Threads was that of Partridge (1991), a primary school teacher, who utilised the time at the end of term when the senior children had finished all their assessments for secondary school, to set up a textiles project for her entire class of twenty-four ten and eleven year olds. Her study focussed on the sort of mathematics used in textiles work to see if the children themselves were aware of the mathematics they were using and she chose textiles as a means of breaking the barrier between school mathematics and 'real-life' mathematics. First she set up a small exhibition of textiles, for which she borrowed the name 'Common Threads', then asked the children to write down any mathematics they could see in it. The children then did various textile activities of their own choosing, using their own designs, after which they were asked to re-examine the original exhibition for its mathematics. Her secondary interests were in the development of the children's design skills and in gender effects, literally to see how boys would react to being asked to sew. The children were asked to keep records of all their designs, to keep a diary and to write a description of their particular textile work. Between them they chose to do knitting, to sew stuffed toys, to weave, to do embroidery of various sorts, to print in batik (wax resist), tie-dye, and with silk screen, to do patchwork, to plait, and to make bags.

Partridge's description of the reaction of the children when asked to identify the mathematics in the work, indicates a view of mathematics already detached from life outside the classroom. Both boys and girls found the display attractive and interesting but the mood changed as they were asked to write down the mathematics that they could see in it.

> There was a great deal of fuss and argument. The children appeared very uncomfortable and confused. They became unconfident and defensive of their understanding of mathematics and many said they had not been taught such maths! There were comments like 'What do you mean by maths?' and 'I can't see nothing.' One boy ... wrote on his piece of paper 'I am frustrated because I have not been taught anything like this before.' They seem worried that it was a test. (Partridge, 1992:72)

Because of their uncertainty, Partridge asked them to write down what mathematics meant to them, rather than the abstract and more threatening question 'What is mathematics?' Five of the twenty four children were unsure and did not answer. Thirteen said that mathematics was about the 'four rules' or about numbers. Three children thought it was about measuring and three recognised problem solving as an aspect of mathematics. Two children, and the most able mathematically, wrote that mathematics had a range of topics within it (Partridge, 1992:73).

Following this analysis, the children did make their comments on the mathematics they perceived in the articles in the display, and Partridge returned to her original plan by asking them again at the end of their needlework project. Making a straight before-after comparison was not possible however, for a number of reasons: Partridge herself had become ill during the project and on her return, still unwell, on the last day of term and the children's last day at primary school, found that they had become unmotivated, that some of the work was not complete and that the classroom had to be evacuated so that a whole new class could move in that day. There was however a sample of fifteen children from the original twenty four for whom it was possible to make reasonable comparisons.

Listing categories of mathematics chosen by the children and the number of mentions in each category from the total of the fifteen children, Partridge's results can be summarised as follows (Partridge, 1992:79):

	Before	After
Shape	5	4
Measurement	8	13
Area	1	2
Pattern	2	2
Symmetry	1	0
Amount required	5	2
Angles	1	0
Colours	3	3
Count/Number	-	3

She notes that the largest difference, in measurement, can at least be partly accounted for by the reduction in the 'before' category of the 'amount required', by children who had all used a lot of measurement in their own recent work. The reduction in both 'shape' and 'symmetry' was surprising 'because both were a significant and recognisable factor in textiles and many children used these mathematical areas in their work' (Partridge, 1992:80). In general she felt that these results were not truly representative of what the children had learned and that lack of time and motivation on the final day had distorted them.

More information on the children's learning was available both from the children's own written evaluations of their work and from Partridge's interviews with them. It is not possible to discuss in detail here the range of different responses of the children, nor was it possible for Partridge to follow them up, but it would seem that the children were already adopting the popular perception of mathematics as sums.

> On the whole, the children did not recognise pattern, shape, symmetry and tessellation though much of the work required these areas. ... To me these areas stood out and I would have thought that the children would focus on

them. This is also evident in the children's interpretations of mathematics —
only two children mentioned shape at all. In general the children do not seem
to view these areas as important mathematical concepts. (Partridge,
1992:108)

There were many contradictions in the data. Although the children identified certain mathematics in their work, they did not in the display, and
vice versa ... It could be that the children were too close to their own
artifacts to be able to look at them objectively. The relationships in the
data seem haphazard and tenuous... It is probable that the children were
not fully aware of the processes that their artifacts went through in the
display and so could not comment as fully as they wished. And Partridge
too recognised the necessity for making the mathematics explicit.

The only gendered comment, a sexist insinuation that since the display
was only a girls' project, no doubt Partridge would be doing a football
project next, came from the school keeper (Partridge, 1992:105). In spite
of her gentle probing, there were no adverse gendered remarks or
behaviour from either boys or girls, indeed there was marked enthusiasm
by some of the boys for the work.

Four boys met a few times after school to do their work together, and one
of them, Ben, commented in his diary: 'I've nearly finished my knitting
but I did not. So my mates come round to my house and we done our
knitting watching a film but I still did not finish it. I'm doing a pattern all
different colours. I'm nearly finished now'. On another occasion the same
group of boys took their knitting to their local park and again there is
testimony to the commitment, involvement and pleasure that needlework
inspires.

The mathematics education literature now reports a steady stream of work
where teachers have taken textile artifacts or activities and used them as
the basis for mathematical work in class. The aim may be to emphasise
that mathematics has always been there in the traditional domestic work of
women and girls, but is as likely now to be aimed at the wider context of
mathematics as an unsung ingredient of other cultural artifacts. The
recognition that mathematics is not in origin or practice an entirely
abstract, institution bound, white, male preserve is appearing increasingly
in classroom practice. Miller (1991) for example, who took her inspiration
from *Cabbage*, used cross-stitch embroidery in her work on a teaching
practice, of introducing the concepts of symmetry required by the National
Curriculum, with first and second year secondary students. Like Mardell
above, Watson (1988) was also inspired by Burnham's (1973) description
of the ingenuity of people who made garments by manipulating whole
rectangles of cloth. Her work provides an example of what can be done by

a teacher without the craft expertise discussed by Paechter above. Using Burnham's book *Cut my Cote* as the resource, Watson's mixed-ability twelve year olds began their prescribed work on area and rectangles, working in groups to analyse some of the designs illustrated in the book. This was followed by discussion, led by Watson, on how garments can be made from whole rectangles. Because this work was an untried area for her, she ensured that several activities were going on at once 'so that if one falls flat there are other things going on around for the students to slot into.' She lists the tasks that developed well and includes in them some of the questions that arose, including her own.

1. In civilisations where cloth is woven at home, people are reluctant to waste any of it. Design a garment which can be made from a rectangle with no wastage. Present the design as a rectangular pattern, drawn to scale so that it would fit you. Give instructions for cutting and sewing, or make a cloth or paper version of it.

2. Draw the net of a T-shirt which could be cut from one piece and be comfortable to wear. Will this shape tessellate? If you had to weave the fabrics yourself it would be economical to weave it in this shape. Find out how many threads to the centimetre there are in cotton shirt fabric and use this calculation to give some weaving instruction for the shape. Can you adapt the pattern so that the head hole is made while you are weaving and not cut out after?

3. As civilizations grow wealthier, cloth can be wasted by cutting more curved designs, sometimes resulting in odd-shaped bits to be thrown away. Do we always get wastage if curved shapes are cut? Imagine you have to make a paper pattern for an armhole and try to represent this curve in three-dimensional space on paper. Compare armhole curves from large and small people. Are they parallel? Will your method of pattern-making work for any curve? Can you use it to cut a piece of linoleum to fit the curved base of a toilet?

4. Unpick the sleeve from a shirt, leaving the body part in one piece apart from undoing the side seam. You will see that the top of the sleeve and the hole into which it fits are curved. Are the curves the same, and what could we mean by 'same'? Are the curves the same length and how could you measure them?

5. Try to draw a pattern for a man's shirt. Measure yourselves so you can draw it to scale. Unpick an old shirt to check. Each piece of shirt has to be cut so that its grain runs in a certain direction. Try to arrange the pieces so the grain runs the same way on all of them but they use the minimum amount of fabric. Can you invent an accurate or approximate way to reduce the size of the pieces so you can make a smaller shirt? What could be meant by 'a shirt half the size'? (Watson, 1988:24)

Watson shares Paechter's concern for the possible trivialisation of the mathematics content. Her mental checklist included the syllabus requirements and, as in the examples quoted by Gorman above, she too 'was impressed by the amount of mathematical language that was being used, and surprised by the number of concepts the work introduced' (Watson, 1988:25). It had not occurred to her to interpret the topic as particularly girl-based until three boys in the class (of twelve-year-olds) complained. It was only after she had described the task as three-dimensional model building in which the nature of the material is particularly significant, that they were willing to become involved. Her work illustrates a genuinely multi-cultural origin in the widespread geometrical skill of garment makers.

The Wider Context

All these teachers were, in Freirean terms, consciously and unconsciously relating knowledge to the process which constitutes it (Mellin-Olsen, 1986:102). Outside England, mathematics teaching using textiles as a starting point has sometimes come as the result of reaction within mathematics education to political, social and racial repression of pupils confined to basic skills curricula, or to no mathematics education at all. Driven by her own experience as the victim of prejudice and of seeing it while teaching in America, Zaslavsky published her book *Africa Counts* in 1973, bringing to many English-speaking mathematics educators of the day, possibly for the first time, the wealth and variety of mathematical history and practice from the African continent. Since then, she has regularly published learning materials for mathematics that begin from the traditional activities of various cultures. One recent publication (Zaslavsky, 1990) takes examples of American folk art, indigenous Navajo rugs and early immigrant patchwork, and uses them for teaching symmetry in class.

In a more explicit policy of developing a Freirean philosophy as part of a national education philosophy, Gerdes, working in mathematics education research and teacher education in Mozambique, also takes inspiration from the work of indigenous weavers and other artisans. Gerdes' work first came to the notice of mathematics educators in Europe in 1986, while *Cabbage* was being prepared, at a seminar in Norway on Mathematics and Culture (Høines and Mellin-Olsen, 1986). At the seminar Gerdes handed out strips of paper, representing Mozambiquan weaving materials, to his professional mathematics education colleagues and confronted them with a number of tasks: to construct a circle given its circumference, to construct angles that measure 90°, 60° or 45° using only such strips, to decide the minimum number needed to plait broader strips than a demonstration model, and to construct a regular hexagon out of them. All failed in the given time, not, as Gerdes pointed out, because they were not good mathematicians but because the problems were non-standard ones in mathematics classrooms. Yet they were routine tasks for illiterate peasants in Mozambique.

Within his political context, Gerdes is crusading not for one gender, but for a whole people. As part of his work in helping to build a national mathematics education system in an immediately post-colonial country where none had existed, Gerdes' aim was first to recognise the mathematics in popular practices before incorporating them into more formal mathematics education. With his international colleagues he made the point that the form of the artifacts made by weaving are never arbitrary. They constituted accumulated experience and wisdom and were an expression of biological, physical and mathematical knowledge.

> There exists 'hidden' or 'frozen' mathematics. The artisan who imitates a known production technique is – generally – not doing mathematics. But the artisan(s) who discovered the technique, did mathematics, developed mathematics, was (were) thinking mathematically ... By unfreezing this frozen mathematics, by rediscovering hidden mathematics in our Mozambican culture, we show indeed that our people, like every other people, did mathematics ... Defrosting frozen mathematics can serve as a starting point for doing and elaborating mathematics in the classroom. (Gerdes, 1986:16,17)

The concept of 'frozen mathematics' has been much argued since, but the work in Mozambique continues with a steady stream of publications illustrating the richness of local weaving and other activities as artifacts of a mathematical culture (see for example Gerdes, 1994, Gerdes and Bulafo, 1994 and Gerdes, 1995).

In a world where the assessment of projects is calculated by a simplistic quantifying of physical outputs, there is no way of measuring the full influence of *Cabbage* and Common Threads. Both resources were designed to stimulate and to be copied; teachers are notoriously inventive and creative and do not have time to write reports and acknowledge sources in addition to the large amount of paper work already required of them. They take, adapt and generate ideas, however, and test, evaluate, develop or reject them in the processes of teaching. Even a count of the enthusiastic letters from teachers, of pictures of children engaged round looms, of published articles, of local and national conference sessions and

Opposite: **Figure 11**: Strip pattern structures of polychrome beaded Zulu armbands, worked by women, in the collection of Paulus Gerdes, and published as part of his ethnomathematics research initiative.

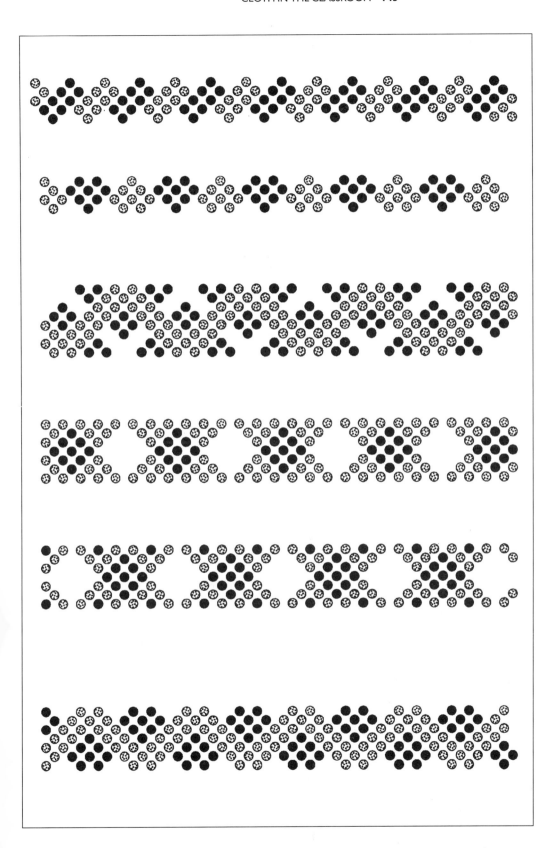

INSET courses cannot provide an accurate measure. Immediate effects however, were wide and deep enough to report them at the Sixth International Congress on Mathematical Education, held in Budapest in 1988. At this congress the rising concern for the social contexts of mathematics was recognised in an alternative session on a rest day for the exploration of the theme of Mathematics, Education and Society. At this day, and through poster presentations throughout the conference, the contribution of Common Threads to international debate on the universal under-participation of girls and the cultural irrelevance of much mathematics education was recognised. A number of requests to borrow Common Threads was made by several countries, but this was not possible since the exhibition had travelled for two years and had finally and irrevocably fallen to pieces. Immediate requests for support for a new version were made to both UNESCO and the British Council, both of whom had representatives at the conference. It was the latter who, with some courage, took up the idea of redesigning Common Threads and through it to uncover the mathematics in traditional women's work in the world context.

References

Benson Alan. (1990) Making a Garment. In Mary Harris (1990) below.

Burnham Dorothy K. (1973) *Cut My Cote.* Toronto: Royal Ontario Museum.

Dowling Paul (1991) Contextualising Mathematics. In Mary Harris (Ed) *Schools Mathematics and Work.* London: Falmer Press.

Gerdes Paulus. (1986) How to Recognise Hidden Geometrical Thinking: A Contribution to the Development of Anthropological Mathematics. *For the Learning of Mathematics.* Vol 6, No. 2 (June)

Gerdes Paulus (1994) *Explorations in Ethnomathematics and Ethnoscience in Mozambique.* Maputo: Instituto Superior Pedagogico Moçambique.

Gerdes Paulus and Bulafo Gildo (1994) *Sipatsi. Technology Art and Geometry in Inhambane.* Maputo: Instituto Superior Pedagogico. Moçambique.

Gerdes Paulus (1995) *Women and Geometry in Southern Africa.* Maputo: Universidade Pedagogica Moçambique.

Gorman Marjorie (1991) Temari Balls. *Mathematics Teaching* Vol 134 March.

Harris Mary (Ed) (1990) *Textiles in Mathematics Teaching. Some experiences of teachers who have used textile activities for teaching mathematics.* London: University of London Institute of Education, Maths in Work Project. (out of print)

Hawkin Wendy (1990a) In Harris (1990) above.

Hawkin Wendy (1990b) In Harris (1990) above.

Høines Marit and Mellin-Olsen Stieg (1986) Mathematics and Culture; a Seminar Report. Rådal, Norway:Caspar Forlag

Lolley Marylynne and Ross Kirsteen. (1990) The Patchwork Quilt. In Harris (1990)

Mardell Jane (1990) Making Shirts with PGCE Students. In Harris (1990)

Mellin-Olsen Stieg (1986). Culture as Key Theme for Mathematics Education. In Marit Johnsen Høines and Stieg Mellin-Olsen (Eds) *Mathematics and Culture, A Seminar Report.* Rådal, Norway:Caspar Forlag.

Miller Jo (1991) Textiles and Symmetry. *Mathematics Teaching* Vol 137, December.

Partridge Danusia (1992) A Mathematical Investigation into Textile Activities. Submitted as a dissertation in partial fulfilment of the requirements for the degree of Master of Science of the Council of National Academic Awards. Polytechnic of the South Bank. Unpublished.

Paechter Carrie. (1990). Patchwork as a Medium of Tessellation. In Harris (1990

Thomas Janet. (1990) Patchwork Fractions. In Harris (1990)

Watson Anne (1988) Cut My Cote. *Mathematics Teaching* Vol 122, March.

Zaslavsky Claudia. (1973) *Africa Counts. Number and Pattern in African Culture.* Connecticut: Lawrence Hill and Company.

Zaslavsky Claudia. (1990) Symmetry in American Folk Art. *Arithmetic Teacher.* Vol 38 No 1. September.

Chapter 8

The Global Village

Introduction

Much of the work of the Maths in Work Project had been in explaining and communicating working mathematical activity beyond limited traditional perceptions, both inside and outside the profession of mathematics education. Common Threads had been particularly effective in breaking down such barriers, with its accessible format, challenging content and happy timing. The effect was to address, in broad terms, most of the issues in mathematics education in the same forum. This also brought with it a message about compartmentalisation in mathematics education.

The variety of roles and issues that Common Threads addressed together reflected changes in thinking in mathematics education, world-wide. In their paper 'School Mathematics of the 1990s', written for the International Commission of Mathematics Instruction, Howson and Wilson (1986) rather naively remark that there is an astonishing uniformity of school mathematics curricula world-wide. 'It is still true that, faced with a standard school mathematics textbook from an unspecified country, even internationally experienced mathematics educators find it almost impossible to say what part of the world it comes from, without recourse to the essentially non-mathematical clues of language and of place-names' (Howson and Wilson, 1986:7). This consistency of mathematics education in spite of wide cultural diversity, had been one of the concerns expressed at the Mathematics Education Congress at which the original Common Threads made its impact outside England. Even without Gramsci's concept of hegemony, the facts of colonial history would lead one to anticipate the extent to which curriculum influence, indeed wholesale transplantation took place in the 1960s and 1970s.

Education as Export

Maravanyika (in press) sketches the history of education in one ex-colonial country, Zimbabwe, the Southern Rhodesia of the colonial era. Here the first African mission school was built in 1859 by the London Missionary Society, eleven years before the first Education Act in England had made education for the English masses possible, but not mandatory. The missionary system expanded using its limited resources and local labour. After 1890 and Cecil Rhodes' occupation, the colonial administration established European education but prevaricated on African education, concentrating on the children of 'the master race' whose education had to be on a par with that of English young gentlemen of the same class, so as to prepare them for positions of leadership. African requirements for education were seen from above as a sort of inferior parallel to English working-class requirements. The basic skills were needed to keep their own communities, whose role it was to supply a colonial society's highly segmented labour market. Rhodes' occupation took place only twenty years after the 1870 Education Act of England and Wales and twenty-seven after the Restricted Code had limited the 'home' working-class curriculum to that considered appropriate to their station. Ironically it was the Church which had argued so strongly for the minimum for working class children 'at home' who, in the form of mission schools, introduced the academic subjects that caused the colonial administrators to complain about 'jumped-up mission-trained natives' (Maravanyika: in press). But the missionaries were also deeply attached to the values of contemporary western life that supported liberal education as well as commerce and administration. They saw little conflict between their own evangelising aims and the imperialist expansion. However unwittingly, they helped pave the way for colonial occupation (Serpell: in press).

In the dual-society philosophy of Southern Rhodesia the relationship between European and African interests was seen as 'mutual but different', described by a Rhodesian Prime Minister as 'similar to one between horse and rider' (Maravanyika: in press). As 'at home', enabling legislation provided grants for African schools against health criteria and the condition that half of the teaching time was spent on vocational subjects, including home crafts for girls, but at a level that would not threaten white artisans. Colonial governments brought in control legislation for age of admission, class size, number of children promoted to higher grades and so on. From 1924 to 1961, British colonial education was overseen by the Colonial Office but education itself was not represented in any official capacity.

The British Government's Board and then Ministry of Education influenced educational plans of colonial governments however, vetting applications for colonial welfare and development grants, and also choosing the people who did the surveys in the colonies. Several of His Majesty's Inspectors sat on colonial advisory committees. The Victorian values of Morant's administration were still widespread. In Rhodesia, policies of 1966 eventually provided access to primary education for all African children, but effectively only those within reach of a school, thus leaving out 4000 children per age cohort without any access. White, Indian and coloured children were to have universal and compulsory education up to the age of 15 but only 12.5% of African children could proceed to African academic secondary schools, 37.5% to a new type of government community vocational junior secondary school, with an 'ecological' curriculum designed to keep children in their villages. The remaining 50% were not accounted for in formal education but, were left to swell the labour pool. By controlling resources and limiting the costs of African education to 2% of GNP (about 10% of what European, Coloured and Indian children received) the indigenous population was consistently and persistently denied access to academic secondary schools. And since Africans had no franchise throughout the colonial era, they had little say in what they did receive. Only in 1979, the year before independence, were the European and African divisions of education unified. Until colonial countries became independent, African education was supply-led and access was deliberately limited and controlled. At independence, countries whose governments had made a commitment to education for all were confronted with a massive and unprecedented problem of social demand, logistics and finance.

The hegemonic history of education has left paradoxical contradictions in the multiple agendas of many contemporary African societies (Serpell: in press). The particular form of the western educational tradition that has been institutionalised in many country's primary schools, is often dysfunctional for both the children and the rural communities, for the agendas of economic progress, for the cultivation of children's intellectual and moral development and for transmission of their culture. When curricula are designed in a way that is alien to other cultural assumptions that, like schooling, contribute to the socialising process, clear discrepancies can arise between curricular and cultural goals. Religion and language are the most frequently quoted examples. The situation is further complicated by the economic power and prestige of those whose success in imported curricula has the effect of alienating them from their own culture, and devaluing it in the eyes of those whose educational aim is to achieve success. Many young people emerge from school with a sense of frustration and lowered self-esteem, to return to subsistence rural living which their school education, aimed ultimately at the academic requirements of an unreachable university, have had to ignore (Serpell: in press).

The legacy of the two sorts of mathematics education has left particular problems. In the late 1950s attempts were being made to bring them closer together but were rather overshadowed by a complexity of moves to revise mathematics education altogether. Employers were becoming involved in the graduate level of mathematics education, as mathematicians themselves were arguing for more algebraic structure within the school subject, to resolve discontinuities between the continuing separate subjects (arithmetic, geometry and algebra) within mathematics education. At the same time there were manpower concerns in the USA and Britain after the launch of Sputnik in 1957, and a worrying shortage of mathematics teachers. One of the results was the 'new mathematics'.

Meanwhile the condition of mathematics education in dependent countries reflected the general state of their education. Gerdes (1986:18) summarises the extreme case of Mozambique, previously a Portuguese colony, in the post-independence era: over-crowded classrooms and the shortage of qualified mathematics teachers: teachers lowly paid and of low social status: lack of teaching materials. In many countries similar conditions prevailed and resulting low levels of attainment were reinforced by hasty curriculum transplantation. The African Mathematics Program was an example. Financed by the Ford Foundation and USAID, it started in 1962 and produced more than 60 'new maths' books. Although 102 out of 186 textbook writers were Africans, the contents and methods of these books were dominated by 'northern'[1] models of mathematics education. The materials were very theoretical, applications were avoided and the language used was strongly formalised. The books were trialed by well-qualified teachers in a few experimental schools and were then introduced on a large scale but with doubtful results. Teachers, parents and politicians protested and in several countries 'modern' mathematics was abandoned in favour of more traditional forms (Gerdes, 1986:18).

Some of the problems of curriculum transplantation had already been exposed by Gay and Cole whose work with the Kpelle people of Liberia had been published in 1967. They describe curriculum materials, including textbooks often several years out of date, complete with pictures of snowballs and circuses, drawn from a culture the children only faintly comprehended (Gay and Cole, 1967:31). Curriculum, teaching methods and language were all completely different from the traditional Kpelle ways of learning: the whole philosophical and conceptual foundation of the Kpelle differed from the American. For the Kpelle, knowledge is the ability to demonstrate mastery of the Kpelle way of life. Truth is the conformity of one's statements and actions to that way of life, and is without substance outside it. Kpelle people recognise that each culture has the right to set its own standards, to recognise knowledge for itself, and to submit to its own truth: truth for them is thus a relativistic matter. This willingness to recognise other people's ways of life and controls of meanings within their own land, made them easy prey to the ignorant and wholesale impositions of another culture. Traditional Kpelle teaching methods rely heavily on imitation and rote learning. The imposition of totally foreign concepts of mathematics on a people who were numerate in their own culture and requirements, made what the foreigners saw as the discovery of fundamental mathematical principles, into a guessing game for the Kpelle. What appeared to the foreigners as inconsistencies of logic, were in reality Kpelle shifts of category. 'Considering the many hours spent in trying to force him to accept an alien content through a methodology which cannot, by its very nature, make that alien content clearly understood, it is remarkable that the Kpelle school child has learned anything at all' (Gay and Cole, 1967:93). Gay and Cole came up with the only possible recommendation for teachers in the circumstances: start with the child's experience and concepts, and work outwards from them.

Curriculum transplantation is not specific to Africa but constitutes a general phenomenon of mathematical under-development (Gerdes, 1986:19). With it comes not only values, but implications of the structures of education for which the curriculum was devised. In the liberal education tradition of mathematics, the requirements of universities ultimately determine what goes on in primary schools. Primary schools mathematics is seen as the foundation for secondary school mathematics, from which a very small minority is creamed off for tertiary mathematics education, with the university view of mathematics controlling the formal mathematics experience of the vast majority of children who leave school in or at the end of the primary stage.

Education itself is never neutral. It expresses the interests of the dominant class, and, in the colonial context, a foreign class. It is structured in the interests of the social and economic élite: it over-emphasises the value of mathematics itself 'with a clear tendency towards over-stating a somewhat romantic importance of mathematics as the builder of clear thinking, as the rigorous science par excellence, and an unconvincing possible practical value.' (D'Ambrosio quoted by Gerdes, 1986:19). As in the cultures from which it is transported, mathematics reinforces power structures, labels different levels of social class and effectively filters out whole peoples through the handy tool of universally recognised results of commercially published examination. The elevated status of mathematics itself has the effect of over-rating the information that tests and examinations can yield and under-rating other measures, while belief in the objectivity of tests and examinations hinders progress in developing alternatives (Ahmed and Williams, 1995). A vast complex of hegemonic forces liberally peppered with commercial concerns, arising in colonial histories and interests, and involving programmes of development aid, international textbook publishing and internationally recognised examination boards, ensures the continuity of mathematics education that surprised Howson and Wilson.

Individual countries of course know this well, and each works out its own solution within constraints ranging from the conditions of aid programmes to the necessity for international recognition of standards while preserving their own cultural values. In every country where I worked with Common Threads, or in which Common Threads was well exploited in my absence, mathematics curricula were or had recently been under review. In Botswana the first move towards modern mathematics came in 1968 (Taole, 1993) and in the early 1970s a UNESCO project was set up to develop the teaching of mathematics and science in the BLS or Boleswa countries (*Bo*tswana, *Le*sotho and *Swa*ziland). A modern syllabus was drawn up and part of the Schools Mathematics Project (SMP) series of the Cambridge University Press was prescribed to go with it. Workcard versions of the SMP books were trialed, with selected schools modifying them for children who found difficulty with them. SMP Boleswa Books E and F were the result, but the scheme was not a success. Teachers did not like them and children continued to have difficulty in understanding the language used in them (Taole, 1993:78). The experience of local curriculum development thrived however and Ministries of Education, Universities and teachers in all three countries worked together to produce their own Projects in Secondary Mathematics (PRISM) books. As Botswana's education system developed, further revisions were made and the country now has its own revised books. Botswana worked through curriculum transplantation to produce its own scheme which reflects its own cultures, in an internationally recognised course, but the costs in human and financial terms were high. Some unhappy memories of Boleswa SMP were still evident in Lesotho where some resistance to Common Threads was shown by some expatriate advisors through a misinterpretation of my work which saw it as advocating a return to a workcard scheme. This mistake was not made by practising teachers, who recognised its potential for enriching textbook experience with some neglected realities of a very geometric culture.

Women's Education

In parts of early colonial Africa the terrain was more difficult to exploit than the farming lands of East Africa. The absence of settlers showed Victorian attitudes to women in a more than usually masculine light, though in both 'settler' and unsettled countries, Victorian values lasted longer than they did in England. Just as the School Board maintained nineteenth century ideology in the education system until half way through the twentieth, so its influence on the Colonial Service under-pinned their maintenance in the colonies, long after the strict systems of social division had begun to crumble in England.

The colonial administrators were not civil servants in the usual sense: they were the government and it was a government by gentlemen in the Victorian sense, for the sources of imperialism are heavily intertwined with the sources of the Victorian code of the gentleman. The Public Schools, followed by Oxford and Cambridge provided the gentleman's training, which was very much influenced by the Victorian interpretation of medieval chivalry. Moral strength was built through physical exertion and the team spirit, and a knighthood from a recently extended range of chivalric orders, rewarded an honourable career overseas. The concept of gentleman and the pattern of behaviour commensurate with it, were rooted in inequality; a gentleman was one of higher rank and fortune as well as stronger character and upbringing. Bradley (quoted by Callaway, 1987) remarked that the theory of indirect rule by a handful of Public School men which controlled the Pax Britannica, was essentially the prefect system writ large, with District Officers as the masters, local Chiefs as the prefects and tribesmen as the boys. It was in the Colonial Service, particularly in disease-ridden terrain like Nigeria, that the young gentleman went through his initiation into full masculinity through ordeals which, as Callaway remarks (1987:6), were real enough. The Service was a thoroughly masculine institution in all its aspects with masculine ideology, military organisation and processes, and elaborate symbols and rituals of power, and it remained Victorian until its death.

Such a hierarchy of gentlemen included necessary less-than-gentlemen (Callaway, 1987:39). In the colonies as 'at home' the administration looked down on the agricultural expert and the railway engineer. So long as there was an Empire, and for many years afterwards, the Liberal Arts retained their social superiority over the Mechanical, everywhere that the colonial process had influence. By the first decades of the twentieth century, Cambridge University with its public school trained graduates and influence in the examination system, was the hub of the masculine enterprise of mathematics education world wide. In the 1920s practically all the chairs of mathematics and mathematical physics in the colonies and India were filled by Cambridge men (Howson, 1982:144).

Public School training of gentlemen also required the total absence of women traditionally from the age of eight[2], and particularly so at the dangerous stage of puberty. 'Woman' was not in the hierarchy at all. She was in a separate category, 'the other', in her own category not of less-than-gentleman, but of non-gentleman (Callaway, 1987:42). Regardless of existing gender relations in the occupied countries, colonial admini-stration with its fervent belief in its own ethnic and class superiority embedded in its power structures, dealt directly with male Chiefs not in a calculated male plot to dispossess African women, but rather an 'ethno-centric and unexamined exercise (in terms of gender) of power relations between two male groups, each with its own prestige structure' (Callaway, 1987:52).

Contemporary views on women were full of conflict however, and even if the records demonstrate the continuing phenomenon of their anonymity or invisibility, they have eventually to admit of the occasional eccentric or totally capable woman; some of the Victorian Lady Travellers (Birkett, 1991) in the former category for example, or Margery Perham or Lady Lugard in the latter. Contemporary views on race were also conflicting, but whether 'The Negro' was seen as an inferior species, or whether he was seen as sharing a common humanity but at a lower evolutionary level, he remained socially far inferior to the English gentleman. In line with general attitudes to women, Negro women were also invisible, no matter what their power and status in their own societies. The stereotypes of the missionary literature, of the oppressed wives and chattels of polygamous households, was the justification for bringing them the 'civilisation' of the colonial power and although for some societies the latter had brought an end to raids, abduction and slavery, it often also drove a wedge between males and females of the same cultural group. Advances in scientific agriculture for example, brought services to men but not for women, even in areas where women were actively involved in farming. As in England, what education there was for the new lower orders, separated boys and girls by curriculum. Science and technology were masculine. Girls had to learn domestic subjects and to sew, for new mistresses and to cover their confident nakedness with a more suitably symbolic femininity. Under colonialism women lost more than did men (Mba quoted by Callaway, 1987: 54).

As in England, women objected. In Nigeria powerful women traders objected to the imposition of taxes without representation, and in one episode in 1929 at Aba in the east of the country, they waged what they themselves called 'the women's war', which the colonial power condemned as 'the Aba riots'. The power and ability of such women was recognised however by several of the colonial women themselves.

> As early as 1905, Constance Larymore rejects this view of the 'down-trodden women of Africa' in her observations in Kabba of the women long-distance traders between Lagos and the Hausa States: 'There is not much that indicates subjection or fear about these ladies, sitting at graceful ease among their loads, or strolling about in the hot sunshine ... Leith-Ross concurs, 'Speaking in general, the women of Nigeria ... correspond little to the widely held idea of the downtrodden slave or unregarded beast of burden'. (Callaway, 1987: 52)

Under the ideologies of colonial rule there was no way however that such ability could be recognised. The complexities of the Yoruba system of numeration for example, now the subject of a literature in English (see for example Zaslavsky, 1973 for an early review), testify to powerful abstract reasoning with an effective system of learning behind it, and were part of the confident capabilities of Yoruba women traders. It was their daughters who were expected to conform in their mission schools, to the same priorities as the English Victorian view of domestic femininity: sewing over sums.

In the case of Nigeria, the lack of education for girls was eventually admitted in the colonial hierarchies and became the subject of 'all out attack' by another group of women, the women education officers of the last decades of the colonial era. From 1909 women's groups in Lagos had campaigned for education for girls, demanding a girls' school along the lines of the newly founded King's College for boys. On being told by the government that there was no demand for girls' education, they had raised £1000 and Queens College was established in 1927 with Nigerian and British women on the staff. Although criticised today for cultural imperialism, the expatriate women education officers who continued the tradition some thirty years later, were acutely aware of that potential themselves, in their attempts to provide an education that would be both academically recognised in the gendered international community, and relevant to the range of cultures in the Nigerian context. Part of the cultural imperialism which they tried to adhere to for example, was to protest about such practices as pre-pubertal marriage. In their fight for recognition of the educability of girls, the campaigners, like Miss Beale and Miss Buss before them, are also accused today of not questioning gender roles transmitted through the curriculum of domestic subjects for girls and agriculture for boys, in a country where much of the food production is carried out by women (Callaway, 1987:241). But there is a considerable difference between recognising a role and being able to do something about it, when the very presence of women in senior educational administration was still under challenge. As one of them remarked, 'It is really quite difficult to handle more than about seven educational revolutions at the same time' (Alexander, 1987).

In the late 1950s when colonial education was at last expanding in the period immediately before independence, colonial values were still pervasive. It was only in the mid 1950s that the West African Examinations Council made its revolutionary plans to include Africa in the geography syllabus for West African schools, to accept local specimens for biology, and set books in literature by African authors. As an undergraduate at University College Ibadan in the late 1950s (an internal college of London University that became the University of Ibadan on Nigerian independence) and just one very junior member of the bottom of a rapidly expanding academic hierarchy, I still occasionally met a colonial wife who expressed shock that I, like everyone else, should live in a hall of residence and attend lectures given by Nigerian academic staff. I was told that it was dreadful for an expatriate girl to 'go native' in such a communist way.

Girls and Mathematics

In general in the colonial countries, the education of girls suffered similar hierarchical constraints to those in England. At higher secondary school levels it matched that of boys but for the vast majority and where it existed, it imposed the traditionally English models of domestic destination. In 1985, the United Nations Conference to mark the end of the United Nations Decade for Women was held in Nairobi. It brought recognition of the complexity of the social structures that keep women subordinated, the realisation that the decade had not fundamentally changed the situation, and that changing it would be no easy matter (Obura, 1991:1). As in all other areas of social and historical analysis, the gender perspective throws a very different light on both the concepts and processes of development. It was generally recognised at the 1990 Jomtien (Thailand) UNESCO Conference on Education for All, that education is both crucial and costly to national development (in Africa it takes 30% or more of national budgets), and that schooling systems have to be more responsive to local and national needs and conditions, including those of large minority groups, of which the largest is women.

Preparation for the Decade of Women Conference, and its press coverage, brought a sharing of information among Kenyan women and a tardy recognition of the role of women in the economy (Obura, 1991:2). In an attempt to fill the information gap on the real role of women in

Kenyan society, and the under-participation of girls in education, Obura undertook a study of the most commonly used school text books and the message they pass to girls on the role of women in society. She asked if the inadequate participation of women in society was due solely to their relative absence from school or if there were additional in-school factors which reduced girls' participation (Obura, 1991:3). In the former case, the drop-out syndrome and low involvement figures for girls are well documented, but in Africa, apart from one study in Zambia, the latter is largely unexplored. Her next question therefore was 'What are the factors leading to girls' apparent withdrawal from learning while at school, and to their minimal participation in education?' (Obura, 1991:3). In spite of national parental support for the education of their daughters, often at very great expense, girls themselves are very well aware of the social conditions of their future; they know that they are not as likely to reach and be maintained in secondary schools as their brothers.

Revision of stereotyping textbooks, school programmes and teaching methods were already high on the agenda of United Nations priorities, but research is poorly developed in the less industrialised world. Yet textbooks have a significance that they do not have in countries that have long had plenty of them.

> In societies new to written materials and where books are scarce, the textbook is often the first book handled by the child. It is highly prized and has commensurate influence on the reader. The book is a source of authority; the teacher, *mwalimu*, is usually the best educated person in the village and is seen to use 'the book' constantly. (Obura, 1991:11)

The very word 'reading' can have a different significance in translation. As Obura points out, it is not clear what distinction is made between 'textbook' and 'book' by people who rarely come into contact with any book. The word 'to read' in Kiswahili, and similarly translated in other Kenyan languages, also means 'to study' or 'to read in school.' In societies where access to radio and print media are scarce, the school textbook is a prominent source of information, and its socialising power has enormous potential (Obura, 1991:11). In Obura's summary, textbooks:

- are sources of information
- are image forming, that is they shape attitudes
- have cognitive and affective effects
- shape learning and teaching
- are prime agents of socialisation
- purvey a growing national culture
- are a durable commodity compared with curriculum change

(Obura, 1991:13)

In addition, textbook publishing is very big business. What then of their effects on books on girls' mathematics education?

Obura and her team systematically analysed three books from the mathematics series that dominates Kenyan primary schools, that written by the Kenya Institute of Education, published by the Jomo Kenyatta Foundation, and recommended by the Ministry of Education. The series is used throughout the country almost to the exclusion of other books, which is not the case with any other subject. Obura's analysis was of five topic areas: the frequency and nature of the appearance of female characters; work/employment roles; sociopolitical roles of males and females: the family roles of males and females; psychological traits of males and females.

At the three school levels of standards 3, 6 and 8, the female presence was 28.3%, 7.1% and 17.4% respectively (Obura, 1991: 28). In an unexpected but logical correlation, the low percentage in book 6 occurs at precisely the stage that mathematical performance diverges between boys and girls. As in the Northam analysis of English texts discussed in Chapter 5 above, where girls and women do appear in the Kenyan texts, they are more often anonymous. Female images are less frequent and less powerful than males. In the work/employment analysis, the females are seen in unpaid work in the home or on the farm. There is no large-scale woman farmer, no woman trader in coffee or cattle, no female in business, no headmistress. In the farm situation, grown females are usually depicted as mother, portrayed at home or buying goods for the family in the market, whereas men are portrayed in action and mobility elsewhere. From the socioeconomic and psychological analyses, the picture is of the active male earning cash, buying land, houses, farms, cattle, vehicles, food, clothing; borrowing and taking loans to develop his financial capacity; saving and investing substantial profits. Women in contrast, are mainly absent from such activities, and when they do appear they are engaged in domestic and other activities perceived as paltry.

> It is hard to escape the conclusion that the mathematics textbooks would force on us: women's passivity and retiring nature are the cause of their marginalisation in society and the reason why development has passed them by in favour of men who display constant eagerness to do things and to participate in a variety of functions in society. The message of these textbooks is persistent, internally consistent and insidious. (Obura, 1991: 37-38)

In the realities of Kenyan life, where 50.4% of the population is female, 30% of families are single parent families headed by females who are necessarily economically active. What and who, asks Obura, is responsible for the fairy tale that the children's most widely used books tell?

Everywhere in the developing world, where girls sit in classrooms, they do so at enormous cost to their nation and to their parents, and they under-achieve in both school and the world of work (Kagia quoted by Obura, 1991:3), apparently just as their mathematics texts expect. Outside the classroom, Obura cites evidence of the general trend in society that living conditions of women are deteriorating; that on an interval scale the literacy gap between men and women is widening, and that in both developed and under-developed countries, increased educational pro-vision has not automatically opened the door of educational opportunity and career advancement to women; poverty itself is becoming feminised. As Obura states, women are at the centre of the debate on development.

In the developed countries, the mathematical education of girls and women has only been an issue since the late 1960s. In 1976, a group of women mathematics educators attending the Third International Con-gress on Mathematical Education protested at the lack of representation of women as speakers, as panel members or as presiders at a congress where nearly half the delegates were women. They established the informal network IOWME, the International Organisation of Women in Mathematics Education with the aims bringing together those concerned with the subject of women and mathematics, of founding branches in as many countries as necessary, of encouraging further research into why so few women study mathematics, and of exploring the job possibilities of those who qualify (Shelly, 1988).

By the Seventh International Congress on Mathematics Education in 1992, the work of IOWME was strong enough to fill a book of research and intervention in gender differences in mathematics education. In the words of its editors, the experience confirmed that gender differences are ... not due to biology but to complex interactions among social and cultural factors, societal expectations, personal belief systems and confidence levels' (Rogers and Kaiser, 1995).

But IOWME as its name states is concerned with women in mathematics education. The significant omission remains women in vocational educa-tion as tutor or student, where the only mathematics education available tends to be numeracy, mathematics' poor relation with its nineteenth century legacy of the rote learned, pencil and paper sums of the education of the workers. The numeracy teaching of vocational education still tends to be characterised by a lack of professional status and support that is now available in mathematics education (Drake and Mardell, 1989, Drake, 1991). Yet further education (in contrast to academic higher education) that categorises both numeracy teaching and much of the educational work of women's groups, particularly those who try to help themselves, is a significant provider of the only education available to women in the poorest countries. Again, the women at the bottom of the heap are short-changed.

The New Common Threads Tour

At the time that Common Threads began its overseas tour, general curriculum disatisfaction in mathematics, in content, delivery and results, had reached the proportions of a world epidemic. The particular issue of gender in mathematics education tended to be seen either as national disaster, or in brave denial of its existence, masking the presence of yet another problem. For in a world rapidly entering the information age, mathematics more than any other subject spearheads the change. Countries vary in their response to the demands and challenges of the transition. As Jurdak (1994) observed, industrialised countries set the transitions as a priority in educational planning, driven by the need to maintain the competitive edge in the world economy. Developing countries on the other hand, are primarily concerned with improving quality and availability of education. 'It is not the demands of the information age that guide their policies but rather the compelling problems of the present' (Jurdak, 1994: 201). In between, the international perspective of the World Declaration on Education for All, had specified the basic learning needs in the emerging economic, social and cultural environments of the 1990s. The reality is a divorce in mathematics education between the industrialised and developing countries, with radical differences between information age mathematical literacy and the still pre-industrial mathematics of impoverished countries. Instead of uniting the world, mathematics education is 'poised to act as a wedge, sustaining and reinforcing the divisions among countries along socioeconomic and cultural lines' (Jurdak, 1994:204). The economic realities are stark, and many countries are bleeding, 'struggling to service a foreign debt [they] can neither afford, nor afford to repudiate' (Mandela, 1996). Those countries most heavily affected are those with high populations under the age of five (Hawes and Stephens, 1990:185) and the educational priority has to be how to achieve more with less. So far as resource allocation for the primary sector goes, and for the vast majority of children this is all they will be offered there is no prospect of avoiding large teacher to pupil ratios, though there is the opportunity for ensuring pupils have more suitable materials. And there is no prospect of a fully qualified teaching force, though there are opportunities to ensure teachers receive effective and professional help and support on the job (Hawes and Stephens, 1990:189). In these circumstances, teacher education and the quality of basic mathematics education in commonwealth countries was the subject of a major initiative of the Common-wealth Secretariat in 1992. (Harris, 1993)

Deep concerns in mathematics education therefore were as high in both developed and less developed countries, albeit for differing reasons, at the time that the Common Threads overseas tour began. Given that Common Threads exposed the challenges in mathematics education that it did, it is not surprising that it was at least able to focus many of the concerns in one forum. The circular sent out by the British Council Mathematics Advisor, David Martin, in the preparatory literature for the tour, listed some of the issues that it could address, including:

- questions of relevance of existing school curricula to the lives of pupils outside school
- gender bias in school mathematics
- problems of integrating mathematics with other school subjects
- the use of familiar outside school activities in mathematics education
- possibilities for mathematics education concurrent with craft training.
(Martin, 1991)

In her outline of the Australian setting prior to the arrival of Common Threads in Perth, Parker (1991) sketched the country's current debate and spoke for many others. 'Arguments linked to Australia's economic competitiveness, to social justice, to the need for a mathematically com-petent citizenry, and to the need to respond to, and anticipate workplace demands, underpin many of the current concerns about mathematics education ... In a strategic sense, it is emphasised that mathematics needs to be pervasive across the curriculum rather than isolated as a separate, possibly unattainable entity.' (Parker, 1991:13). New Zealand had similar concerns and an active programme of developing mathematical work from indigenous Maori culture (for example Knight, 1984, Robertson, 1989), and those of its more recent South Pacific immigrant population (for example Hosack and Nagy, 1993). In Norway, the mathematics education community under the inspiration of the late Stieg Mellin-Olsen had long promoted what they were calling 'folk mathematics' (Mellin-Olsen, 1987). In Denmark an informal group of academics from different disciplines concerned with the education of mathematics teachers con-vened as 'The Circle' to develop the pedagogy of mathematics as a cross-cultural subject. In Thailand, the Philippines and Malaysia, and most of the African countries, education ministries had policies for developing curriculum materials from indigenous resources.

Overleaf: **Figure 12(i)** and **Figure 12(ii)**
Mathematics of the Poor. Women's weaving and sewing from Bangladesh.
From the *Cabbage* pack.

পাখা

বাংলাদেশের সিলেটে বেত, বাঁশ অথবা কিছু হেঁকে জোঁক্রা পাখা বানানো হোলাকার বাঁশের ফ্রেমের মধ্যে পাখাগুলি জোড়া হয়। এই সিলেটি পাখাগুলির বুনুনির ছোট ছোট চৌঁকোয় ভাল করা নকশা কেমন সেটা বোঝার জন্য কাগজের নখরা চুঁকরো ব্যবহার করুন।

নানা রংয়ের কাগজের চুঁকরো নিয়মানুগাবে ব্যবহার করলে নকশাগুলির কি পরিবর্তন হয় সেটা লক্ষ করুন।

আপনার নিজের কিছু নকশা তৈরী করুন এবং তাদের শ্রেণী ভাগ করার জন্য একটা উপায় বের করুন।

Fan

In Sylhet, in Bangladesh, people weave fans from strips of cane, bamboo or reeds. The fans are fixed to circular frames made of bamboo. Use strips of paper to investigate the woven tessellations on these Sylheti fans.

Note what happens to the tessellations when you use different colours strips systematically.

Make more weaving patterns of your own and devise a way of classifying them.

MiW Cabbage
Drawing by Mary Harris
© Maths in Work

Naksha

Nakshi Kantha means "embroidered, patched cloth." Bangladeshi women make them by sewing together old saris and other cloths, then embroidering them with the coloured threads pulled from the saris.

They use many designs but they always put a circular design in the centre. The circular design represents the lotus flower with its very many petals. The women sew the outline of their designs, then fill them in by using different stitches, threads and colours.

Choose a number of petals and design a lotus for nakshi kantha.
When you have made some lotus designs you may like to try SMILE 1731, (Rose) on the micro.

MiW Cabbage
Drawing by Mary Harris
© Maths in Work

নকশা

নকশী কাঁথার মানে হলো "এমব্রয়ডারী করা [ফোড়াতানি দেওয়া কাপড়]"। বাংলাদেশী মহিলারা পুরনো শাড়ির সাথে অন্যান্য কাপড়-চোপড় জোড়া লাগিয়ে এই কাঁথা তৈরী করেনে পুরনো শাড়ি থেকে বিভিন্ন রংয়ের সুতা খুলে নিয়ে তার ওপর তাঁরা এই এমব্রয়ডারী করেনে

এমব্রয়ডারীতে তাঁরা বহু ধরনের নকশা করেন কিন্তু তাঁরা সব সময়েই ঠিক মাঝখানিয়ে একটা [গোলাকার] নকশা বানান। এই [গোলাকার] নকশাটি পদ্মফুল ও তার বহুসংখ্যক পাপড়ির প্রতীকা প্রথমে মহিলারা তাঁদের নকশার একটা রূপরেখা সেলাই করে দেন। তারপর নানা রকমের সূঁচ, সুতা এবং রং ব্যবহার করে তাঁরা এই রূপরেখাটি ভরাটি করেনে

কয়েকটি পাপড়ি বেছে নিন এবং নকশী কাঁথার জন্য একটা পদ্মের নকশা বানানা কয়েকটি পদ্ম নকশার পর আপনি হয়তো SMILE 1731 [গোলাপ] মাইক্রোতে বানানোর চেষ্টা করতে পারেনা

The countries that hosted the new Common Threads were Australia, Bostwana, Brazil, Cameroon, Canada, Denmark, Kenya, Lesotho, Malawi, Malaysia, New Zealand, Nigeria, Norway, Pakistan, Philippines, Singapore, Sri Lanka, Swaziland, Tanzania, Thailand, Turkey, Uganda, Zimbabwe. In each one, mathematics education was undergoing or had recently undergone overhaul and in most, the situation of women in education and development was the subject of concern, if not of governments, then of women's groups themselves.

Notes

1 Again it is difficult to find an appropriate term. Gerdes use of 'northern' is more accurate, but the term 'western' is more widely used.

2 The habit of the English upper classes of sending its small sons and sometimes daughters away to be 'big house' is much older than the Victorian era. One Venetian visitor to England in 1500 noted it askance. (Bowen, 1975 II:326).

References

Ahmed Afzal and Williams Honor (1995) Mathematics for the Twenty-first Century – Whose Priority? Paper read at the DICE International Conference on Partnerships in Education and Development: Tensions Between Economics and Culture. London: University of London Institute of Education May 24-26. (unpublished)

Alexander C L H (1987) Personal communication. Before her marriage, Dr C L H Geary had been Chief Woman Education Officer in Northern Nigeria , appointed in 1948 after ten years as Principal of Lahore College for Women.

Birkett Dea (1991) Spinsters Abroad. Victorian Lady Explorers. London: Victor Gollancz.

Bowen James (1975) A History of Western Education Volume II. Civilisations of Europe. London: Macmillan.

Callaway Helen (1987) Gender, Culture and Empire. European Women in Colonial Nigeria. St Anthony's/Macmillan series. Basingstoke: Macmillan

Drake Pat and Mardell Jane 1989. Beyond 16-Maths in the Workplace. Mathematics Teaching Vol 126 March p 26 and 27

Drake Pat (1991) 'Maths in the Workplace': Some Issues Arising out of the Development of a Resource Pack. In Mary Harris (Ed) Schools, Mathematics and Work. London: Falmer Press and Philadelphia : Taylor and Francis.

Gay John and Cole Michael (1967) The New Mathematics and an Old Culture. New York: Holt, Rinehart and Winston.

Gerdes Paulus (1986) On Culture, Mathematics and Curriculum Development in Mozambique. In Marit Johnsen Høines and Stieg Mellin-Olsen. Mathematics and Culture, a Seminar Report. Rådal:Caspar Forlag.

Harris Mary (1993) Improving the Quality of Science and Mathematics Education – The Role of Higher Education. Report on a Planning Meeting 26-29 May. London: Commonwealth Secretariat

Hawes Hugh and Stephens David (1990) Questions of Quality: Primary Education and Development. Harlow: Longman

Howson Geoffrey (1982) A History of Mathematics Education in England. Cambridge: Cambridge University Press

Howson Geoffrey and Wilson Bryan (1986) *School Mathematics in the 1990s*. ICMI Study Series edited by A G Howson and J-P Kahane. Cambridge: Cambridge University Press.

Hosack John and Nagy Dénes (1993) South Pacific Symmetries. In Symmetry: Culture and Science, *Quarterly Journal of the International Society for the Interdisciplinary Study of Symmetry*. Vol 4 No 4 p 341-344 and 429-432.

Jurdak Murad (1994) Mathematics Education in the Global Village: The Wedge and the Filter. Selected Lectures from the Seventh International Congress on Mathematical Education. Québec 17-23 August 1992 p 199-210. Québec: Les Presses de l'Université Laval

Knight Gordon (1984) The Geometry of Maori Art-Weaving Patterns. *New Zealand Mathematics Magazine* Vol 21 No 3 p 80-86

Mandela Nelson (1996) Presidential address to the Houses of Parliament. London: *Independent Newspaper* July 12th.

Maravanyika Obert (in press) Community Financing Strategies and Resources within the Context of Educational Democratization: the case of Zimbabwe. In Fiona Leach and Angela Little (Eds) *Schools, Culture and Economics in the Developing World: Tensions and Conflicts.* (temporary title) New York: Garland Publishing Inc

Martin David (1991) *Common Threads*. Circular GEN/886/52. London: The British Council.

Mellin-Olsen Stieg (1987) *The Politics of Mathematics Education*. Dordrecht: Reidel

Obura Anna (1991) *Changing Images: Portrayal of Girls and Women in Kenyan textbooks*. Nairobi: ACTS Press.

Parker Lesley (1991) Mathematics and Textiles: Recognising Mathematics where it can really count. *Cross Section* Vol 3 No 2 July p 13-15

Robertson Ailsa (1989) *Patterns of Polynesia*. Auckland: Heinemann Education.

Rogers Pat and Kaiser Gabrielle (1995) *Equity in Mathematics Education: Influences of Feminism and Culture*. London: The Falmer Press

Serpell Robert (in press) Local accountability to rural communities: a challenge for educational planning in Africa. In Fiona Leach and Angela Little (Eds) *Schools, Culture and Economics in the Developing World: Tensions and Conflicts.* (provisional title) New York: Garland Publishing Inc.

Shelly Nancy (1988) A brief history of IOWME. In Heleen Verhaage (Ed) *IOWME Newsletter* Vol 4 No 2 p 3-5

Taole James (1993) Mathematics Textbooks in Botswana. In Leda Stott and Hilda Lea. *Common Threads in Botswana* p 78 and 79. Botswana: The British Council

Zaslavsky Claudia (1973) *Africa Counts: Number and Pattern in African Culture*. Westport, Connecticut: Lawrence Hill.

Chapter 9

A Worldwide Web

Introduction

Different people have different perceptions of mathematics and mathematics education. With the exclusively layered range of experiences it has offered over several hundred years, it is hardly surprising that perceptions differ among people both inside and outside the profession (Harris, 1989). The traditionally defensive communication by the profession with those outside it, is reflected in chronic lack of outside awareness of the paradigm shifts within.

In any exhibition, form and content are interlinked, and mathematics education is an unusual subject. An exhibition designed by professional designers specifically for an overseas tour intended to last for two years, is inevitably a different thing in both form and content, from one put together by a professional educator, for a stay of about ten days in a particular gallery. In the case of my original, I had been able to expand the exhibits and their captions, until I felt that a topic had been adequately covered or I ran out of gallery space. Professionally constructed display stands, designed for ease of setting up and taking down, yet sturdy enough for frequent freighting by air, sea and a good many roads, are necessarily expensive and naturally limit display space. In the context of what I shall call the new Common Threads, interest in hosting it from 23 countries meant that two sets were made for parallel tours, and both had to be made within budget.

For both structural and security reasons, it was no longer possible to display large textiles, though the British Council Design and Exhibitions Department, DPX, commissioned some superb photography and provided perspex shielded showcases in which small textiles items could be displayed. Each copy of the new Common Threads eventually consisted of four sections, Number, Codes, Geometry and Symmetry, each with one display stand of three panels and one showcase. An introductory stand and an empty showcase were also provided so that, as in the original, local articles could be included in the fabric of Common Threads as it toured. It was also possible to use the backs of the stands for local displays.

The much reduced size compared to the original obviously meant a reduced exhibition, but more significant educationally, a mathematics education artifact was now perceived through the eyes of another discipline and another institution. DPX felt that the level of mathematics in the original had been too high and that my captions were both too extensive and too difficult for people for whom English was not their first language. I was concerned however that the countries hosting the new Common Threads thought they were getting the original, indeed all had been sent a copy of its catalogue. Without thinking of possible future developments, I had simply handed over the title. I was also ignorant of the literature of exhibition design and could only counter its research evidence that people do not read long captions with my own evidence, that in the case of the original Common Threads, they had. In addition DPX had to work to the requirement of a house style, a controlled language designed not to embarrass the social, educational, political and diplomatic circles in which the Council works overseas, whereas the essence of my original had been to confront the anodyne. But Common Threads was now part of the establishment and subject to what might be called Mellin-Olsen's Law, that 'whenever a radical idea is absorbed by an establishment, it is converted into something which does not disturb the status quo too much' (Mellin-Olsen, 1993:1)*.

The New Common Threads Tour

The new Common Threads was launched in London in July 1990, looking spectacularly beautiful and well maintaining its original multicultural content, but with its mathematical content reduced and my relationship to it unclear. As a British Council exhibition it was subject both to their practised administration of travelling exhibitions, and to different local interpretations of what it was actually about. In spite of carefully drafted, and redrafted briefing papers by the Council's Mathematics Advisor and myself, there was still a wide range of interpretations between a majority of hosts who saw the point and took the challenge, and one extreme where it was found almost impossible to prepare for an exhibition that addressed three pigeon-holes at once. Political forces also affected the tour, at macro and micro levels. In one location, anti-British activity in a country close to the Gulf War temporarily closed down all the Council's activities; in another, rioting students closed the university, though local mathematics educators still ran a reduced programme in the schools' sector. In two others, changes in Council staff prevented preparations being put into effect or resulted in changed policies and so prevented follow up. The greatest problems occurred where Common Threads was seen as an exhibition rather than as an educational resource. Lead times in preparing for the latter are necessarily much longer than those for preparing the former, since they involve progressions in teaching and the diaries of people often committed many months in advance. Intense frustration was caused when communications were delayed on the former assumption, until it was too late to be fully effective on the latter. Different perceptions of what mathematics education involves remain a universal problem.

At the time of the tour, country Directors of the British Council had considerable autonomy in policy and budgets, though more funding was available in developing countries than in developed ones. The Scandinavian and Antipodean countries for example could only ship the exhibition and provide travel grants for me as a Visiting Consultant, whereas in developing countries there were sometimes funds, at the Director's discretion, for employing me to run a particular educational programme. My relationship with Common Threads was variously interpreted on a scale ranging from the inaccurate extremes of 'that knitting woman' to 'expert mathematician', and I could only work with Common Threads at all, if invited. In spite of the complexities of communication however, it was possible for me to work in thirteen of the twenty three countries in a variety of programmes, often adapted or extended after I had arrived. In several countries, particularly those who were only budgeted for travel grants, the Director passed Common Threads and myself to the mathematics education community, keeping in touch through correspondence and reports; in others they went out of their way to provide the sort of close support and assistance that made short visits maximally effective.

Throughout the nearly three years in which Common Threads toured, it proved that an interactive exhibition can be a very economic way of providing INSET (In-service education for teachers) to large numbers of teachers. It also provided a focus for debates on gender and vocational issues, for curriculum development and, through my associated workshops, practical experience in the design of locally-sourced learning materials. A single consultant who can continue to run an educational programme while sharing local conditions of chronic water shortage, absence of power, violent storm and hazardous travel (and all four at once) also makes a cost-effective resource.

Focus on Schools

In Norway, Denmark and New Zealand, textiles were already being used in mathematics education, and here Common Threads provided a focus and a boost for existing work, and a stimulus for extending it. In Bergen Teacher College three students were given the task of developing Common Threads in the Norwegian context, as a marked module of their course. They translated the catalogue and all the captions, made a collection of Norwegian textiles, designs and artifacts with accompanying mathematical analysis, and added some existing worksheets to an exhibit that over-flowed the empty showcase. They also worked with a group of oral-history researchers preserving and reconstructing national costumes in danger of dying out. Characteristically these costumes include panels of cross-stitch embroidery of particular symmetrical designs, and elaborate head-dresses of linen, needing the construction of three dimensional wooden forms over which the linen is shaped by steaming and starching. The feedback after Common Threads had moved on, noted that 'we work on as usual but now have more points of reference ... Common Threads fulfilled its ambition to unite women from different cultures in mathematics to an amazing degree. Harris' point that it is possible to break the pyramidal structure of mathematics by a exhibition such as this, in such a way that visitors can contribute and discuss mathematics issues, were confirmed every day of the exhibition' (Mellin-Olsen in Harris, 1995). Two years later, it had been remembered as 'an original and powerful initiative to promote mathematics education in developing countries and inner cities', in both of which staff of the college were heavily involved. By the second country, the tour was already educationally justified.

The tour of Denmark took place immediately before the tour of Norway and it was in preparation for it that members of *The Circle* (see previous chapter) had translated the catalogue and worksheets. They also translated the whole of *Cabbage* before passing it on to Norway. As in all countries where the mathematics education community was involved in planning the visit, the empty showcase was filled with local artifacts, inviting mathematical analysis of their design and construction. Mathematical tasks for visitors were provided to ensure that school children really used the exhibition. The backs of the stands displayed mathematical activities deriving from traditional Danish motifs in which Viking spiral formations featured strongly. *Håndarbejde* (handwork) is compulsory in Danish schools for grades five and six, boys and girls, and the feedback from this level in particular indicated that Common Threads had 'opened a lot of eyes to cross-curricular work ... to what was all around us ... and to new things' (Danish feedback in Harris, 1995). A tangible souvenir is the book *Matematik og Håndarbejde* (Mathematics and Handwork) by three teachers (Bjerg et al, 1992), in preparation by the time of the Common Threads tour, but further inspired by it.

As in the Scandinavian countries, the New Zealand tour, which I was unable to join, was coordinated by a working party of mathematics educators, in this case supported by the New Zealand Royal Society and with sponsorship from a commercial textiles company, and five of the country's six Science Centres acted as hosts. The catalogue was expanded with extra worksheets of locally sourced activities, articles on the mathematics of knots and braiding, a book list provided by the National Library of New Zealand, and follow-up activities for children. An exhibition of spirolaterals was added, including a worksheet on generating them through the computer program Logo. Common threads were extended further in exhibits of Maori weaving and the South Pacific craft *Tivaevae*, with worksheets exploring and developing their mathematical basis.

The most effective use in the tour of its own exhibition, by the British Council itself was in Botswana. The Council's Education Department worked with the Department of Mathematics and Science Education of the University of Botswana, with local craft and education organisations (including special needs) and the National Museum and Art Gallery of Botswana, in what became a mathematical celebration of Botswana culture. Hilda Lea, of the University's Mathematics and Science Education Department, had contributed to the original Common Threads by choosing and mailing locally-made baskets that displayed particularly interesting symmetries. Such baskets already had a world reputation and in the new Common Threads, they came home again in an international exhibition to a fine mathematical welcome. Additions were provided in the form of weaving, beadwork, more basket work, pottery and examples of house-making and decoration, many from the collections in the Botswana Museum and Art Gallery which displayed Common Threads. The University's Mathematics and Science Education Department added mathematical displays, of Fibonacci numbers in plant life, of spiral forms in animal life, of symmetry and fractals, of triple junctions in nature, and of geometry in African hairstyles, house decoration and animal footprints (Stott and Lea, 1993), raising the level of mathematics in Common Threads again.

Two permanent records were also made. The Arts Project Officer of the National Gallery organised a running mosaic workshop, where groups of school children worked with motifs taken from Common Threads. The

Overleaf: **Figure 13**: Botswana baskets, home again in Gabarone.
From the original Common Threads exhibition

final mosaic was presented to the British Council and now hangs in their Gabarone office. In recognition of the whole event, the Council published an 82 page booklet written by Leda Stott the Council's Education Officer and Hilda Lea, which recorded and developed some of the work that had been added to Common Threads, and in a generous act of reinforcement and continuity, the Council gave a copy to every secondary school in the country.

Possibly the most pronounced curriculum effect however, was in Thailand. Here the Ministry of Education's Institute for the Promotion of Teaching Science and Technology (IPST), is responsible for revising and updating science, mathematics and technology curricula, for promoting innovations in teaching and learning, for promoting research into teaching methods and other aspects of curriculum development, and for promoting relationships among other institutions at national and international level. The particular policy of the British Council in Thailand was to use my visit to assist in their co-operation with IPST, to help stimulate discussion on the secondary school syllabus and to raise awareness of the importance of mathematics in everyday life (Moss in Harris, 1995). The Head of the Mathematics Section of IPST, Dr Patrakoon Jariyavidyanont, and her team translated the catalogue and a number of worksheets, but they also set up their own mathematical exhibition of the Thai textiles *Mud-Mee* and *Kit*. In an inspired choice both exhibitions were displayed together in a department store which provided a working weaver and set up a selling display of local textiles. In addition, the Company gave space and hospitality in its training department to our workshops, which were also open to the public. Both exhibitions were staffed by mathematics undergraduates from Chulalongkorn University, who acted as guides and gave impromptu mathematics lessons to interested shoppers. In Bangkok, department stores act as social centres; they are air conditioned and they contain food centres in which it is possible to eat cheaply and well. The location and the company's copious advertising inside and outside the store meant that members of the public who would not normally shop there were able to enjoy a mathematical experience with plenty of assistance on hand if required.

Workshop Practice

It was in Thailand too that the IPST team and I developed workshops along the lines outlined in Chapter 5 above, that were to become the most productive part of my INSET work in many countries. In England, obviously enough, I had been working in a language, cultures, and to syllabuses and examination systems with which I was familiar. In other countries all three conditions were different and in Thailand, as in some other countries, there was some scepticism on the part of both the British Council Education Officer and some of the mathematics education professionals, about the effectiveness of workshops with students used to formal pedagogy in a hierarchical social system. It was my role however to interpret Common Threads and its theoretical background, to work to government policies of more open and interactive pedagogy, and to help ease the passage from textbook dependence to environmentally re-sourced, teacher made materials. I was also less sceptical about the perceived language and culture problems, not least because I had the complete support of the bilingual and professionally experienced Dr Patrakoon and her team. With the translations that her team had already done, the preparation and evaluations that we did together, and with her willingness to work alongside me there were no insuperable difficulties, though the task was undeniably demanding. My own routine preparatory programmes of immersion in the language and culture of the country I am about to visit, though obviously never full enough, also helps considerably in confirming to audiences that my intentions are to interact and share knowledge and practice, rather than to play the role of lofty visiting expert.

For workshops themselves, introductory passages can be translated beforehand and reproduced as handouts. The bulk, and the chief value of the communication that generates the richness of the mathematics, is between the teachers themselves, and much of the feedback can be handled through the internationally recognised symbols and diagrams of mathematics. Pedagogical points are better discussed amongst teachers and their own advisors in their own context, and suggestions for following up particular theoretical points in the international academic literature can be made with written references. Goodwill consciously fostered by the format of the workshops does most of the rest. This is not to undervalue the professional co-operation of colleagues, but to stress that there is infinitely more genuine communication in a relaxed workshop setting than in a formal lecture in a foreign language. In the particular case of Bangkok, after I had speeded up my introduction on one occasion, on the grounds that it was to be followed immediately by Dr Patrakoons' translation, I was asked to slow down again because many of the teachers had understood what I was saying, so long as I abided by the golden rule of international communication in a shared context: speak slowly, gently and clearly.

Workshops were in three parts, a brief introduction explaining the theoretical background to Common Threads and the workshop, the performance of a practical task as a group activity, and feedback. The ideal sized group for maximum involvement is five or six. Beyond that, groups tend to isolate individuals or break into smaller groups. The number of groups that can be accommodated in a single workshop depends on the size of the available space and the time for feedback. The latter needs from three to five minutes per group, before the final, general discussion that dwells on the particular needs or wishes of the group as a whole. The performance of the task is the core of the workshop, for it is there that the particular relevance of mathematics is explored. Teachers are given an article to design, or an artifact to analyse and possibly reconstruct, depending on the needs of the group previously discussed with tutors; the ideal is to use some object or task from the teachers' own culture as a starting point. In workshops held in the exhibition itself, this was usually a textile item, but it some locations away from it, we used a cardboard boxes. In Malaysia I sometimes used the ball of the game *Sepak Raga* played all over South East Asia, and woven from three layers of cane to produce a spherical tessellation of pentagons. In one African country, we used the wire mesh fence outside the window (a tessellation of quadrilaterals) and the plant growing up it (symmetrical growth, the Fibonacci series and spirals). In the textiles context, a rich activity that can be adapted to local textiles and presented on a chalkboard, or by scratching it in the sand, is the one called Mats, adapted from the Bags of the *Cabbage* pack, that had proved to be such a rich resource in England. (See Chapter 5 above). Its usefulness on the tour is indicated by its translation into Danish, Norwegian, Thai and Turkish.

Because the tasks centre on everyday things, and because teachers are asked to discuss their work as they do it, the atmosphere is always relaxed but productive. Under such circumstances, teachers think about their own thinking and learn about their own learning, being responsible for both, in extreme contrast to formal pedagogies that rely on higher authority for both learning content and approval. The teachers' analysis of their own performance is the major contribution to the feedback discussion. By then they usually need no convincing that what they have been doing is a mathematical activity, and discussion can focus on particular points of classroom practice, syllabus relevance or materials development.

Naturally a single workshop of this type cannot of itself change a curriculum or a school, but it can and it does open eyes and minds to change. Workshops can cater for large numbers of teachers, and the fact that so many teachers attended in the case of Bangkok, opened discussion across the secondary school system. Feedback after three years indicated that at every national mathematics conference since Common Threads, there has been a fresh exhibit of a mathematical activity sourced in Thai textiles. This suggests not only an increased mathematical interest in the textiles themselves, but mathematical analysis within the context of daily life outside the formalities of classrooms.

Extending the Web

Since workshops explore mathematics in the environment, the mathematical analysis reflects the interests and initiatives of the members; they are therefore easily adapted to a range of levels of mathematics. In East Malaysia, for example, another country with an enormous richness of woven textiles, it was possible to respond to the Director's policy of spreading workshops across as many aspects of mathematics education and parts of the country as was possible in a week. A bonus over her existing experience of working with the mathematics education community, was her knowledge of the textiles of Sarawak and a good relationship with experts in the Sarawak Museum, who generously lent unique items from their ethnographic collection for the Malaysian context of Common Threads. While the enriched exhibition was running, I worked with both staff and students in teacher training, with curriculum developers, with associations of teachers of mathematics, and in urban and rural schools. In Penang, in Peninsular Malaysia, the same policy was pursued, and I worked from an equally generous Ethnographic Museum at the Universiti Sains Malaysia. Here I lectured and ran workshops in teacher training colleges, at the ASEAN (Association of South East Asian Nations) Regional Education Centre in Science and Mathematics (RECSAM), in the exhibition itself and at a Saturday morning, multicultural women's group.

In even less time in Kenya, through the progress of adapted workshops and talks arranged by the Council's Cultural Affairs Officer, himself an ex-inspector of schools, 'a good exhibition was transformed into a highly educational event' (Edmundson in Harris, 1995). A programme of training teachers to develop their own materials was already operating in the primary and secondary teacher centres in Nairobi and it was possible to link this initiative to teaching in the exhibition itself with its rich addition of Kenyan textiles. I was also able to introduce the idea of learning mathematics through textiles teaching, to the very active national group, Women in Development, though there was no possibility of following it up.

In Nigeria, the pattern of workshops was again adapted, this time with a joint group of textiles students and mathematics teachers, who worked together for a week. Because of its emphasis on textiles, Common Threads had been booked into the Yaba Institute of Technology in Lagos, rather than into a setting more accessible to school mathematics educators. The mathematics teachers who joined the group presented themselves unannounced, having seen the report on the opening of Common Threads on the nine o'clock news the previous evening. It was the first workshop in which textiles and mathematics educators had worked together and the maturity of the members in opening their own discipline to the other, together with the local educational tradition of questioning until satisfied, made a particularly invigorating set of workshops. By the end of the week the group had generated a collection of worksheets for primary schools about the mathematical activities of Femi the weaver, which I took home to draft in fair copy before mailing them back for translation, as Common Threads left Lagos for other parts of the country.

Equal energy and enthusiasm was offered, as in so many African countries, by women active in women's development: Mrs Okunna, Deputy State Governor of Lagos; Mrs Oredugba, President of Nigerian Women in Mathematics; Dr Ugbebor of the Department of Mathematics of Ibadan University and Mrs Akinkugbe, Chair of Lagos State Commission for Women, jointly and severally extended the audience for Common Threads. The meeting they arranged with the Minister of Education, came too late however to involve the teacher-training arm of mathematics education, and secondary mathematics educators.

In the small country of Swaziland where the mathematics education community already had a long and profitable relationship with the Council, workshops could focus on materials development in which the curriculum development team was already involved. Makhosazana Madondo of the National Curriculum Centre for example, was preparing materials for primary schools taking as one of her sources the geometric beadwork that is widely worn with traditional dress and appears in all public buildings and in many homes in ubiquitous portraits of the King. In Swaziland too, I witnessed a perfect impromptu mathematics lesson using no resources other than a piece of string, a piece of chalk and of course the skills of the teacher. On a fleeting visit to a school on the road to a distant teacher training college, I was accompanied by Mprophet Sihlabela of the Secondary Mathematics Materials Fund. I gave an impromptu lesson to two classes, about the mathematics in their school ties and socks. After my presentation Mr Sihlabela produced a loop of string from his pocket, familiar to all the children as the raw material of the shapes and forms of their string games. In one such game, the string is formed to represent a varying number of fields and gates. Using the mathematical names of the shapes, *quadrilaterals* and *triangles*, and working from the children's responses, he recorded a column of figures for each while manipulating the string in the way all the children knew. He then announced that, as *quadrilateral* and *triangle* were rather long words, he would use q and t instead, and invited the children to help him find a way to write down a short sentence that would always give the number of fields and of gates, no matter how many there were on the string at any time. The children left after a memorable algebra lesson, with a formula for their string game in terms of q and t, and the enthusiasm to look for other formulae in their other games.

Focus on Women

Workshops were not confined to the schools sector. In many countries Common Threads also became a powerful resource for work with women's groups, and in several African countries the impact on the latter was as strong as the lack of possibilities of follow-up were frustrating. In Kenya, Lesotho and Zimbabwe, as in many African countries, women's groups run a range of programmes including those aimed at training skills for self-sufficiency. Many programmes teach dressmaking and other textiles crafts and all suffer from low status and chronic lack of funding, particularly in comparison with available vocational courses for men. Some also run numeracy courses, sometimes assisted by expatriate volunteer tutors from an aid programme. These volunteers tend to come from a craft or further education background and almost characteristically, further education tutors of numeracy tend to have mathematics education experience that is limited and traditional (see Chapter 8 above), though that is now changing. In textile courses with women's groups, the potential for recognising and developing the mathematics that is already an integral part of the needlework is enormous, but tutors generally do not have the training and experience with which to exploit it. In addition, many courses follow a craft-oriented syllabus leading to examinations which tend to impose the traditional view of low-level mathematics as applied arithmetic skills, that is as skills to be learned outside the textiles context and then applied. In two craft centres in different countries, volunteer tutors were sceptical about the whole idea of teaching mathematics and textiles together, and quoted to me what they saw as the unsurmountable difficulty, that to take the textiles examination, students had to be able to 'do percentage shrinkage'. This pedagogic imposition and its effects its discussed in Chapter 10 below. On a fleeting visit however, simply discussing the mathematics that the women were doing as they worked, was revelation that, whatever their previous experience, they did have some mathematical competence even if they could not perform irrelevant tricks of pencil and paper algorithm.

Gender differentials in expectation and resourcing were already of some concern to the Director of the British Council in Zimbabwe. In another inspired placement, the Sheraton Hotel in Harare sponsored both Common Threads and my accommodation, displaying the exhibition in an open area of the hotel where members of the international public would see it as they

passed by. These included business, government and academic visitors attending meetings and conferences, one of which, by happy
chance, was on women's development in
Southern Africa. Living above the exhibition
allowed me to host impromptu seminars in
the evenings and to repair some of the now
well-travelled artifacts overnight. Like Robin-
sons Store in Bangkok, the Harare Sheraton
acts as an informal social centre, in a city
rather freer of traditional cultural boundaries
than many in the region. On one occasion,
two cohorts of about twenty-five members of
a woman's vocational course, whose qualifications for membership was poverty, arrived
simultaneously to see Common Threads,
instead of with the two hour separation that
had been planned. As the hotel staff supplied
refreshments with the same courtesy with
which they treated their four star guests, we
took artifacts from the show cases to examine,
and sat on the floor to explore the tessellating
patterns on the Sheraton's carpet. All the
women were members of sewing or other

Figure 14(i): Common Threads on tour
Shopper studying mathematics. Bangkok

textile courses and had an understanding of the construction of the textiles
on display that is unaffected by illiteracy, and once more some traditional
perceptions of mathematics education evaporated under the women's
capable hands. On such occasions, lack of a common spoken language is
less of a problem than it might appear to be. Knowledge of the parameters
of the task is already shared and the women's more highly educated and
therefore bilingual tutors were on hand to help with questions. This ability of
women to communicate co-operatively through the task in hand, in contrast
to the hierarchical reception of rules about it, has already been discussed in
Chapter 5 in the context of the work of Gilligan (1982) (see also Harris,
1990).

Although most of my effort was in the schools sector, there was as much
effective consciousness-raising in the field of women's work, both in Harare
and in Bulawayo, the two centres where Common Threads was displayed. In
the latter many local artifacts were added, notably the renowned geometrical
bead work of the Ndebele people. In his feedback, two years after the visit of
Common Threads, the Director Zimbabwe wrote 'the exhibition seemed to
me to be one of the most thought-provoking of its kind we have in the British

Figure 14(ii): Common Threads on tour
Mathematics on the floor. Harare Sheraton, Zimbabwe

Council... It was the launching point for what looks like a serious attempt to be made over the coming years to tackle the problem of the very small number of girls going into mathematics education in Zimbabwean schools. The exhibition was also a major talking point in mathematics education circles ... [and it] also had a major impact on women's affairs. Since Common Threads, we have developed considerably our work with women's groups' (Elborn in Harris, 1995).

From Uganda also, which I did not visit, came a clear statement of a refreshed recognition of women's work. I have no way of knowing to what extent the mathematics education community was involved, but the feedback from the Council's Information Officer informed me that, in its policy of working closely with women's organisations and encouraging more female participation in the country's development, 'this exhibition helped our work no end' (Bewulira-Wandera in Harris, 1995). The same feedback described how the status of women's work was changing:

> Until very recently basket making, weaving etc was done by the women during their leisure time rather than as a commercial venture. But slowly the women were beginning to get involved in trade, as they realised that they could make some money to supplement the family's income. Unfortunately, though these crafts did bring in money they were still considered to be part of the women's 'gossip sessions' because though beautiful, the way the women make them so effortlessly, gave the impression that you could make them blind-fold. (Bewulira-Wandera in Harris, 1995)

The effect of Common Threads had been that 'practically overnight, these crafts makers who are predominantly women, were accorded the respect they deserve.'

In Nigeria in particular, the question was repeatedly raised of follow-up to the exhibition and its associated INSET. Without the resources of an educational initiative to support and sustain it, the undoubted effects could fade. In Botswana, this need had been answered by the involvement of the mathematics education community from the beginning of the tour, and by the material published at the end of it. Here and in Denmark and

Norway, New Zealand, Swaziland and Thailand it was sustained by the mathematics education community itself. These were all educational initiatives however, pigeon-holed separately from women's initiatives. Though the potential for joint educational and economic development was present in most countries, it was not possible to achieve or even begin to plan for without funding support, lack of which eventually prevented the Zimbabwe initiative. In other countries it prevented planned projects from getting off the ground or ranked them second to more urgent health programmes.

Common Threads, Common Responses

The country that did have the resources and initiatives to address all the problems that Common Threads addressed, is Australia, a Commonwealth of States which guard their educational independence. It is also a country that tends to see itself as cut off from the rest of the world, yet contributes more than most to mathematics education, not least to work on gender issues, for example in the work of Burton (1986 and many others), Leder (1992 and many others) and Willis (1989 and many others). Australian women are also in the fore-front of the work on numeracy and women, for example Johnston (1992) and Marr and Helm (1992).

On its arrival in Perth, Common Threads was described as being at the 'cutting edge' of mathematical education (Willis in Harris, 1995). Some of the materials of the Maths in Work Project and those associated with Common Threads, were already in use through the usual international networks of mathematics education, and the good offices of Dr Jan Harding, a science educator, who had run a preparatory seminar on Common Threads using my materials, at a conference on girls and science at Curtin University. The opening of the Australian tour at the Technology Park at Curtin was marked in the national and State media, and helped launch a three week programme with schools, academic colleagues and craft groups. In Melbourne, Common Threads was the theme of the annual conference of the Mathematical Association of Victoria. In Hobart it was used to stimulate closer links between mathematics and the widespread pursuit of textiles crafts in Tasmania, and to revive interest in indigenous mathematics. In Canberra it was used for cross-curricular initiatives and cross-institutional links, and between university and school mathematics. In Sydney it was displayed in the Powerhouse gallery where it was opened by the Head of the Science Unit of the Australian Broadcasting Corporation and where it attracted widespread public and media attention. Although no academic programme had been prepared for my visit to Sydney before Common Threads arrived, there was time to make a videotape covering the theoretical background.

Feedback from the Australian tour described clear cases of changed perceptions of mathematics and progress in curriculum and teacher development. Writing from Adelaide where Common Threads had arrived at the end of a school term, Will Morony, then Curriculum Development Officer, acknowledged the contribution of the Adelaide Embroiderers' Guild, and that the staging of the exhibition in the Education Department had resulted in policy makers seeing 'the human face of mathematics, possibly for the first time' (Morony in Harris, 1995). Changing perceptions can be a slow and sometimes painful process, and Morony's sensitive description of the underlying frustrations and small rewards, will resonate with mathematics education professionals, everywhere in the world.

> There is substantial prejudice against mathematics in the community and many people carry the scars of their own experiences at school. Things are terribly slow to change in schools, but often there is a blindness to improvements that have been made. The exhibition, with its celebration of people's mathematics in context, and the attendant beauty of the results, provides a vivid picture of what is possible when exploring the mathematics of textiles. This in turn opens people's eyes to other, less spectacular, advances in mathematics in schools. The picture of mathematics as something human is painted in many ways in schools and, although there is a long way to go in the practice and content of mathematics curricula, I think we should be encouraged by how far we have progressed. Part of this is to change the opinions of the cynics and I believe that the visit of Common Threads to Adelaide is an important event in this. My intuition here is borne out by a number of conversations with people outside the field who were very impressed by the exhibition. That I considered it as an exciting adjunct to what we are already doing – and could cite numerous initiatives – was salutary to those who considered that mathematics has not changed since their time at school. Small steps ... always small steps. (Morony in Harris, 1995)

In Western Australia, one visitor to Common Threads, left me an anonymous note about her own craft work:

> I have always believed myself to be rather a 'dud' in the area of maths ... I thought I used my eye to give my work balance and set the position, but I was actually measuring in a precise way. I looked for satisfying balanced shapes but what I was actually doing was counting spaces on either side of my design. I wanted evenness in my work and my understanding of symmetry gave me this (Anon in Harris, 1995).

Gwen Egg, a well-known Tasmanian weaver and teacher who contributed to Common Threads in Hobart, also wrote of changed perceptions:

> it made me look at my work in a new way [and] ... I am still thinking about it. I still refer to the basket which I made for the exhibition as my 'maths basket' ... when invited to teach weaving in schools I am [now] much more likely to discuss mathematical concepts with my students and to see my teaching related to other areas of the curriculum. I am clearer with craft students about why I use particular weaves or achieve particular patterns. (Egg in Harris, 1995)

Lasting effects were recorded by a senior mathematics teacher from South Australia; Common Threads activities were in use 'in quite a few mathematics and arts faculty areas areas round the State' (Oxenberry in Harris, 1995).

End of Term

In spite of my lasting and substantiated concern about the reduction of the mathematics content of the new Common Threads, and continuing differences in perception of mathematics education between administrators and different professionals, this small, interactive resource achieved substantial educational development, with many implications for further work. An exhibition that attracts and holds visitors' attention to its subject is a prime consideration, and I found myself gladly crediting DPX with the beauty of the new Common Threads as often as I found myself trying to restore some of its mathematics. I have records in feedback of only two negative reactions. In Dr Harding's workshop in Perth, some men walked out, but no reason is given. In the Philippines, one senior woman mathematics educator remarked that the exhibition did not impress her much 'because it looked pretty much like the displays in our shopping malls' (Nguyen in Harris, 1995), but this may say more about the status of shopping malls in Manila and of academic mathematics for those who have had to fight hard to achieve it, than about an exhibition whose point may have been missed. The alliance of Common Threads to a department store in Bangkok had delivered a very potent message. From further detail in the same feedback, it is also clear that low levels of mathematics in the exhibition had influenced the judgment. Her point that 'very often people in textiles handicrafts ... create beautiful accurate work without knowing mathematics, is discussed in further in Chapter 10 below. This particular feedback too was not wholly negative, recognising the 'strength of Common Threads lies in the greater possibilities of cross-curricular work and in the development of materials that will address gender problems' (Nguyen in Harris, 1995).

In countries in which women are expected to maintain a traditional feminine role, working with women teachers could sometimes be difficult, not because of any lack of competence of the teachers themselves, but because of social expectations on their behaviour. For example in one location it was difficult to draw any response from women teachers, until I joined them in women-only groups and worked alongside them. Here responses of male tutors to women's obvious mathematical activity was contradictory and spoke of individual sensitivity rather than cultural imperative. One male tutor remarked with obvious pleasure that he had had no idea that his women teachers could be so creative and that he would use this talent in future. Another, however, responded with some aggressive and destructive questioning that reduced the women to silence again. It was clearly a gendered response, since the questions were directed only to the women in the whole group including me. In discussion after the episode, the women explained that they were quite used to this, that they had been delighted to have been consulted in the workshop, but that they had been even more delighted to see me respond to the questioning as a mathematics education professional, in a way that was impossible for them, because they were perceived first and foremost as women. The lack of logic in the situation was obvious to everyone except the perpetrator; women teachers are expected to stimulate and enthuse pupils but must not show the same characteristics themselves. It was only one incident but a powerful one and one that will be recognised by many women for the devastating effects it can have, not only on the confidence of the teachers so treated, but on the confidence of the children they themselves teach.

Although problems of mathematics education differ across the world, it was the commonalities expressed in the context of Common Threads, which seemed to emphasise stronger similarities than differences and perhaps counter some of Jurdak's (1994) pessimism noted in Chapter 8. Nearly all problems and questions raised at the end of lectures and workshops were not unique to a particular country, though questioners were nearly always convinced that they were. No country, including England, was happy with its mathematics education, and in every one, when I asked what the major concern was, I received the same responses: that so many children fail; that so many girls do not participate beyond a certain point; that curricula are too academic for the substantial majority of children; and that curricula are irrelevant to the culture and working lives of ordinary people. In all countries too, there was concern centring on examinations, as if examination was the main point of educating people.

In nearly all countries I was asked at some stage to give a formal talk at a level that included policy makers, an indulgence that allowed me to offer the opinion, that in a small world with too many and too gross differences, and mathematics education whose chief characteristic seems to be that it fails most people, we have to abandon the archaic élitisms of control and open it up to embrace the talents and aspirations of all people by sharing knowledge, skills and expertise. No one country, continent or culture has the ownership of mathematics or mathematics education or the intellectual or moral right to impose it on any other. In the past when this had been attempted, the results have been disastrous for all but a few. Such a view contains more than romantic idealism, for there is good reason to believe that culturally rooted pedagogy can be a cost-effective challenge to the current expense of the alternative of hardware dependency that can dominate a teacher-training budget (Thomas, 1995). There is good reason too, to believe that an inexpensive resource along the line of Common Threads and its workshops, could share and support locally grown initiatives. Common Threads spoke to economic self-help groups as much as to practising teachers, curriculum developers and academics. It questioned the mismatch between the mathematics of schools and the lives and work of ordinary people; it did speak to large numbers of working teachers and working women, and to large numbers of people whose experiences of mathematics had been irrelevant, unhappy, short-lived or non-existent as well as to those for whom it had been considerable. It spoke to designers and makers of teaching materials whether in classrooms, curriculum development units or in distance learning, and it spoke across the curriculum divide between schools and work. It did change attitudes, raise awareness, widen viewpoints and stimulate fresh views.

The tours of the two copies of the new Common Threads ended in places that express its range between radical and mundane. One set was donated to Science World in Vancouver where it finally came to rest, to be displayed in a modern scientific setting in a country of rich cultural diversity. The other more battered copy ended its days in an air freighter's shed on the fringes of Heathrow airport, where a member of DPX staff and I retrieved the artifacts that had survived, and put together a reduced, working set of display stands which were donated to a West London charity in a final act of British Council generosity. The backs of the stands are now fronts which display information to those who currently work with learning difficulties, while occasional passers-by can, by looking at what are now the backs, still interest themselves in some of the mathematics of ordinary every-day life.

Note

* I have taken the liberty of converting this remark of the late Stieg Melin-Olsen into a law, as a tribute to a radical mathematics educator without equal.

References

Bjerg Mette, Engraf Lars and Eskilden Hanni. (1992) *Matematik and Håndarbejde*. Samsø: Forlaget Matematik.

Burton Leone (1986) *Girls into Maths Can Go*. Eastbourne: Holt, Rinehart and Winston.

Gilligan Carol (1982) *In a Different Voice: Psychological Theory and Women's Development*. Cambridge Mass. and London: Harvard University Press.

Harris Mary (1989) Basics. In *Mathematics Teaching* Vol 128.

Harris Mary (1990) Embroidery for Tourists. In Mary Harris (Ed) *Textiles in Mathematics Teaching*. London: Maths in Work Project, University of London Institute of Education (Out of print)

Harris Mary (1995) Common Threads Feedback MSS. Unpublished.

Johnston Betty (1992) *Reclaiming Mathematics*. Sydney: Language and Literacy Centre, University of Technology.

Jurdak Murad (1994) Mathematics Education in the Global Village: The Wedge and the Filter. Selected Lectures from the Seventh International Congress on Mathematical Education. Québec 17-23 August 1992 pp199-210. Québec: Les Presses de l'Université Laval.

Leder Gilah C (1992) Mathematics and Gender: Changing Perspectives. In D A Grouws (ed) *Handbook of Research on Mathematics Teaching and Learning*. New York Macmillan.

Marr Beth and Helm Sue (1992) *Breaking the Maths Barrier: A Kit for Building Staff Development Skills in Adult Numeracy*. Sydney: Language and Literacy Centre, University of Technology.

Mellin-Olsen Stieg (1993) Opening Address. In C Julie, D Angelis and Z Davis (Eds) *Political Dimensions of Mathematics Education 2 (PDME2) Curriculum Construction for Society in Transition*. Cape Town: Maskew Miller Longman.

Stott Leda and Lea Hilda (1993) *Common Threads in Botswana*. Gabarone: The British Council.

Thomas Elwyn (1995) Seminar Discussion. DICE International Conference, Partnerships in Education and Development: Tensions between Economics and culture. University of London Institute of Education 24-26 May 1995 (unpublished but see Thomas (1996) below).

Thomas E (1996) Developing a Culture Sensitive Pedagogy: Tackling the Problem of Melding Global Culture within an Existing Cultural Context. *International Journal of Education and Development* Vol 16 No 4 (forthcoming)

Willis Sue (1984) *'Real Girls Don't Do Maths': Gender and the Construction of Privilege*. Victoria: Deakin University.

Chapter 10

Women, Mathematics and Work

Introduction

Throughout the world it is women and girls who underachieve in mathematics. Mathematics is the study above all others that denotes the heights of intellect. Throughout the world, the activity that most clearly denotes the work of women, in both the unpaid, domestic sphere and in paid employment, is work with cloth. Work with cloth symbolises women as empty-headed and trivial. Yet constructing cloth, decorating it during construction and converting it into garments, is work that cannot be done without involving spatial and numerical concepts that are the foundations of mathematics.

Work with cloth also represents the economic exploitation of women, maintained by justifications in the form of accepted myths of the feminine stereotype (Elson, 1983). Women naturally have nimble fingers (though they are not encouraged to train as brain surgeons); women are not technically minded and cannot cope with machines (except in war time when they are needed to operate the factories); women do not need to support a family, their wages are pin money (even when the father is absent, unemployed, sick or just plain mean); women workers are docile and compliant (except when they are trouble-makers). The cloth industries depend most on female labour and are the most persistent perpetrators of the myths. Textiles is one of the most visible arenas in economic competition between states, as multinational industries shift capital between low-wage countries, and as sub-contracting chains link the world in networks of illegal workshops and poor and unprotected homes. Women's work with cloth is crucial to world economies and there are strong vested interests in not recognising the skills involved. All the common threads of women, mathematics and work currently combine to tie women down.

Gender and Mathematics Revisited

Mathematics is indeed a powerful subject. It provides the figures on which political, commercial and aid policies and planning are researched, reported and analysed. It is the means for pricing resources, paying personnel, monitoring results. It is the language through which international bankers with no spoken word in common can communicate. It is the chief tool of manufacturing industry and scientific and technological research. It is the provider of models, the arbiter of progress, the measure of success.

With power goes control. Probably the most widespread use of mathematics is in failing people, for mathematics as a selection device is the critical filter to economic, educational and professional advancement. Its chief use as such is not so much because it is useful however, but because it is a powerful selector, taking the role of now discredited intelligence tests but without attracting their criticisms (Willis, 1989:35). Mathematics certainly has the power to intimidate (Buxton, 1981) and indeed is used on occasion 'to produce mystification and an impression of precision and profundity' (Koblitz quoted by Willis, 1989:37).

Many adults, taught when young to revere mathematics, learned rules and processes they did not understand but which they learned to trust implicitly. Without much understanding of, for example, why long division works and only hazy memory of how to do it, they demand that today's children should also acquire the respect and rules they acquired. As in the late nineteenth century, demand for such 'basic skills' is made in the late twentieth by a small group of unaccountable and unelected people with little or no experience of research, theory or practice in state education (Brown, 1993:98), who dominate educational policy and have acquired considerable public support in England and Wales. These 'cultural restorationists' (Ball, 1993) 'seem intent on imposing the 'curriculum of the dead', where the dead are white, male and, if at all possible British' (Brown, 1993:101). As in the Victorian era, they see knowledge as an existing canon, an epistemology of remote and inert facts, techniques and opinions of revered forefathers, with an advocated pedagogy recognisable in the Gradgrind method of Charles Dickens' lampoon. The resulting dead curriculum comes in neatly packaged coffins, to be assessed by the pencil and paper measures beloved of administrators for the easiest ranging of bodies in layers. The model favours those who were brought up in it, indeed it particularly favours those who do not question it (Keddie, 1971:155), so that among a small élite it remains self-perpetuating.

What is ignored is its history of failure with the majority outside the small group for which it traditionally caters. As Brown (1993:103) points out, until recently 60% of British pupils responded to it by leaving school at the earliest opportunity, for learning seen as passive reception of knowledge and ideas, and the 'hard slog in memorising this and continual tests' (Brown, 1993:103) fits ill with the enquiring nature of young people. It is the latter that is motivating, the valuing of knowledge won by personal enquiry and owned as understanding, not by the red ticks or crosses of authority. The learners who fail to win the required number of red ticks, or acquire too many crosses, leave school with their mathematical confidence destroyed. And it is unlikely that they would submit themselves to more of the same torture in future. Prepackaged rote-learned pedagogy has not been shown to be very successful in enhancing student learning (Brown, 1993:104).

Professional mathematics educators generally set themselves more positive agendas, in ongoing research and debate. They focus attention more on the processes of learning, and epistemologies that emphasise their flexible structures, in contrast to the rigor mortis of a dead curriculum. They follow the belief that the study of how children construct and de-construct their own knowledge and the influence of context on these processes, is likely to shed more light on the nature of knowledge than any armchair, philosophical theory. The study of children's interactions with computers sheds more (Papert, 1980). The cultural restorationists seem unaware of the evidence of the effectiveness for mathematical thinking (in contrast to test performance) of more flexible teaching, from and in contexts that have meaning for learners, and of their assessment by means that respect ongoing interactions of teachers and pupils (Brown, 1993:110).

One of the effects of pressures from cultural restorationists has been to push girls back again from a pedagogy which had been shown to have increased their involvement in mathematics. The 1970s saw a number of government supported initiatives in mathematics education which sought to redress gender, social class and cultural imbalances in mathematics and science (Smart, 1996 and Chapter 5 above), but from 1988 and the Education Reform Act that introduced the National Curriculum, these began to evaporate. The Cockcroft Report on the teaching of mathematics in schools, published in 1982, advocated more practical, investigatory work and discussion amongst pupils. These methods proved to be particularly beneficial to girls, though HMI reports of the end of the 1980s pointed out that the sensitive and perceptive teaching that benefited girls, benefited all children. As Willis (1989:32) reminds us, the traditional masculinity of mathematics reflects a particular construction of masculinity that is also inappropriate for a great many boys. Focusing on the attainment of girls had also led to some revealing analyses of the nature of mathematics and mathematics learning. It was in this context that the work of Walkerdine and her colleagues at the Girls and Maths Unit was published (Walkerdine, 1989). Girls' attitudes and learning were shown to benefit particularly, not just from more interactive, investigatory teaching, but also when work was placed in relevant contexts. They were shown to suffer disproportionately when exposition and discussion were neglected (Smart, 1966).

The introduction of new school-leaver examinations in the late 1980s had also benefited girls. The new examinations adopted the philosophy propounded by the Cockcroft Report that examinations should not undermine the confidence of candidates and that they should demonstrate what candidates can do, not what they cannot. A new unified examination replaced the previous overlapping two-tiered system that had already graded candidates before they entered them, and introduced the assessment of ongoing coursework. The Girls and Mathematics Unit had found that girls were more likely to be entered for the lower level examination even when they performed better than boys who were entered at the higher level, for reasons already noted in Chapter 5 above. Removal of the entry disadvantage, and girls' better performance on coursework than boys, together reduced the previous differences in performance. At the end of the 1980s however, the reactionary changes in the education system described so graphically by Brown (1993), succeeded in removing the gains girls had made, by their insistence on a return to 'traditional values' of rote-and-test learning, and the elimination of coursework assessment. 'In six years all the agencies promoting equality were curbed or disbanded. A curriculum that pays no service to equal opportunities is being institutionalised and testing improvements have been withdrawn. Gender issues are no longer considered important: girls' performance is expected to fall again' (Smart, 1996). Smart cites work which suggests that the reversal of policy of one government that took place between the 1970s and the 1990s was due less to concerns with social justice and equality or empowering women than to an economic strategy to deal with shortages of skilled labour, notably scientists and engineers. By the time the first cohorts had graduated, the country was in recession, there were fewer jobs available and women were less welcome. There was no longer an economic need to encourage them into mathematics and the government talked again about traditional family values: it was time for women to go home again.

Ethnomathematics

There is agreement amongst all but the most reactionary, that the context in which mathematics is learned and is practised, affects, if it does not determine, how it is understood and how it is performed. If mathematics is the product of human inventiveness, in contrast to a body of infallible knowledge waiting to be discovered (see Chapter 5), then there are implications for all knowledge, that which rests on the certainties of an infallible mathematics and that which concerns the place of mathematics and its learning in society. As Ernest (1991:xii) notes, mathematics as a body of infallible knowledge can bear no social responsibility. The under-participation of women and some class and cultural groups, and its role in the distribution of wealth and power are irrelevant. If it is a social construct however, then it is as fallible as any other human activity and it becomes another process of coming to know, not a finished product. There are of course many different conceptualisations of the relationships between various categories and definitions of context, and it is within these that the cultural anthropology of mathematics is defined by Gerdes (1997) as *ethnomathematics*. As he points out, it is not new to look at mathematics like this. He cites an essay by Keyser of 1932, which defends the thesis that the type of mathematics found in any major culture is a clue, or key, to the distinctive character of the culture as a whole. Thirty years before Gay and Cole (1967 and see Chapter 8), Raum (1938) published his *Arithmetic in Africa*, based on his course of lectures in the Colonial Department of the University of London Institute of Education, and advised that 'education cannot be truly effective unless it is intelligently based on indigenous culture and living interests' (Raum, 1938:4). Fifty years on from Raum, D'Ambrosio, called by Gerdes 'the intellectual father of ethnomathematics', proposed an ethnomathematical programme as a way of tracing and analysing how knowledge is generated, transmitted, diffused and institutionalised in different cultural systems. His 1985 definition of ethnomathematics is that 'which is practised among identifiable cultural groups such as national-tribal societies, labor groups, children of a certain age-bracket, professional classes and so on' (D'Ambrosio, 1991).

Under such a definition, the academic mathematics of institutional education, and the mathematics of women who sew, are both examples of ethnomathematics among many (Harris, 1987). The institutionalisation of one élite ethnomathematics at the end of the nineteenth century, and its world spread, effectively devalued all others then and since. But, argues D'Ambrosio, before and outside school, almost all children become 'matherate', that is they develop the 'capacity to use number, quantities, the capability of qualifying and quantifying, and some patterns of inference' (Gerdes, 1977 quoting D'Ambrosio). From summaries of research that viewed mathematics as a cultural product, Bishop (1991) identified six universals that appear to be carried out by every cultural group ever studied: counting, locating, measuring, designing, playing and explaining.

In D'Ambrosio's argument, the mechanisms of schooling replace these forms of ethnomathematics with the codified and formal school mathematics which make a very efficient way of instilling in children a sense of failure and dependency (Gerdes, 1997). The hasty curriculum transplantations of the 1960s (see Chapter 9) had the same effect: they negated African, Asian and Amerindian mathematics. Ethnomathematical activities, now 'fighting back' in these regions, are recognised in terms that contrast academic and pre-academic mathematics with indigenous, spontaneous, oral, oppressed, non-standard, hidden, frozen, folk or socio-mathematics.

There is now a considerable body of research that covers a wide range of ethnomathematical activities and mathematical topics; probabilities in traditional games; geometries in art, architecture and design, in woven and plaited mats and baskets, in coiled baskets and mats, in roof rafters and on house walls, in metal working and body drawing, in sand drawings and threshold designs; in the arithmetic and number work of street and market traders and supermarket shoppers, of carpentry apprentices, fishermen, tailors, weavers and carvers, in reckoning and the methods of trackers; and in the mathematics of story puzzles and riddles (see Gerdes, 1977 for an up to date review). In the analysis of mathematics in textiles available to the Maths in Work Project while setting up Common Threads, the titles Symmetry, Number, Creativity, Information Handling and Problem Solving, arose as clear, if overlapping, categories and testify to the range of mathematical activity they clearly involved (Chapter 6).

The arbitrary selection and formal and symbolic methods of school mathematics set it apart from mathematics outside school in many ways. Historically and consciously, traditional liberal mathematics education is disconnected from how people think and what they do in their daily lives, indeed from all the circumstances in which mathematics is actually used. It teaches people not to believe in their own capability but to rely on authority and it teaches them to disdain the work of their hands so that they do not recognise the mathematics they are using in their daily work, and do not accept that their daily work can be mathematical. As Paechter (1993:41), quoting Young, remarks, pupils are classified and curricula and examinations are differentiated by the extent to which non school knowledge has to be incorporated into the learning situation; 'the more non-school knowledge a student requires, the less 'able' he or she is perceived to be.' The historical facts of the building of an entirely separate system of elementary education for the intended workforce, and of using the education system as a whole to allocate people to different levels in the economy, still has effects in the reciprocal ignorance of two sorts of mathematics education. A vast array of workplace mathematics remains invisible to the hegemonies of formal education, economic planning, development programmes and mathematics education research.

The 1970s research projects dear to employers (see Chapter 5), on the mathematical skills of workplaces, supported the liberal education assumptions of the association of low social status with arithmetic, of arithmetic as low level mathematics and the association of both with work deemed unskilled (see Chapter 5). Even the use of the word *skill* in the vocational context, emphasises its contrast to the liberally educated whole person as if there was a disjunction between hand and brain that characterises the labouring classes (Paechter, 1993:43). Thus from the ranks of the cultural restorationists come demands for the skills of *numeracy*, a truly nineteenth century conception of the late twentieth century, bastardised from the idea of literacy and applied chiefly to the 'ignorant' lower orders. There is no generally agreed tight definition of numeracy, but as literacy means something like access to the written word, numeracy means something like access to the written number, rather than for example access to drawn geometry. The emphasis on written number in numeracy leads to assumptions that people who are illiterate are also innumerate (see Chapter 2). In adult education and aid programmes throughout the world, literacy takes precedence over numeracy on the assumption that the latter needs the former, and numeracy programmes consist mainly of teaching the sort of written sums that are dictated by the commercially published and imported examinations (see Chapter 8). In such numeracy, the counting and measuring of Bishop's list predominate, while the visual, spatial and philosophical items remain as activities of the more socially privileged mathematics in spite of their obvious appearance in the work women do outside the numeracy class. D'Ambrosio's pre-school matheracy and categories on Bishop's list are rendered invisible, both because their owners are illiterate to begin with, and because the processes of assessment of 'vocational' numeracy education are those of the controlling liberal education tradition.

The imposition makes invisible the vast differences between the ethno-mathematics of school and that of workplaces, not only its content but the way in which it is done. In school, mathematics is done alone, for to ask a colleague what to do is cheating. Work on the other hand is usually a social activity, to ask a colleague what to do is common sense. Mathematics in school is usually entered through written instruction: at work it often results from spoken ones. In school, examples are imported, selected, edited, revised or invented to illustrate some particular mathematics being learned: at work the need for mathematics is generated by the context. In traditional schooling, the answer is right or wrong as determined by the authority of the teacher or answer book: at work the answer depends on what is wanted and there is sometimes no right answer at all. In school the accuracy of the answer is specified: at work it depends on what is required. In school, the numbers in problems are often 'cleaned up' and variables removed so as to make it easier to obtain the right answer: in work the numbers are those of real life, recurring decimals and awkward fractions and all. In school, significant variables in the problem are often indicated with the problem: at work, part of the problem is to select the variables that matter from everything else that is going on. In school particular symbols and language must be used: in work symbolism is often dependent on context, and non-standard units and rules of thumb abound. Work mathematics is everything school mathematics is not.

Workplace ethnomathematics is limited in its techniques because it draws on narrow resources, but it can be highly creative because it is not bound by formal rules or abstract criteria. It is particularistic because it is context bound, though broader than ad hoc knowledge, unlike academic mathematics which aims to be culture free. It operates through metaphors and symbol systems which can be culturally unique, unlike the symbols of academic mathematics which are condensed through an acknowledged, universal form of rationality. School mathematics with its symbol systems and generalisations is more obviously powerful: workplace and home ethnomathematics is more clearly meaningful. The educational task of Common Threads, indeed of all the work of the Maths in Work Project (see Chapter 5), had been to try and make the meaningful more general and the general more meaningful (Carraher, 1991).

Ethnomathematics in Practice

There was long an assumption, born of psychological theories of learning, that arithmetic learned in school is 'literally carried away from it to be applied at will in any situation that calls for calculations' (Lave, 1988:4). Conventional cognitive psychology with its origins in a positive epistemology of science and the division of the disciplines, sees continuity of activity across settings as a function of knowledge stored in memory and general cognitive processing. It treats cognition and culture as units of analysis that can be isolated, with culture reified as particular pieces of knowledge. Lave preferred a social anthropology, seeing cognition as a complex social phenomenon, a nexus of relations distributed over, not divided between mind, body activity, and culturally organised settings. Mathematics education research stands accused by Eisenhart (1988) of this sort of division and of the resulting limited way in which it has entered the lives and activities of those it has studied. Lave's work tried to understand mathematical problems in the same way as do her subjects, for example in the case of shoppers in a supermarket. They showed virtually error-free arithmetic within their shopping problems, compared to a much poorer performance in matched arithmetic in the formal context of tests. The arithmetic used by shoppers was not 'applied' to their problems in the methods of arithmetic lessons, but rather grew out of them in form and content. The arithmetic practice was quite specific to the situation and appeared as what Lave calls a 'gap closing process' that draws the problem and its already anticipated form of solution, closer together. It was the iterative use and the monitoring of these processes by the shoppers that accounted for their extraordinarily high level of successful problem solving in practice (Evans and Harris, 1991:207). For them, everyday practice involved a multiplicity of reasons for choosing particular items to buy: calculation of best value per ounce was one activity among many others in pursuit of their criteria for what they wanted. Their arithmetic was more structured by, than structuring of, the shopping activity.

Dowling's (1991) model (see Chapter 7) develops some theoretical work of Lave, and in presenting it, takes issue both with the utilitarian approach of the Cockcroft Report and the 'mathematical anthropologists' like Gerdes, Bishop and D'Ambrosio. To him, the utilitarian approach of Cockcroft serves to stress the separation of school from work mathe-matics by defining non-mathematical practices in mathematical terms. The only sort of understanding recognised by the mathematical anthro-pologists is their own elaboration of the specifically mathematical descrip-tion of the worker's activity. The fact that the workers do not see it thus themselves, is taken to signify their lack of understanding. Dowling (1991:103) quotes an example from Cooley. An aircraft company engaged a team of highly qualified mathematicians to try and define a method of drawing a particular engine part. In two years of working on the extremely complex shape they failed. 'When however, they went to the experimental workshop ... they found that a skilled sheet metal worker, together with a draughtsman had actually succeeded in drawing and making one. One of the mathematicians observed 'They may have suc-ceeded in making it, but they didn't understand how they did it''.

To Dowling the anthropological approach is the opposite to the utilitarian. It celebrates everyday practices in their mathematical activity, but again this is the view of the researchers, not the practitioners. In spite of his strong antiracist and anti-colonial stance, Gerdes is still interpreting what people do in terms of European mathematics and he remains Eurocentric. That he wants to find mathematics in basket-weaving at all, says Dowling, is the result of the hegemony of European rationalism. Though emphasising the much deeper analysis of the mathematical anthropologists than that of the utilitarians, the latter are still reductionists while the former are naive. The judgemental hegemony of mathematics still holds and Dowling's model offers reasons why. The work of Common Threads was to challenge the hegemony from within, in Dowling's terms, by dissolving the walls between the cells of the model (see Chapter 7) by using their several discourses at the same time. This was the policy behind the Common Threads workshops and the main reason for the length of the captions of the original exhibition (see Chapter 6). It is not an unusual thing for people who are both mathematics educators and textiles workers to do. For example a correspondence between Hawkin, Jones and Perks (1991) relishes both their mathematics and their embroidery with an increase in involvement in both. It is not unfair to Dowling to suggest that perhaps his model too, comes from someone with more experience of mathematics education than needlework.

Fasheh (1990) works to a complete separation, in principle, of institutional mathematics from the mathematics of everyday life, in a wholesale rejection of the role of mathematics as an agent of hegemony. He contrasts the Western mathematics he learned and taught in this Third World environment, with that of his illiterate mother. His own teaching bore all the hallmarks of good mathematics teaching, pupil involvement and discussion, clubs, magazines and revitalised curriculum and materials. She was a dressmaker who regularly took rectangles of cloth and without paper patterns or any other written instruction, converted them into well-fitting garments. This manipulation of shape, pattern, order, relationships and measurement was beyond his comprehension. His mathematics was a matter of manipulating symbols and concepts; hers consisted of breaking a whole into smaller parts and constructing a new whole that had its own style, shape and size and that had to fit a specific person (Fasheh, 1990:2). Mistakes in her mathematics entailed practical consequences: mistakes in his did not. The value of hers related to her own community: his related solely to the symbolic power of Western hegemonic culture. Indeed it depended on it entirely and it made hers invisible. Yet mathematics was integrated into her work as it never was into his: it lacked the structure and theory of his to be sure, but his lacked practice, relevance and a context. Neither knowledge was praxis, for each lacked one part of the 'dialectical relationship between life and mental construction, between practice and theory, between the work and our consciousness of it, between reality and our perceptions of it' (Fasheh, 1991:22). He had originally been attracted to mathematics because of its explanatory powers, its claims to higher intelligence, universal truths and absolute laws, and to pleasurable, ethical, intellectual and useful practices, and he responded to accusations of the abuse of mathematics and science in warfare for example, as the abuses of people, not of the mathematics and science. It took a war on which he was on the losing side, to see the central function of mathematics and science as that of creating power and generating hegemony. For the victory was due not to moral but technological superiority. Education can do either of two things: it can either introduce hegemony into the community or it can reclaim and develop what hegemony has made invisible (Fasheh, 1990: 25). Fasheh's current educational programme is to reclaim, through community education, people's sense of worth and ways of thinking, and to facilitate their ability to articulate what they think and do about it as a foundation for autonomous action.

Such knowledge is 'owned knowledge' (Paechter, 1993:56). It is not simply something that is learned well: 'it is that which contains within it the potential for effective and group action [for] it positions its possessor as an acting subject able to use her or his knowledge in a dynamic way'. It has the power of counter hegemony, through conscious cultural change. It may be difficult to effect within the wholly hegemonic context of school classrooms, but outside them it offers an emancipatory tool, ready for action. In practice, Knijnik (1993) for example, reports her work with landless peasants in Southern Brazil who use education as a strategic weapon for land reform. They know they need technological knowledge, but to serve their own cause, not to follow those of hegemony. Knijnik works at the interface between academic and popular knowledge, helping to develop a pedagogy through which the people can interpret and codify their knowledge and 'acquire academic knowledge and establish comparison between these two different types of knowledge, in order to choose the most suitable one, when they have real problems to solve' (Knijnik, 1993:150).

Women's Work Revisited

The exploitation of women's work in the international textiles industry is now well documented. Joekes (1985) for example, details the conditions in factories in Morocco, where the cultural context differs from the Asian countries, where most similar factories are, and where most of the abuses have been recorded. The relationship between technology and power in the context of women's work in textiles has also been well documented, for example by Cockburn (1985) and Holland (1991). Research in factories in England during the preparation of *Cabbage* and Common Threads showed that gendered abuses of labour were still far from eliminated in England (Harris, 1991). As the real cost of fashion in swinging London continues to be borne by such exploited women the world over, the only redress has to be through the sort of political action now undertaken by the Clean Clothes Campaign of SOMO (1996:2), the Centre for Research on Multinational Corporations based in Amsterdam.

The gendered division of labour in textiles work is not just a matter for factories or sweatshops however, it is also a development issue. As newly independent colonies joined the world's economic system, development was first seen as economic growth and industrialisation, with the richer countries injecting capital and technical assistance. Under such schemes economic growth was supposed to take off and the ensuing benefits trickle down so that eventually poverty would be eliminated. By the 1970s it was clear that this was not working and the first rethinking of the model concluded that this was because the *human factor* had been omitted (Mosse, 1993:11). The human factor was seen as people consuming development not producing it, and people were not seen as both men and women. The Women in Development movement began in the 1970s with the realisation that 'expecting a country to develop towards modernisation with the female half of its population unable to take full part in the process, was like asking someone to work with one arm and one leg tied behind their back' (Østergaard, 1992:xii). The Gender and Development movement followed with a more objective analysis that admitted that the functions of men and women in the 'receiving' countries differed substantially from those in the 'donor' countries, though 'donor' is hardly the word to describe one side of a relationship that has left the other in a state of overwhelmingly unpayable debt. Development still seems often to be little more than an extension of the relationship that countries used to have with their colonial masters.

In spite of changes in thinking about development, many gender stereotypes remain in the workings of recent models which emphasise self-reliance in the context of participatory democracy. The forces of patriarchy remain strong and males still dominate in all of societies' powerful roles: military, education, business, health care, advertising, religion. 'Women work, women's priorities, women's lives, have not counted on the agendas of the Third World's national planners' (Mosse, 1993:151). Thus development projects can still carry culturally inappropriate ideas on the sexual division of labour, with the western middle-class family pattern clearly legible between the lines (Østergaard, 1992:1). There is some debate as to whether colonialism increased gender inequalities that already existed or introduced them (Mosse, 1993:24 and Chapter 8). Certainly the European concept of housewife has been and is still influential in many development programmes that include textiles work and education, and it is to be remembered that *housewife* was the curriculum aim for most girls, (see Chapter 3) at just the time when curricula were being exported wholesale. This entirely European conception of male and female roles was behind trickle-down theory, with its assumption that the men in receipt of aid, being decent chaps, would pass it on down the family.

The idea that women do not work was of course ludicrous to societies in which families do not eat unless the women farm. Nevertheless the conception encouraged an increase in the number of textiles and handicrafts projects, reinforcing existing vocational programmes in which women were taught to sew the sort of missionary needlework with which middle class European women liked to decorate their dining tables and bathrooms. Meanwhile, small scale industrial projects of aid programmes with their own sexual exclusions in labour, produced more unemployed women for whom handicraft projects seemed, to donors, like a suitably female occupation. But almost all such projects are geared to limited and unreliable markets for tourists, or for the export of decorative, non-essential items whose market evaporates in the recessions of the countries which import them. Their effect is to make further ghettos for women, keeping them outside 'mainstream' development, and steering them back into unpaid or poorly paid domestic economies again.

The resulting, limiting effects on women's lives were obvious in some of the women's projects visited on the Common Threads tour. In one for example, an expatriate woman made much of her training of local women weavers to make the wall hangings that are fashionable in some European countries. The trainees sat at vertical looms copying pictures of touristic bowdlerisations of their own environment, romantic little thatched houses shaded by what looked like far from indigenous coconut palms. In reality, the culture of the trainees includes a widespread use of geometry. The women decorate their own houses with a range of geometric patterns, and their traditional overgarment is a blanket that also carries geometric designs. These however are imported nowadays through the textiles industry of a nearby highly developed country. My suggestion that the women could perhaps weave their own geometries into their own blankets, where they would be explored by their own children in a continuity of their own cultural richness, rather than following the insulting fantasies of foreigners in exchange for pitiful wages, was heard askance.

It remains ironic that the traditional work of such women is so often used in teaching the higher levels of the abstract mathematics of Western hegemony. Traditional peasant embroideries from Hungary for example, are used in teaching group theory to university undergraduates (see Chapter 6) and mathematics has long been used as a way of categorising the symmetries of textiles woven by just the sort of people that aid projects can so easily patronise (Washburn and Crowe, 1988 for example). There is no suggestion that the weavers themselves are consciously following a particular piece of European nineteenth century mathematics while they work. On the other hand, the maker of a coiled basket in Botswana or Uganda (Chapter 9 and Figure 14) could not produce a basket at all if her work was entirely mindless. The coils of such baskets are formed from short lengths of local fibres, bound together in such a way that the diameter of the coil is kept constant during the construction. The three dimensional symmetry of the basket is maintained during the entire process of manufacture, otherwise it will not be much use as a basket. The designs worked into it as work progresses are also symmetrical: they are not worked onto the finished article, but are part of the whole conception and construction. The proposition is made again, that there is much mathematical thinking in such basket work and that it would be empowering and emancipatory for the workers themselves for it to be accredited. What prevents this happening is mathematics education hegemony that does not recognise the sheer complexity of what the weavers are doing, or else interprets it in the literary culture of mathematics education, without any practical knowledge of it. Such work is of course impossible to convert into written instruction.

Some vocational centres visited during the Common Threads tour taught numeracy with the broad aim of providing textiles trainees with the skills with which to run their own businesses. In all those visited, the numeracy being taught was that entirely separate, pencil and paper subject so beloved of the cultural restorationists. The syllabi and examinations were also controlled from England, and were sometimes imposed by the conditions of an aid agreement. This numeracy is of course the tool that book-keeping requires for when the qualified textiles workers come to run their own businesses, and as such is justified as a subject to be taught, but it stood in complete contrast to the obvious matheracy of the local cultures and their vibrant geometries over which their missionary needle-

Figure 15: Traditional cross stitch patterns of the type
used by hargittai and Lengyel (see Chapter 6) for
teaching group theory to university undergraduates.

work lay like a limp rag. The history of adult education in developing countries brings additional baggage. One legacy has been stepwise instruction related to age, and institutionalised 'as intrinsically suited to an immature mind' (Serpell: in press). Much of traditional adult education has become a condescending process in which the teacher is obliged to direct students along a predetermined path. The visible result is often the bizarre situation in which mature women are ranged in rows and trained to manipulate written symbolic algorithms for skills that have been on skill lists since the seventeenth century and are most renowned for everyone's inability to remember how to do them once examination day has passed.

In two vocational centres in two countries the enthusiastic analysis by trainees of their own designs during Common Threads workshops was promptly squelched by expatriate volunteer tutors, who told me sharply that I was wasting the women's time since it would not help with 'doing percentage shrinkage' (see Chapter 9). This 'doing' apparently had nothing to do with cloth, but was an item on the syllabus of the only available means of publicly acknowledging the women's skills. It seemed to be entirely unassociated with the practical business of taking two equal lengths of the same cloth, shrinking one and finding a generally applicable way of comparing it with the other. No amount of their experience of the behaviour of cloth when washed compared to the value of their ability to push a pencil over paper in the only way that would satisfy the examiner.

Brief participatory observation sessions, where I worked with trainees both as dressmaker and mathematics educator, showed clearly that in the course of their work, they used most of the items on any basic numeracy syllabus from craft examination stables (though not percentage shrinkage). In spite of this obvious usage, all that the available examinations achieve in reality, is to feed the trainees back into the bottom of another hierarchy, this time that of numeracy examinations. Interestingly enough, the practical numeracy of the male carpentry students in the same institutions was somewhat less than that of the dressmakers yet it was accreditable as such. That and the 'workmanlike' overalls issued to them, made a further contrast with the women who worked in their own clothes, doing what women do. Even the pursuit of the possibility of exploring the accreditation of the embedded mathematics of the women seemed to drive them back down again, for it would require an application for aid, and there was no accessible category of aid provision that encompassed women, mathematics and work at one and the same time. To expect the women to advance themselves through numeracy examinations was to expect them 'to liberate themselves using the very instruments of their oppression' (Paechter, 1993:34), for the accreditation was still tied to the ankles of that superior liberal education view of mathematics to which they could never hope to aspire, because the hurdles of the hierarchy that had so long disdained them and their work were just too high.

It remains possible however to convert swords into ploughshares if there is both an option and the means to do so. Back in England, under a project of the Women's Institute, the largest women's organisation in England and Wales, with its own comprehensive education programme and its own college, three participatory studies were conducted in courses for curtain and blind-making, knitting, and machine patchwork respectively. As anticipated, the skills embedded included most of those found on a numeracy syllabus and the on-task talk was as full of mathematics as that of Gorman's (Chapter 7) children. The aim as before was to try and find a way of accrediting this mathematical thinking and action through some sort of dual coursework assessment, the method that had been shown to favour girls (Smart, 1996 above). The possibility of devising a unique accreditation was explored but that would have meant peer-group appraisal. It would be unlikely that an existing peer-group for such a radical proposal could have been convened, and there was no will to go through the lengthy and frustrating processes of arguing one into existence. The last thing anybody wanted was to have to go cap in hand to a hierarchy again. The problem solved itself by redefinition. The very act of talking about the mathematics they were doing as it arose during the courses, was enough to illustrate their mathematical skill to people who had been brought up to believe they had none, and to raise enough confidence in both course members and tutors to take forward the idea of talking about the embedded mathematics as it arose in *all* textiles courses, and of laying on additional courses that were openly about mathematics. The redefinition had been in terms of confidence and, unlike the women in development programmes, these had the economic security in which to deploy it. They could afford simply to ignore examination and assessment altogether and pursue the mathematics of their birthright in any way they wished, including taking examinations if they wanted to. For the rest it is not so easy.

As recently as 1994, Downs described his experience as a student teacher on mathematics teaching practice when, in failing to be the aggressive bully that he was expected to be, he was seen as a failed mathematician. 'Changes are still desperately needed to the way that mathematics is both perceived and taught' (Downs, 1994:21). All educational change is notoriously slow and difficult (see Chapter 9), but as Fasheh remarked 'schools of education and ministries of education usually fall behind what is happening and what is needed' (Fasheh, 1995). Changes are happening, and forms of assessment that cultural restorationists decry,

but which nevertheless fill the demands of their war cry to raise standards, are already available (Brown, 1993:119). International discussion on similar methods in adult numeracy have at last begun (Coben, 1994). And if the work of one small subversive project can demonstrate that by using the common threads of women, mathematics and work, the confidence bred out by two millennia of social conditioning can be revived, then so can another.

References

Ball S J (1983) Education, Majorism and the 'Curriculum of the Dead'. *Curriculum Studies* Vol I No 2 p 195-214.

Bishop Alan (1991) Mathematics Education in its Cultural Context. In: Mary Harris (Ed) *Schools Mathematics and Work.* London: Falmer Press.

Brown Margaret (1993) Clashing Epistemologies: The Battle for Control of the National Curriculum and its Assessment. Inaugural Lecture given by Margaret Brown, Professor of Mathematics Education at King's College London, 20 October 1993. In *Teaching Mathematics and its Applications.* Vol 12 No 3 pp97-112.

Buxton Laurie (1981) *Do you Panic about Maths? Coping with Maths Anxiety.* London: Heinemann Educational Books.

Carraher David (1991) Mathematics in and out of School: A Selective Review of Studies from Brazil. In: Mary Harris (Ed) *Schools, Mathematics and Work.* London: Falmer Press.

Coben Diana (compiler) (1994) *Proceedings of the Inaugural Conference of Adults Learning Mathematics: A Research Forum.* London: Goldsmiths College.

Cockburn Cynthia (1985) *Machinery of Dominance: Women, Men and Technical Knowhow.* London: Pluto Press.

Cockcroft D W (Chair) (1982) *Mathematics Counts. Report of the Committee of Enquiry into the Teaching of Mathematics in Schools.* London: Her Majesty's Stationery Office.

D'Ambrosio Ubiritan (1991) Ethnomathematics and its Place in the History and Pedagogy of Mathematics. In Mary Harris (Ed) *Schools Mathematics and Work.* Basingstoke: Falmer Press.

Dowling Paul (1991) Contextualising Mathematics: Towards a Theoretical Map. In: Mary Harris (Ed) *Schools, Mathematics and Work.* Basingstoke: Falmer Press.

Ernest Paul (1991) *The Philosophy of Mathematics Education.* London and New York: Falmer Press

Eisenhart Margaret A (1988) The Ethnographic Research Tradition and Mathematics Education Research. *Journal of Research in Mathematics Education.* Vol 19 No 2 pp 99-114.

Elson Diane (1983) Nimble Fingers and Other Fables. In Wendy Chapkis and Cynthia Enloe (Ed) *Of Common Cloth: Women in the Global Textiles Industry.* Amsterdam: Transnational Institute.

Evans J and Harris M (1991) Theories of Practice. In: Mary Harris (Ed) *Schools, Mathematics and Work.* Basingstoke: Falmer Press.

Fasheh Munir (1990) Community Education: To Reclaim and Transform what has been made Invisible. *Harvard Educational Review* Vol 10 No 1 p 19-35.

Fasheh Munir (1995) A Personal Reflection on the DICE International Conference on Partnerships in Education: Tensions between Economic and Culture. University of London Institute of Education. London 24-26 May. Unpublished.

Opposite: **Figure 16**: Poster prepared by the author for the Maths in Work Project.

Frankenstein Marilyn (1989) *Relearning Mathematics: A Different Third R – Radical Maths.* London: Free Association Books.

Gay John and Cole Michael (1967) *The New Mathematics and an Old Culture.* New York: Holt, Rinehart and Winston.

Gerdes Paulus (1997 forthcoming) Survey of Current Work in Ethnomathematics. In Arthur B Powell and Marilyn Frankenstein (Eds) *Ethnomathematics: Challenging Eurocentrism in Mathematics Education.* New York: SUNY Press.

Gerdes Paulus (1995) *Women and Geometry in Southern Africa.* Maputo: Universidade Pedagógica Moçambique.

Harris Mary (1987) An Example of Traditional Women's Work as a Mathematics Resource. *For the the Learning of Mathematics* Vol 7, No 3, p 26-28.

Harris Mary (1991) Postscript: The Maths in Work Project. In: Mary Harris (Ed) *Schools, Mathematics and Work.* Basingstoke: Falmer Press

Hawkin Wendy, Jones Lesley and Perks Pat (1991) Cross Stitch Maths Part 1 In: *Mathematics Teaching* 136. Cross Stitch Maths: Part 2 In: *Mathematics Teaching* 136.

Holland J (1991) The Gendering of Work. In: Mary Harris (Ed) *Schools, Mathematics and Work.* Basingstoke: Falmer Press.

Joekes Susan (1985) Working for Lipstick? Male and Female Labour in the Clothing Industry in Morocco. In Afshar Haleh (Ed) *Women, Work and Ideology in the Third World.* London: Tavistock Publications.

Keddie Nell (1971) Classroom Knowledge. In: M Young (Ed) *Knowledge and Control.* West Drayton: Macmillan.

Knijnik Gelsa (1993) Culture, Mathematics, Education and the Landless of Southern Brazil. In: C Julie, D Angelis and Z Davis (Eds) *Political Dimensions of Mathematics Education 2* (PDME2) Curriculum Construction of Society in Transition. Cape Town: Maskew Miller Longman.

Lave Jean (1988) *Cognition in Practice.* Cambridge: Cambridge University Press.

Mosse Julia Cleves (1993) *Half the World Half a Chance. An Introduction to Gender and Development.* Oxford: Oxfam.

Østergaard Lise (1992) *Gender and Development, A Practical Guide.* London and New York: Routledge.

Paechter Caroline F (1993) Power, Knowledge and the Design and Technology Curriculum. London: Unpublished PhD Thesis. King's College, University of London.

Papert Seymour (1980) *Mindstorms: Children, Computers and Powerful Ideas.* Brighton: Harvester Press.

Raum O (1938) *Arithmetic in Africa.* London: Evans.

Serpell Robert (in press) Local Accountability to rural communities: a challenge for educational planning in Africa. In: Fiona Leach and Angela Little (Eds) *Schools, Culture and Economics in the Developing World: Tensions and Conflicts* (provisional title). New York: Garland Press.

Smart Teresa (1996 forthcoming) Gender and Mathematics in England and Wales. In Gila Hanna (Ed) *Towards Gender Equity in Mathematics.* Dordrect: Kluwer Academic.

SOMO (1996) *The Clean Clothes Campaign.* Amsterdam: Centre for Research on Multinational Corporations (SOMO in Dutch acronym).

Walkerdine Valerie (compiler) (1989) *Counting Girls Out.* London: Virago Education in association with the University of London Institute of Education.

Washburn Dorothy K and Crowe Donald W (1988) *Symmetries of Culture: Theory and Practice of Plane Pattern Analysis.* Seattle and London: University of Washington Press.

Willis Sue (1989) *'Real Girls Don't Do Maths'. Gender and the Construction of Privilege.* Victoria: Deakin University Press.

Index